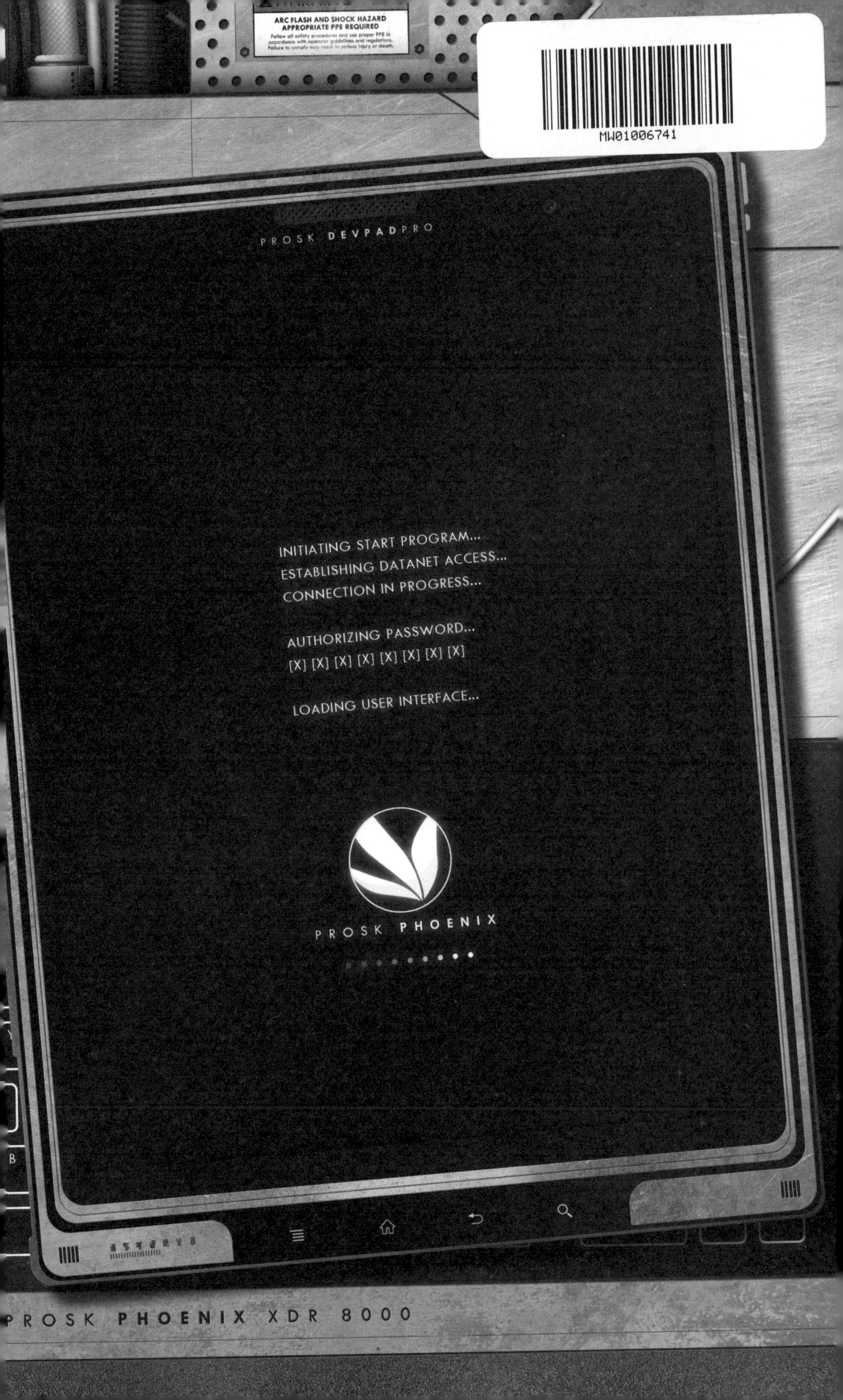
ARC FLASH AND SHOCK HAZARD
APPROPRIATE PPE REQUIRED
Follow all safety procedures and use proper PPE in accordance with operator guidelines and regulations. Failure to comply may result in serious injury or death.
PROSK DEVPADPRO
INITIATING START PROGRAM...
ESTABLISHING DATANET ACCESS...
CONNECTION IN PROGRESS...
AUTHORIZING PASSWORD...
[X] [X] [X] [X] [X] [X] [X] [X]
LOADING USER INTERFACE...
PROSK PHOENIX
PROSK PHOENIX XDR 8000

HAWKEN:
GENESIS

ARCHAIA ENTERTAINMENT LLC
WWW.**ARCHAIA**.COM

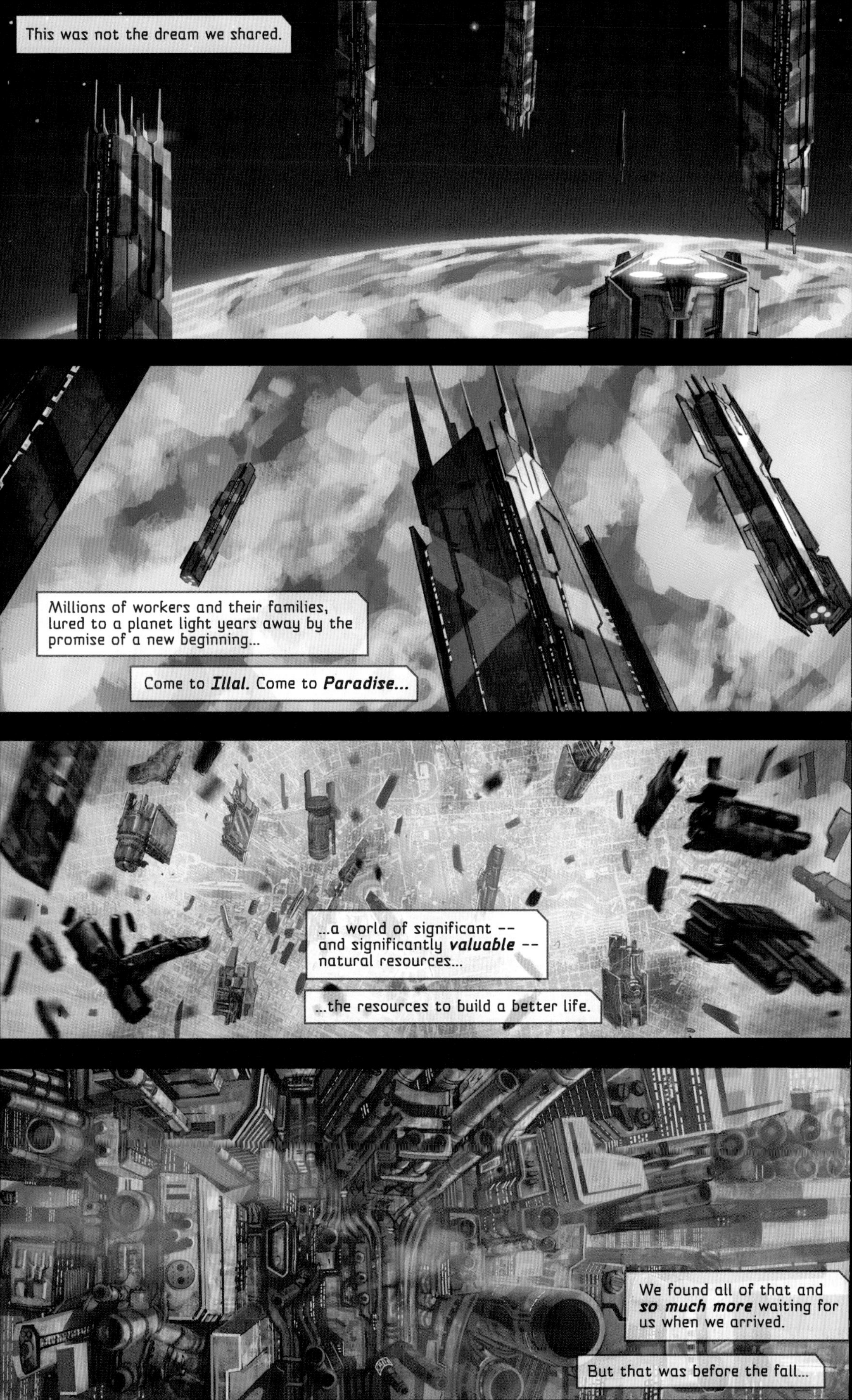
This was not the dream we shared.
Millions of workers and their families, lured to a planet light years away by the promise of a new beginning...
Come to ***Illal.*** Come to ***Paradise...***
...a world of significant -- and significantly ***valuable*** -- natural resources...
...the resources to build a better life.
We found all of that and ***so much more*** waiting for us when we arrived.
But that was before the fall...

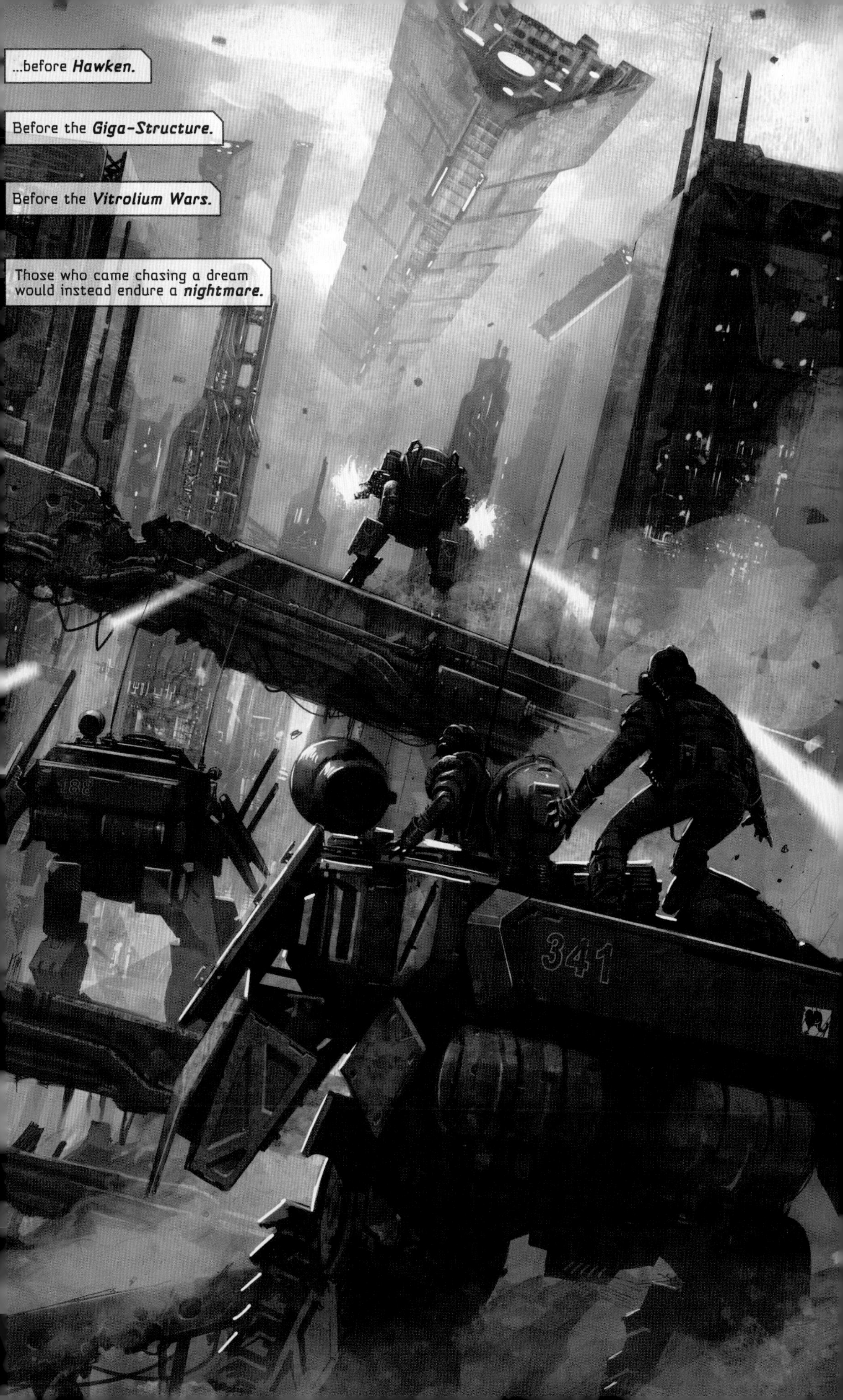
...before *Hawken.*
Before the *Giga-Structure.*
Before the *Vitrolium Wars.*
Those who came chasing a dream would instead endure a *nightmare.*
188
341

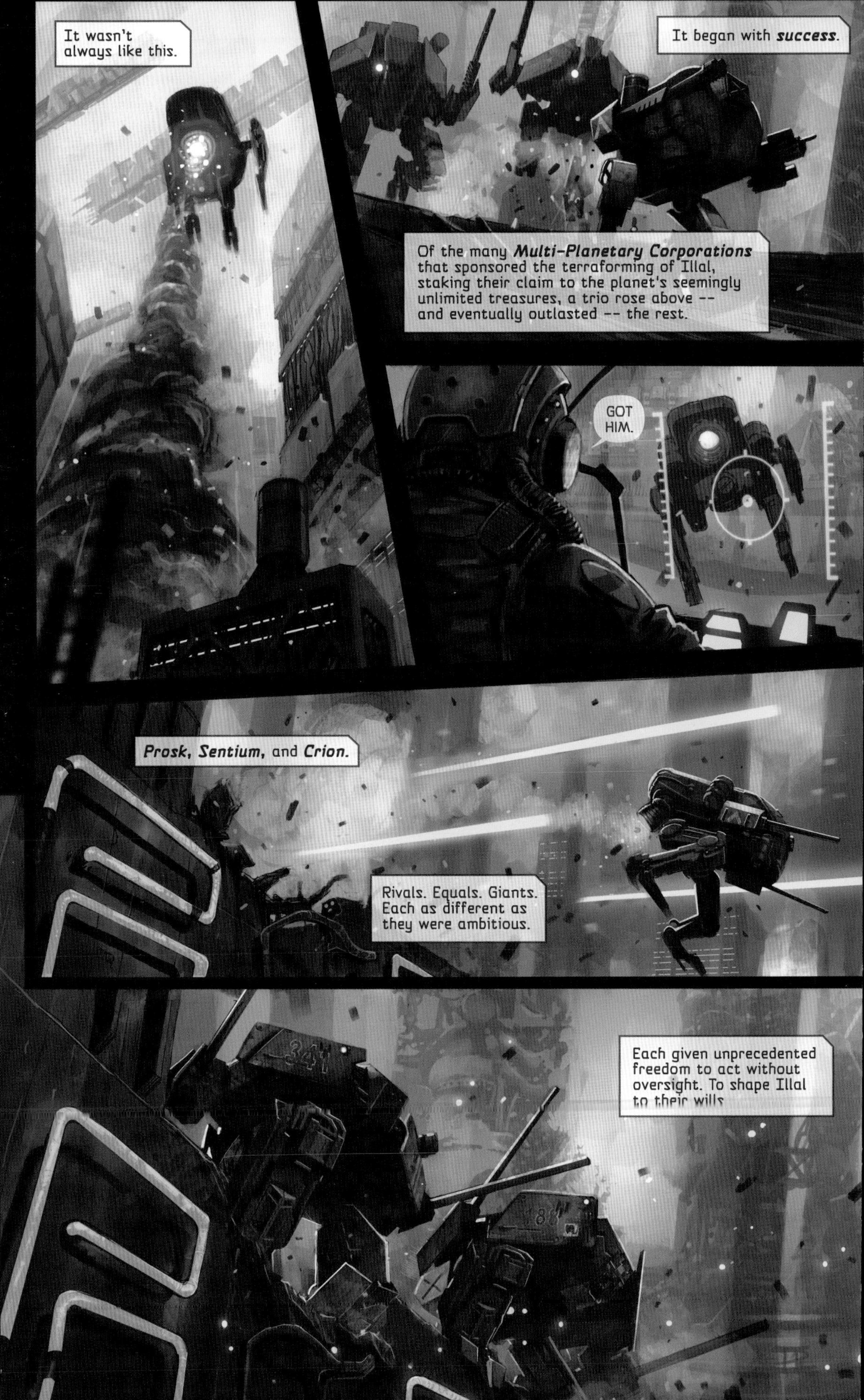

It wasn't always like this.
It began with *success*.
Of the many ***Multi-Planetary Corporations*** that sponsored the terraforming of Illal, staking their claim to the planet's seemingly unlimited treasures, a trio rose above -- and eventually outlasted -- the rest.
GOT HIM.
Prosk, ***Sentium***, and ***Crion***.
Rivals. Equals. Giants. Each as different as they were ambitious.
Each given unprecedented freedom to act without oversight. To shape Illal to their wills

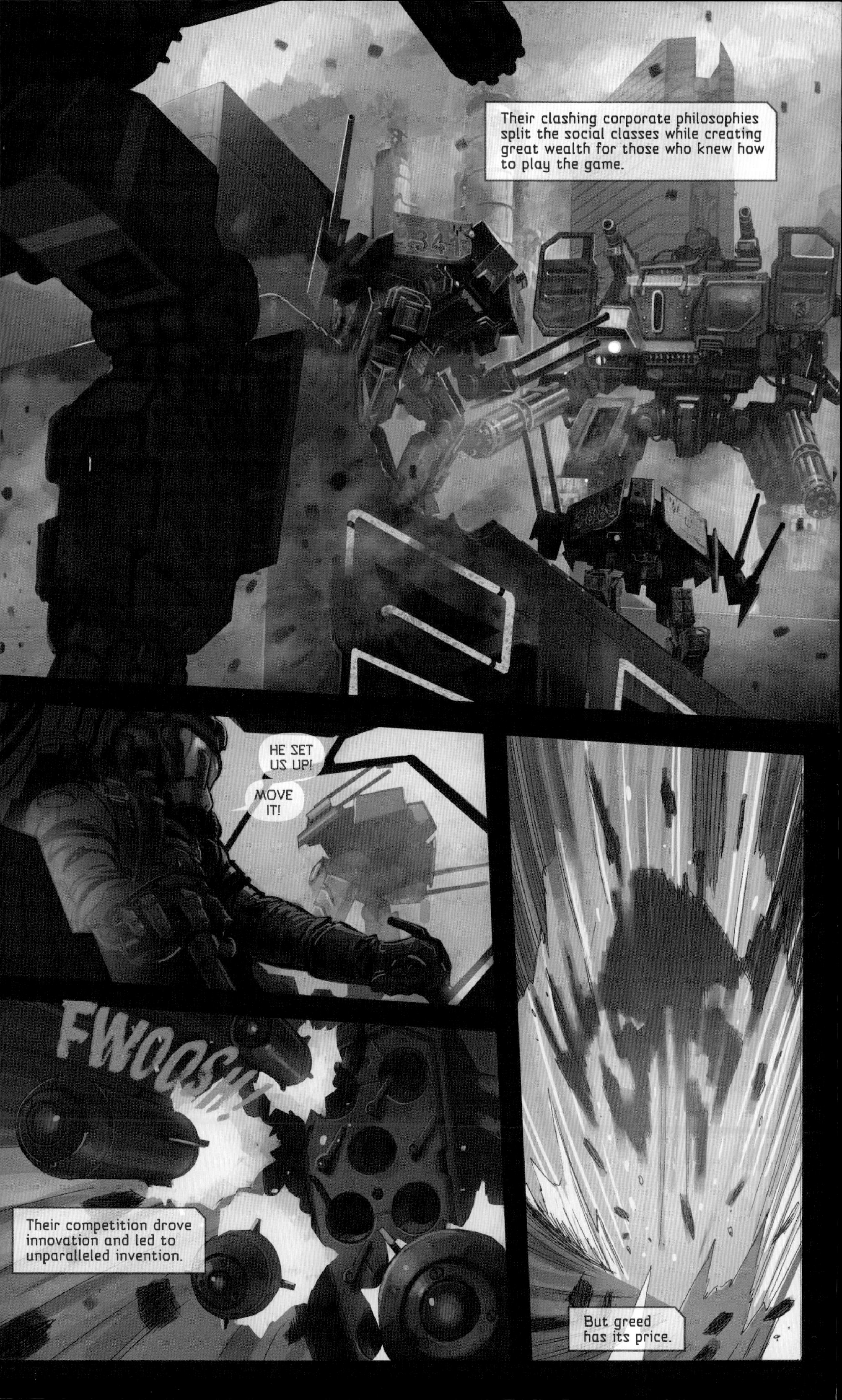

Their clashing corporate philosophies split the social classes while creating great wealth for those who knew how to play the game.
HE SET US UP!
MOVE IT!
FWOOSH!
Their competition drove innovation and led to unparalleled invention.
But greed has its price.

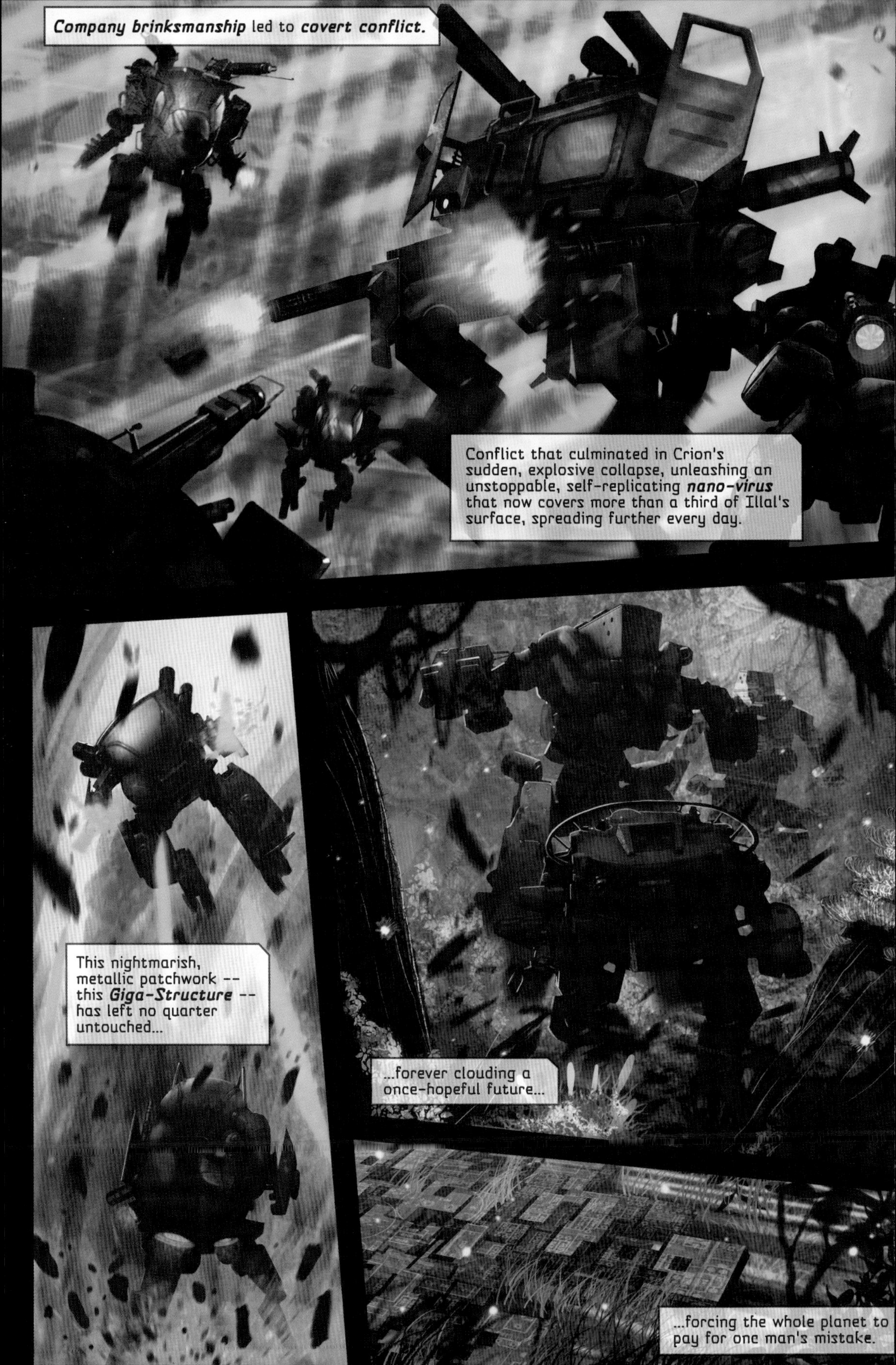
Company brinksmanship led to ***covert conflict.***
Conflict that culminated in Crion's sudden, explosive collapse, unleashing an unstoppable, self-replicating ***nano-virus*** that now covers more than a third of Illal's surface, spreading further every day.
This nightmarish, metallic patchwork -- this ***Giga-Structure*** -- has left no quarter untouched...
...forever clouding a once-hopeful future...
...forcing the whole planet to pay for one man's mistake.

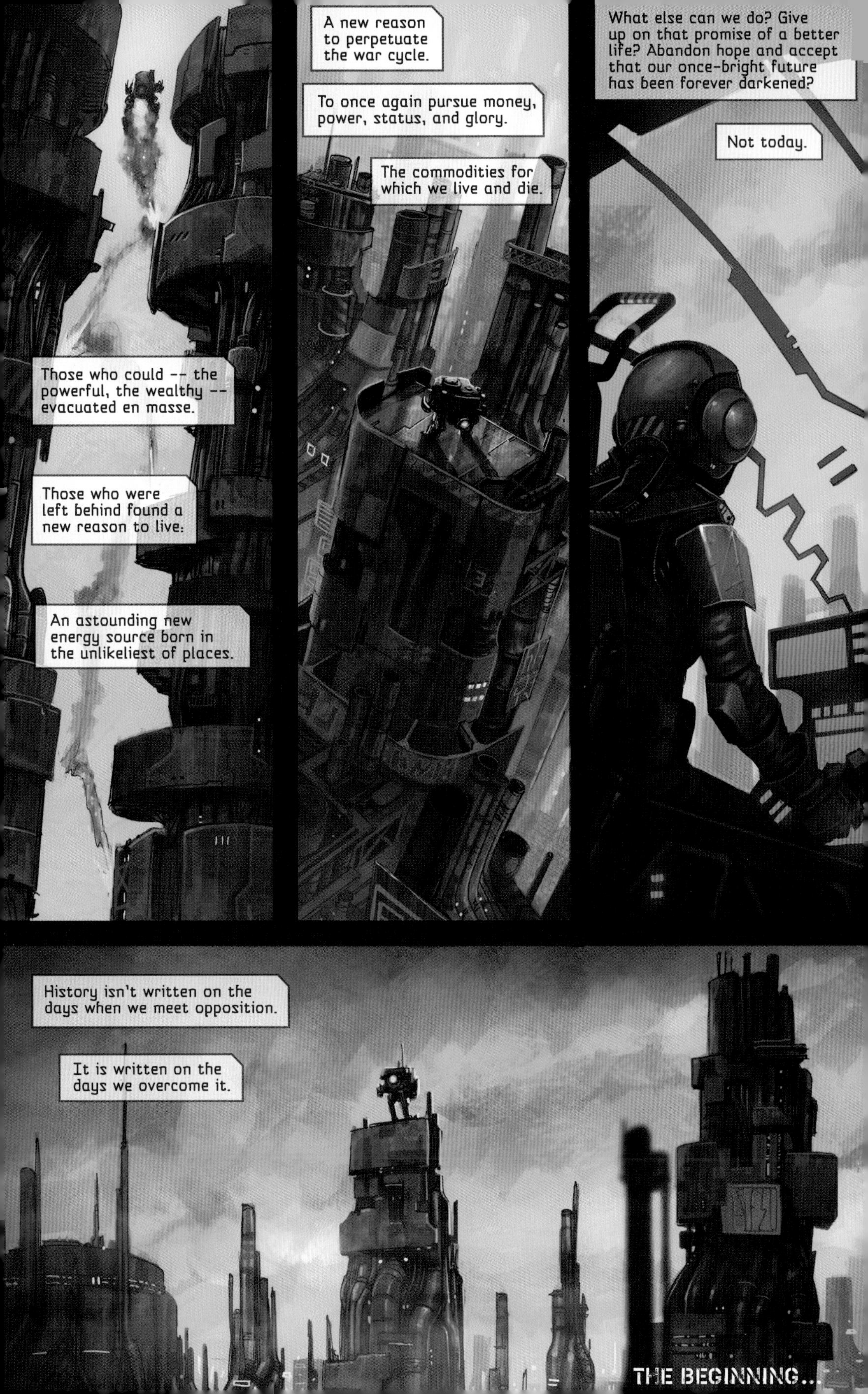
Those who could -- the powerful, the wealthy -- evacuated en masse.
Those who were left behind found a new reason to live:
An astounding new energy source born in the unlikeliest of places.
A new reason to perpetuate the war cycle.
To once again pursue money, power, status, and glory.
The commodities for which we live and die.
What else can we do? Give up on that promise of a better life? Abandon hope and accept that our once-bright future has been forever darkened?
Not today.
History isn't written on the days when we meet opposition.
It is written on the days we overcome it.
THE BEGINNING...

HAWKEN:

COVER & CONCEPT BY
KHANG LE

STORY BY
DAN JEVONS, MILES WILLIAMS, & KHANG LE

WRITTEN BY
JEREMY BARLOW

LETTERED BY
DERON BENNETT

INTERSTITIAL STORY MATERIAL BY
ANDREW NIELSON & HEATHER NUHFER

DESIGN BY
SCOTT NEWMAN

EDITOR
MIKE KENNEDY

PRODUCER
CULLEN THOMAS

TRANSMEDIA PRODUCER
DJ2 ENTERTAINMENT

EXECUTIVE EDITOR
JOE LEFAVI

ASSISTANT EDITORS
**REBECCA TAYLOR
& ANDREW NIELSON**

TRANSMEDIA PRODUCER
QUIXOTIC TRANSMEDIA

Archaia Entertainment LLC
Jack Cummins, *President & COO*
Mark Smylie, *Chief Creative Officer*
Mike Kennedy, *Publisher*
Stephen Christy, *Editor-in-Chief*
Scott Newman, *Production Manager*
Mel Caylo, *Marketing Manager*

Meteor Entertainment, Inc.
Mark Long, *CEO*
Torrie Dorrell, *CRO*
Paula Cuneo, *VP, Transmedia Marketing & Promotions*
Wes Harris, *VP, Transmedia Publishing*
John Williamson, *Producer*
Shannon Gerritzen, *Senior Manager, Global PR*
Danielle Davis, *Marketing Manager*

Adhesive Games
Khang Le, *Creative Director, Co-Founder*
Jonathan Kreuzer, *Technical Director, Co-Founder*
Dave Nguyen, *Designer/Artist, Co-Founder*
Christopher Lalli, *Animator, Co-Founder*
Jason Hughes, *Producer*
John Park, *Lead Concept Artist*

DJ2 Entertainment LLC
Dmitri Johnson, *CEO*
Dan Jevons, *CCO*
Cullen Thomas, *SVP*
Amitabh Klemm, *Creative Director*

Published by **Archaia**

Archaia Entertainment LLC
1680 Vine Street, Suite 1010
Los Angeles, California, 90028
www.archaia.com

HAWKEN: GENESIS Original Graphic Novel Hardcover. March 2013. FIRST PRINTING.

10 9 8 7 6 5 4 3 2 1

ISBN: 1-936393-92-1
ISBN 13: 978-1-936393-92-3

GENESIS

TABLE OF CONTENTS

PR
FR

PROSK PORTAL EXTRANET BROWSER

Welcome to Illal | IWN - Illal World News

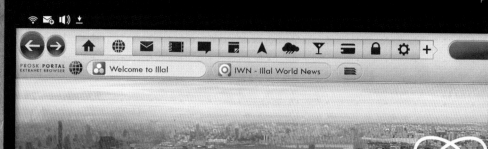

WELCOME TO ILLAL

A NEW WAY OF **BUSINESS.** A NEW WAY OF **LIFE.**

A historic milestone in Mankind's exploration of the stars. A bustling colony of industrial innovation an imagination. A bold new world for a bold new way of life. Here on Illal, experience a renaissance of moder commerce and culture combined, where the happiness of each citizen is more than a pursuit. It's a promise.

A momentous beginning. With the United Terran Authority's unprecedented decision to ratify the 2296 MP Terraforming Incentive Provision, Mankind earned the right to seek its own destiny in the great unknown. Four years late nine visionary multi-planetary corporations (MPCs) invested in the Illal Development Initiative (IDI) – a landmar conglomerate that financed the first corporate-sponsored and privately terraformed space colony in human histor 150,000+ volunteers and pioneers from every facet of society – from leading engineers and entrepreneurs to commo working-class families eager for a new start – boarded over 20,000 individual transports bound for the mineral-rich soil this amazing, untouched planet to found a new, model civilization destined to become the envy of the entire universe.

The next evolution of modern civilization and civic duty. Abandoning the melting pot mentality commo to so many UTA colonies, our Illalian founders pioneered an innovative 'interlocking' urban planning techniqu allowing the disparate architecture of various corporations to fit tightly together, saving valuable space whil contributing to the functional and commercial strength of the greater whole. While we welcome an endless arra of beliefs and cultures, we are all equals under the banner of Illal and collectively bound by its fate. Here we believ that the prosperity of a nation and the well-being of its people are one and the same. Thus Illal is not ruled by sovereign governing body, but maintained by a dynamic corporate coalition under the vigilant guidance of a on-planet UTA regulatory commission and peacekeeping force. Together they ensure that everyone's commercia socioeconomic and political agendas serve the same goal -- the betterment of Illal and its citizens.

TRAVEL TIPS | BE **PREPARED.** BE **PROSPEROUS.**

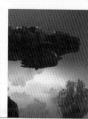

Each colony city requires its own tourist and immigration visa. Titan is known for its longer wait times. Complications with visa or customs can be addressed by contacting the UTA INS department, located on Illal's orbiting moon colony. INS can be conveniently reached via Illal Custom's lunar-ladder transport facility

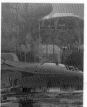

Make sure to visit d quarterly report cyc festivities follow the or loss. Be sure to c currency into scrip strongly impact scrip even a meager inve prior to the PQRs co

256 GB
MEMORY STORAGE
XDROE FLAT SPACE

ARC FLASH AND SHOCK HAZARD
APPROPRIATE PPE REQUIRED
Follow all safety procedures and use proper PPE in
accordance with operator guidelines and regulations.
Failure to comply may result in serious injury or death.

PADION

14 2332

9:36AM

PORTAL POWERED BY **PHOENIX**

Search

File   Edit   View   Favorites   Tools   Help

+ EXPLORE   + TRAVEL   + CONNECT

+ VISIT THE ASHIHAN FORESTS

UTA IMMIGRATION
     NEUTRALIZATION
     SERVICES

LEARN MORE ▶

HOME | TRANSPLANET VISA APPLICATION | MPC GUIDE | EMPLOYMENT OPPORTUNITIES

Take ownership over your community's future. In order to become a legal resident on Illal, you must first be granted Patron status – a unique combination of citizen and shareholder. Illal forgoes the antiquated universal credit-based monetary system in favor of a proactive, investment-related currency. All citizens of Illal must buy and trade in corporate stock ("scrip"). To become a Patron, Illalian citizens must personally invest (financially or via employment) in the success of one of our many thriving MPCs (touch here for investment details and packages). When an MPC enjoys a profitable quarter, the value of its scrip increases, and so too does the wealth and prosperity of its many shareholders. As a result, Patrons of Illal boast a stronger sense of community and resolve than anywhere else in the Terran Hyper-Republic. When your employer, your coworker, or your neighbor succeeds, so do you… transforming every citizen's pursuit of financial stability into more than just a personal goal, but also a national objective of valuable socioeconomic significance.

A land like none other in the galaxy. Home to multiple proud generations, Illal boasts the fastest growing industrial-technological economy in the galaxy, fueling the advancement of our self-sufficient, self-regulating civilization ever forward towards our ultimate utopian ideals. Setting a new standard for Mankind, we are maturing more each day, with an ever-evolving presence in the galactic super economy.

Offering lush accommodations, a thriving, exciting culture, and generous Patron incentives, the Illalian Promise is more than just a dream. It is a new way of life for every UTA citizen seeking a renewed sense of societal purpose and value. Whether you aim to start a new career, build a business or raise a family, here on Illal we want you to succeed. For the success of our colony is fueled by the prosperity of its people, and only together can we thrive.

WELCOME TO ILLAL | ONE **PROMISE.** ONE **PURPOSE.** ONE **PEOPLE.**

DISCOVER MORE ▶   SHARE THIS OPPORTUNITY ▶

public
ad, the
f profit
aveling
. PQRs
es, and
C scrip
nancial

Our natural atmosphere is low in oxygen and high in carbon dioxide and other harmful gases, so be sure to [ ] well inside the designated breatha[ ] of your current Colony City[ ] our landmark Atmospher[ ] designed and maintained[ ] Crion Solutions. Touch h[ ]

Illal i[ ]
United T[ ]
your he[ ]
repor[ ]
with[ ]

PROSK PHO

ILLAL IDENTIFICATION KEY
IDENTIFICATION NO. 1.01.06819.019984RVD-62RSD102.3A

PRESS

UTA United Terran Authority | Illal Immigration Neutralization Services

UDID: 120RTDG49075JF989947DH47577811
CARTHRIGHT, MARION
DOB: 08.03.2306
SEX: FEMALE
HEIGHT: 5' 10"   HAIR: BLACK
WEIGHT: 168 lbs   EYES: BLUE
                      MPC: PROSK

PATRONAGE: 12 MONTHS
CITIZENSHIP: 8 MONTHS

7A

PROSK

WHICH MPC IS RIGHT FOR ME?

OPPORTUNITY THROUGH **DEDICATION**. PROSPERITY THROUGH **LOYALTY**.

THE ILLALIAN SUPERPOWERS While Illal boasts over 25 colonies, home to 9 separate MPCs, almost two-thirds of our population are Patrons for one our three most prominent MPCs: Sentium, Prosk and Crion. Dubbed by locals as "The Big 3", these corporate giants and the megacities they sponsored are the oldest and largest influences on Illalian commerce and culture, each offering its own perks and quirks for prospective Patrons.

SENTIUM CORPORATION One of the leading manufacturers of luxury-grade personal and freight transports, Sentium's unmatched engineering and attractive design have made the iconic *Sentium* swoosh a sought-after status symbol. Based in Titan City, voted #17 on UTA's "Top 50 Cities to See Before You Die," Patrons enjoy a posh, fully-automated campus worthy of Sentium's luxury brand. Many applaud the "perfect balance of corporate innovation and cultural refinement," with its "striking architecture," "soothing gardens," "superb restaurants," and "star-studded premieres." With a menial workforce of largely drones, Titan residents consist mostly of high-ranking professionals seeking a "higher-class lifestyle" of comfort and security. While moguls and millionaires find paradise, critics argue that Sentium's *Superior Technology Demands Superior Minds* motto fosters an "elitist immigration policy" where "climbing the corporate ladder is a politician's game" often stunted by "too many glass ceilings."

PROSK INDUSTRIES From home computing to personal transports, Prosk is a household name throughout the galaxy. Priding itself on human craftsmanship above automated excellence, Prosk produces affordable and reliable products for the common citizen. Infamous for its "entrepreneurial spirit" and "industry versatility," Prosk's ever-expanding product line evolves with its consumers. Branded as a "haven for ambitious businesspersons," many members of the Prosk Board boast "startling success stories with meager beginnings." Ascend the ranks, uncover untapped niches in the market, and earn a seat in the boardroom "through blood, sweat, and scrip alone." This "work hard, live hard" mentality fuels Prosk's constant innovation, not to mention the "never-ending nightlife" of Andromeda, Illal's industrial urban jungle and center of operations for Prosk. While this "wild," "tenacious," and "cutthroat" environment isn't for everyone, Prosk is a choice "home to countless bright lights and big dreams."

CRION SOLUTIONS Since their 2074 Nobel-winning patent for the fusion impulse engine, Crion has been "an unstoppable force of technological evolution" since Mankind first took to the stars. Artificial intelligence. Transparent carbonite. Medical breakthroughs in cryobiology, nano-genetics, and preventative care. Top thinkers in every scientific and technical field push the envelope here in Crion's bleeding-edge laboratories. While Crion will "take scrip from anyone," over-confident Patrons may struggle in an "alarmingly ruthless" job market. Crion's top-secret R&D facilities employ a "merciless weeding process" favoring "only the most forward-thinking minds." More of a gated community than an open colony, tourist trap Praxis Valley is home to Crion and its annual UTA Innovation Summit. This "futuristic wonderland" is famed for "off-market first looks," as radical and "often untested" scientific and medical advances stru down Crion's catwalk years before hitting public retail shelves and pharmacy counters.

QUESTIONS? Tap to chat with a UTA Immigrations and Neutralization Services (INS) representative. ▶

Rygel, Paragon, and more Tier Two MPCs ▶

PROSK DEVPADPRO

FRIDAY, JUNE 14 2332

1:42PM

PROSK PORTAL EXTRANET BROWSER — Forge Drive - IWN Serv... | IWN - Illal World News — PROSK PORTAL POWERED BY PHOENIX — Search|

Author: Marion Carthright <id4662>

Subject: **UNDERSTANDING THE FINE PRINT OF THE ILLALIAN SOCIAL CONTRACT**

Submission Date: 17.03.22.06.14.2332

Submission Draft: First

Submission Status: REJECTED (NO FURTHER DRAFTS NECESSARY)

IWN Illal World News

Everyone keeps telling me about the "Illalian Dream", the promise that every patron of this grand social experiment matters. That not only are we granted the right to pursue our own ambitions, but that the Illalian construct – a synergy of corporate agendas and personal aspirations the likes of which we've never seen – somehow *needs* us in order to thrive. Nine MPCs possessed enough capital to literally *buy* a planet, and (at least) *lease* enough UTA officials to pass the IDI Act in the first place. And after merging into this behemoth, marauding the market with the hubris and tact of a Spanish conquistador, I'm supposed to believe that our economy hinges on how many muffins my bakery manages to sell? If anyone reading still believes in the Illalian Dream, here's my advice: WAKE UP.

Mind you, the "dreamers" out there aren't wrong. This radical social experiment has been a success. Just don't swallow the PR line about Illal's growth being "fueled by the prosperity of its people." Contrary to any claims in your Patron Agreement, Illal is and will always be fueled by the same modus operandi propelling Manifest Destiny since cavemen first sparked rock to tinder: capitalism, corruption, and good old-fashioned greed.

Free to flee the strict moral code of the Hyper-Republic, our founding fathers are now key players in this burgeoning super-economy. Once shackled by the UTA's Scientific Ethics Commission, Crion's oft-controversial research now charges ahead with 200+ patents annually. Meanwhile abundant access to cheap natural resources and even cheaper labor have transformed Sentium and Prosk into manufacturing giants, aggressively expanding into lucrative markets such as transportation and mid-range tech with unprecedented profit margins. Leading the charge, Illal's Big 3 may indeed be setting a new standard for Mankind, but skeptics must ask what kind of standard they're setting… and *for whom*.

Since the onset of civilized capitalist society, corporations were bound by law. And those laws were written by and for the people and upheld by governments with the people's best interests in mind. With the IDI Act, MPCs can now terraform and colonize their own planets, and govern them under their own laws. And the inaugural product of this historic ruling – Illal – is a place where I, among many, fear corporate interests have gone too far.

Who will safeguard our liberties if this experiment fails? The UTA's token force here? Not likely! Many wonder if we're prepared should resources dwindle, unions crumble, and economies collapse. Black markets have already surfaced, offering Patrons low-cost alternatives to Illal's corporate-centric public trade. What might occur on the day when the needs of Illalians and their MPCs conflict? What happens if MPCs begin to ignore even their own low safety standards? Or stop fairly paying staff? What chaos might unfold if Prosk and Sentium turn their armed transports upon each other... or *us*? Sources more than whisper of corporate warfare becoming *literal* (not figurative) practices. With the MPCs so focused on their own agendas, our benefactors may not value the casualties lost in the name of "progress".

So is Illal truly "progress" for Mankind? Or is this a promised land of opportunity for the MPCs alone? As the reality of the Illalian Dream surfaces, I can only hope that the MPCs scoot over and share the bed. Because the slide-out sofa that we've been given is a tad small and smells like my grandma. Still, I gather the believers do have something to smile about. We're not out in the cold and chained to the doghouse. Not yet anyway.

100%

PROSK DEVPODEXP

FRIDAY, JUNE 14 2332 — 1:42AM

Forge Mail | Inbox — Marion Carthright @MC.IllalWorldNews

From: Harold Gutherson <@editor.IllalWorldNews>
Re: Your Rejected Article

SEND | REPLY | DELETE — 10:28AM

I know you're upset Marion, but you must understand that the MPCs control the news cycle here. Even the devices upon which we write it are leased. You go for the jugular, they shut you down, and the only people who suffer are us. To serve the truth, play the game and try to subtly debunk the system from within. Until there's a better way, it's the best we can do.

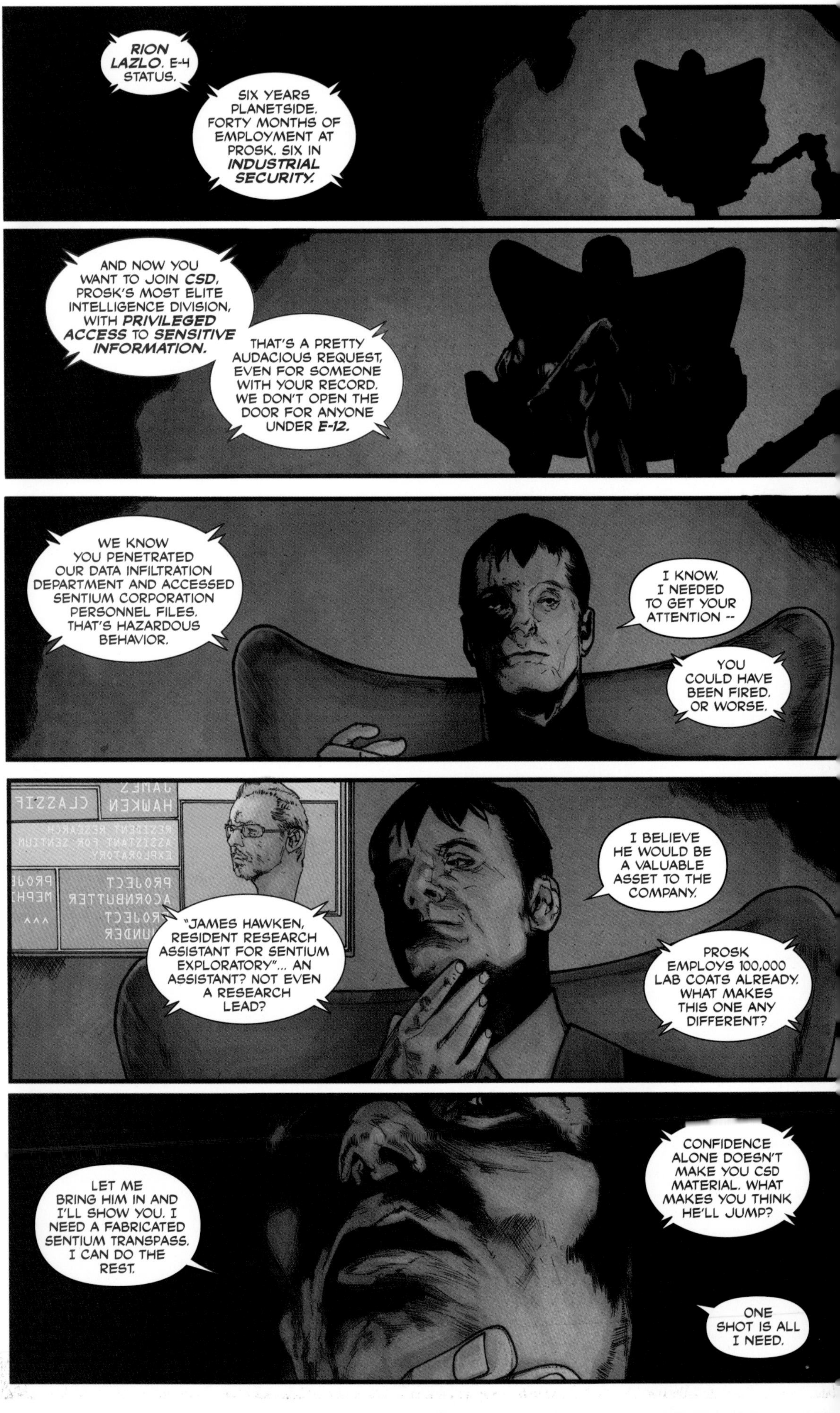
RION LAZLO, E-4 STATUS.
SIX YEARS PLANETSIDE. FORTY MONTHS OF EMPLOYMENT AT PROSK. SIX IN INDUSTRIAL SECURITY.
AND NOW YOU WANT TO JOIN CSD, PROSK'S MOST ELITE INTELLIGENCE DIVISION, WITH PRIVILEGED ACCESS TO SENSITIVE INFORMATION.
THAT'S A PRETTY AUDACIOUS REQUEST, EVEN FOR SOMEONE WITH YOUR RECORD. WE DON'T OPEN THE DOOR FOR ANYONE UNDER E-12.
WE KNOW YOU PENETRATED OUR DATA INFILTRATION DEPARTMENT AND ACCESSED SENTIUM CORPORATION PERSONNEL FILES. THAT'S HAZARDOUS BEHAVIOR.
I KNOW. I NEEDED TO GET YOUR ATTENTION --
YOU COULD HAVE BEEN FIRED. OR WORSE.
I BELIEVE HE WOULD BE A VALUABLE ASSET TO THE COMPANY.
"JAMES HAWKEN, RESIDENT RESEARCH ASSISTANT FOR SENTIUM EXPLORATORY"... AN ASSISTANT? NOT EVEN A RESEARCH LEAD?
PROSK EMPLOYS 100,000 LAB COATS ALREADY. WHAT MAKES THIS ONE ANY DIFFERENT?
LET ME BRING HIM IN AND I'LL SHOW YOU. I NEED A FABRICATED SENTIUM TRANSPASS. I CAN DO THE REST.
CONFIDENCE ALONE DOESN'T MAKE YOU CSD MATERIAL. WHAT MAKES YOU THINK HE'LL JUMP?
ONE SHOT IS ALL I NEED.

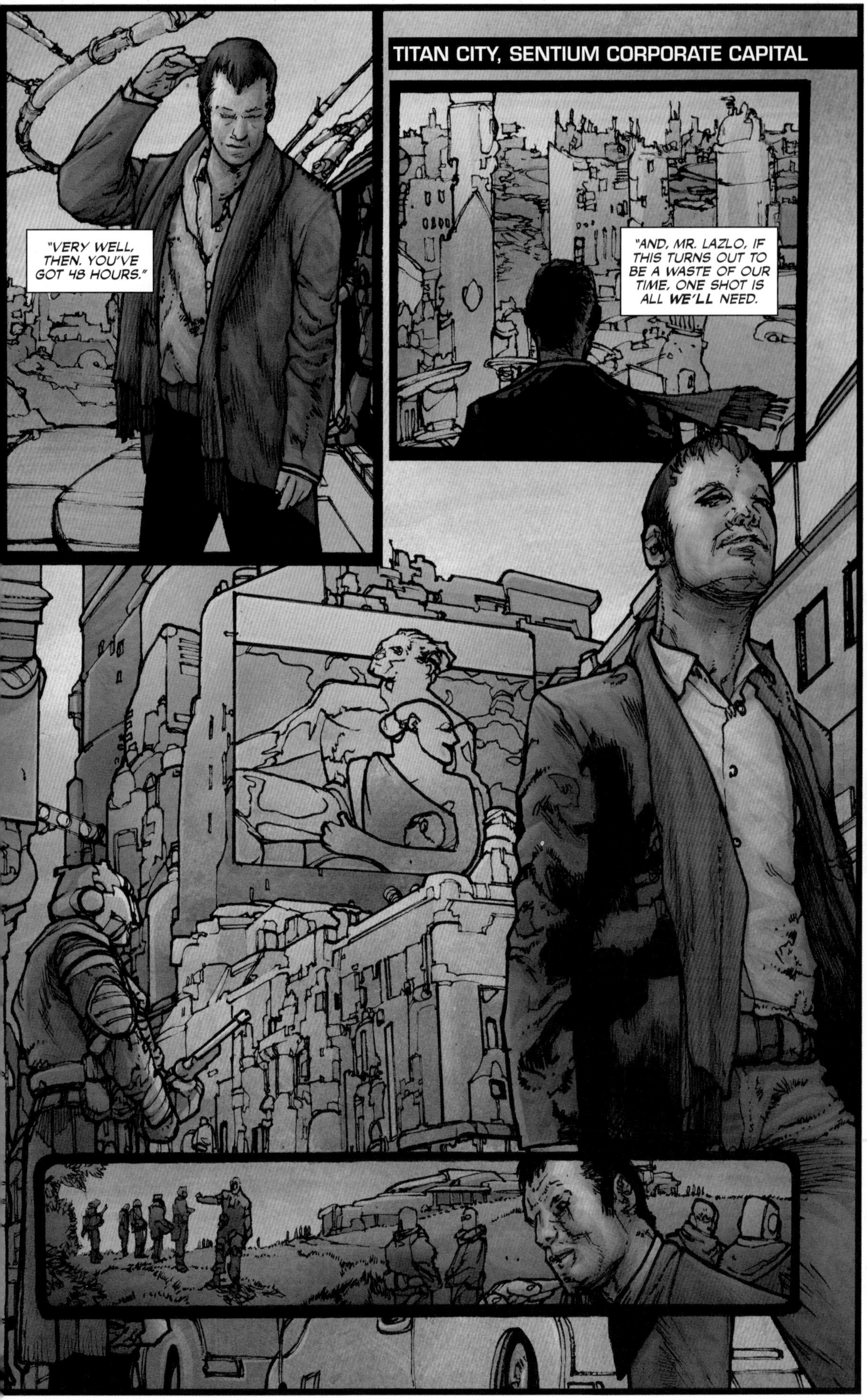
"VERY WELL, THEN. YOU'VE GOT 48 HOURS."
TITAN CITY, SENTIUM CORPORATE CAPITAL
"AND, MR. LAZLO, IF THIS TURNS OUT TO BE A WASTE OF OUR TIME, ONE SHOT IS ALL WE'LL NEED.

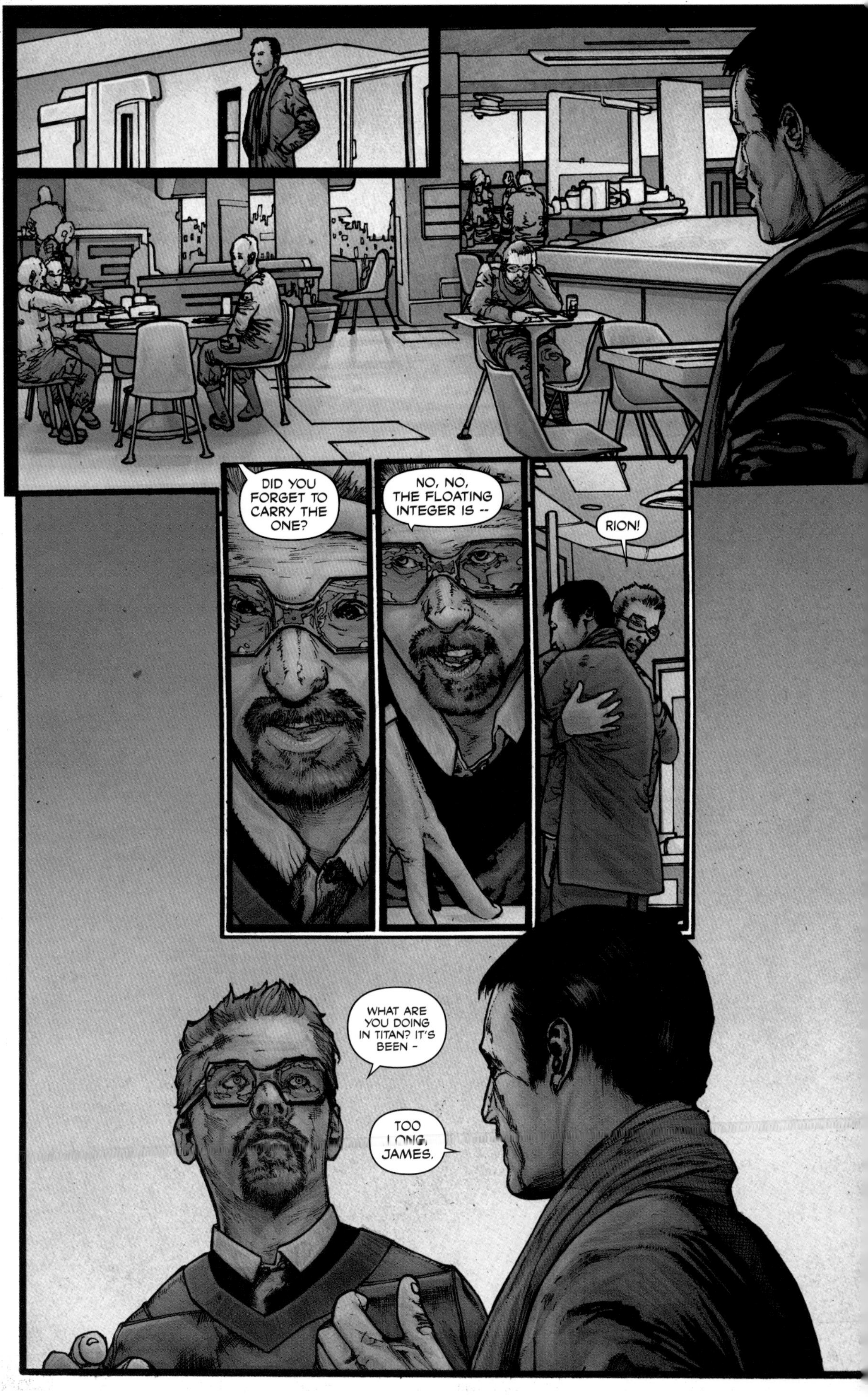
DID YOU FORGET TO CARRY THE ONE?
NO, NO, THE FLOATING INTEGER IS --
RION!
WHAT ARE YOU DOING IN TITAN? IT'S BEEN -
TOO LONG, JAMES.

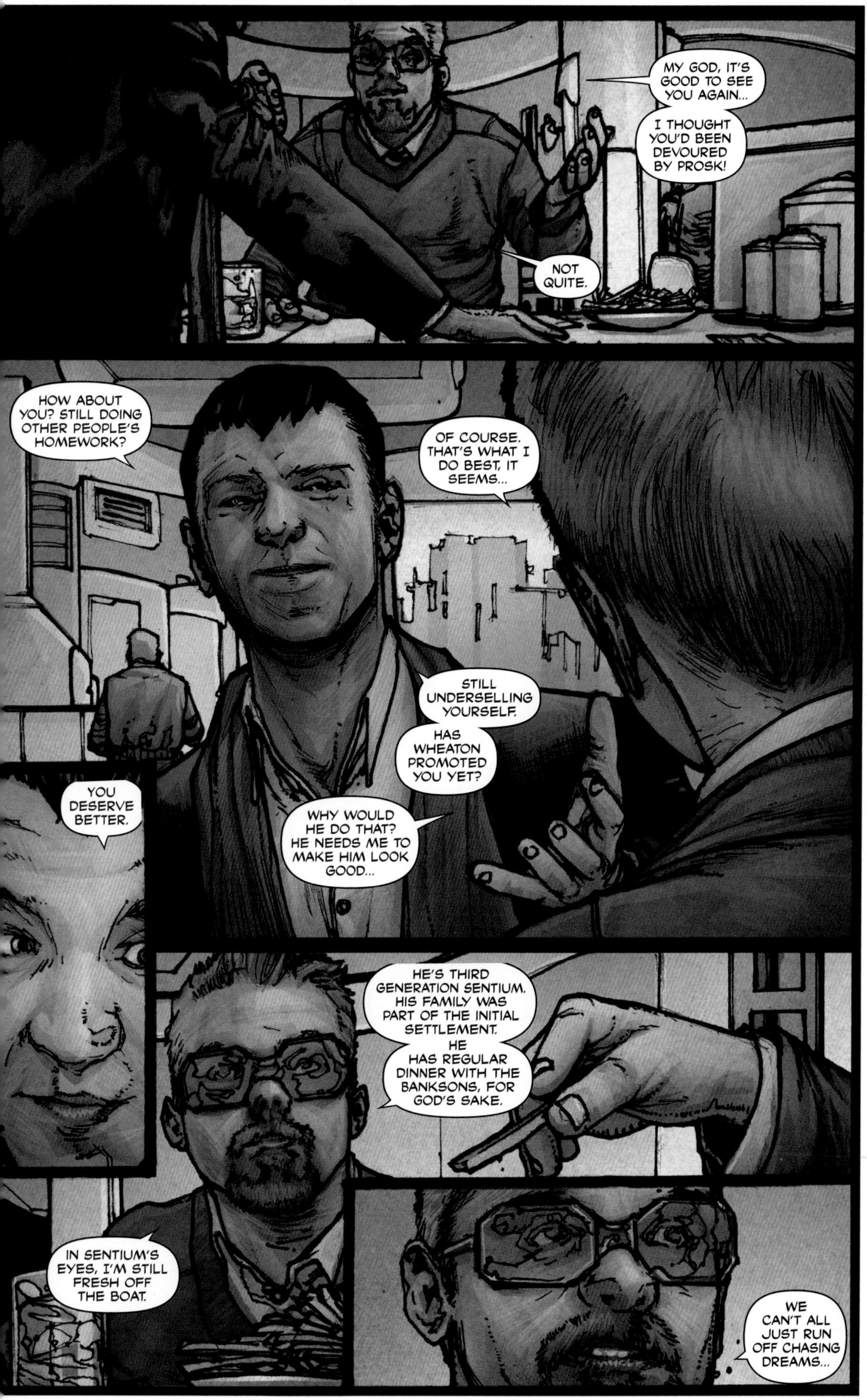
MY GOD, IT'S GOOD TO SEE YOU AGAIN...
I THOUGHT YOU'D BEEN DEVOURED BY PROSK!
NOT QUITE.
HOW ABOUT YOU? STILL DOING OTHER PEOPLE'S HOMEWORK?
OF COURSE. THAT'S WHAT I DO BEST, IT SEEMS...
STILL UNDERSELLING YOURSELF.
HAS WHEATON PROMOTED YOU YET?
WHY WOULD HE DO THAT? HE NEEDS ME TO MAKE HIM LOOK GOOD...
YOU DESERVE BETTER.
HE'S THIRD GENERATION SENTIUM. HIS FAMILY WAS PART OF THE INITIAL SETTLEMENT.
HE HAS REGULAR DINNER WITH THE BANKSONS, FOR GOD'S SAKE.
IN SENTIUM'S EYES, I'M STILL FRESH OFF THE BOAT.
WE CAN'T ALL JUST RUN OFF CHASING DREAMS...

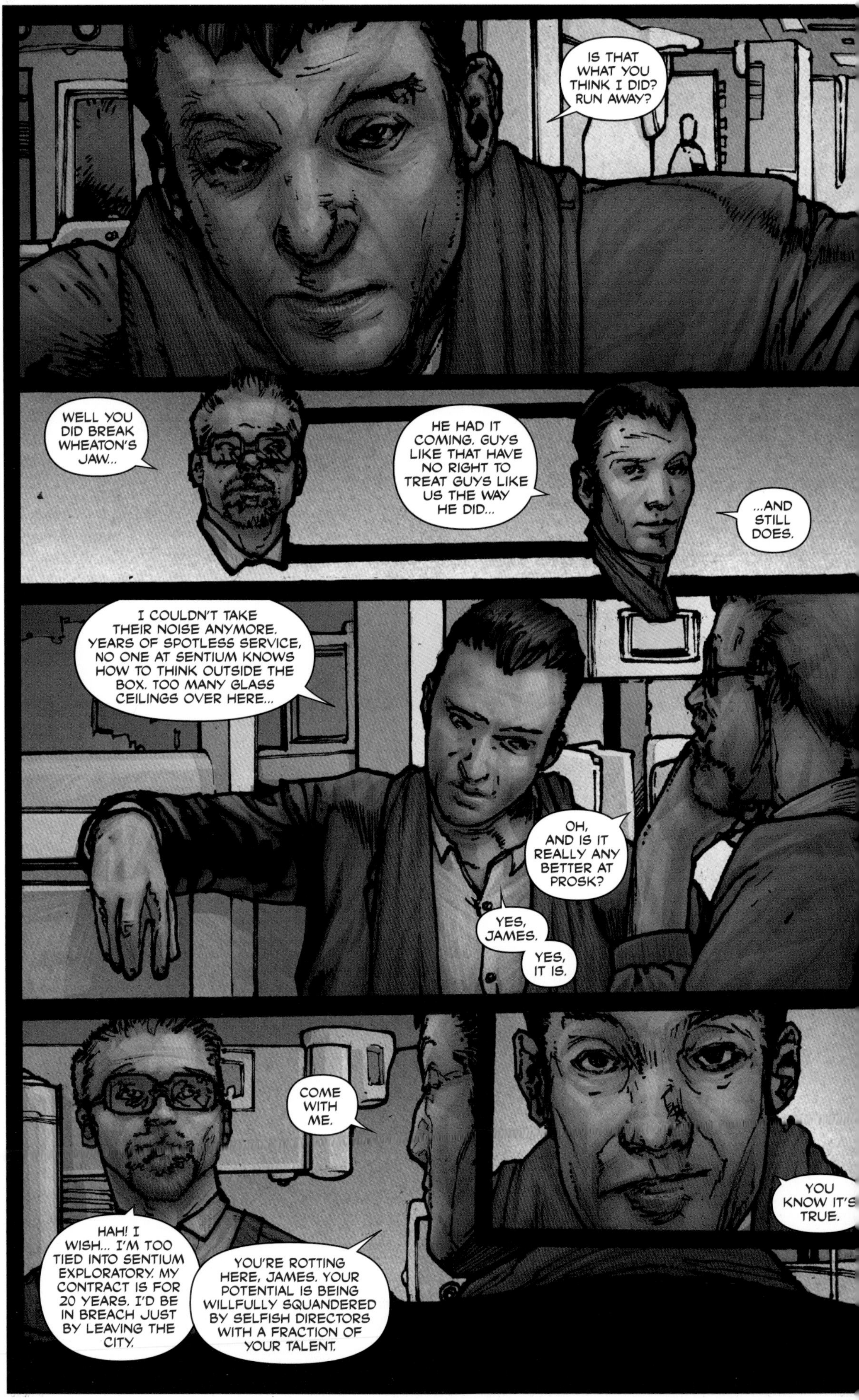

IS THAT WHAT YOU THINK I DID? RUN AWAY?
WELL YOU DID BREAK WHEATON'S JAW...
HE HAD IT COMING. GUYS LIKE THAT HAVE NO RIGHT TO TREAT GUYS LIKE US THE WAY HE DID...
...AND STILL DOES.
I COULDN'T TAKE THEIR NOISE ANYMORE. YEARS OF SPOTLESS SERVICE, NO ONE AT SENTIUM KNOWS HOW TO THINK OUTSIDE THE BOX. TOO MANY GLASS CEILINGS OVER HERE...
OH, AND IS IT REALLY ANY BETTER AT PROSK?
YES, JAMES.
YES, IT IS.
COME WITH ME.
YOU KNOW IT'S TRUE.
HAH! I WISH... I'M TOO TIED INTO SENTIUM EXPLORATORY. MY CONTRACT IS FOR 20 YEARS. I'D BE IN BREACH JUST BY LEAVING THE CITY.
YOU'RE ROTTING HERE, JAMES. YOUR POTENTIAL IS BEING WILLFULLY SQUANDERED BY SELFISH DIRECTORS WITH A FRACTION OF YOUR TALENT.

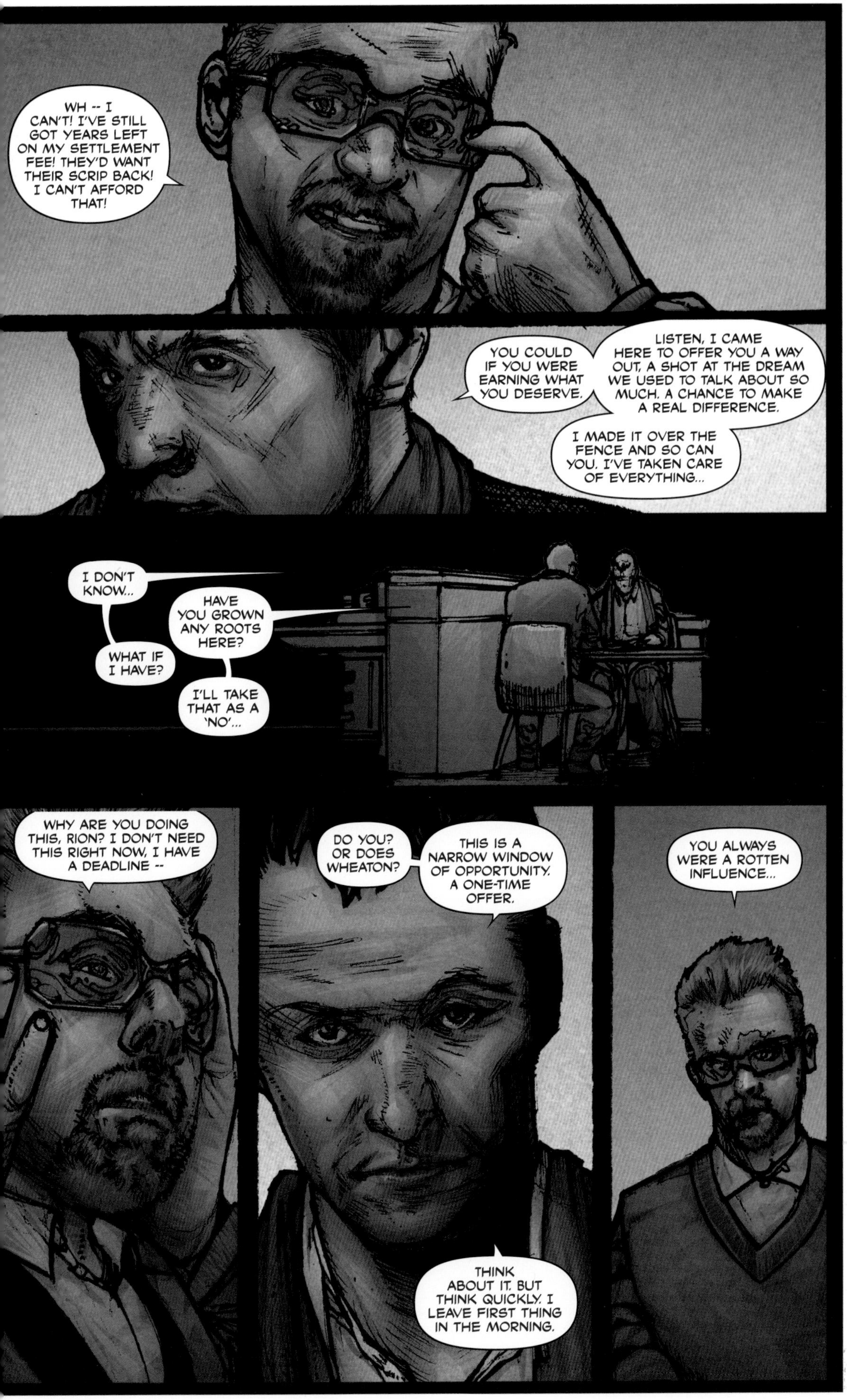
WH -- I CAN'T! I'VE STILL GOT YEARS LEFT ON MY SETTLEMENT FEE! THEY'D WANT THEIR SCRIP BACK! I CAN'T AFFORD THAT!
YOU COULD IF YOU WERE EARNING WHAT YOU DESERVE.
LISTEN, I CAME HERE TO OFFER YOU A WAY OUT, A SHOT AT THE DREAM WE USED TO TALK ABOUT SO MUCH. A CHANCE TO MAKE A REAL DIFFERENCE.
I MADE IT OVER THE FENCE AND SO CAN YOU. I'VE TAKEN CARE OF EVERYTHING...
I DON'T KNOW...
HAVE YOU GROWN ANY ROOTS HERE?
WHAT IF I HAVE?
I'LL TAKE THAT AS A 'NO'...
WHY ARE YOU DOING THIS, RION? I DON'T NEED THIS RIGHT NOW, I HAVE A DEADLINE --
DO YOU? OR DOES WHEATON?
THIS IS A NARROW WINDOW OF OPPORTUNITY. A ONE-TIME OFFER.
THINK ABOUT IT. BUT THINK QUICKLY. I LEAVE FIRST THING IN THE MORNING.
YOU ALWAYS WERE A ROTTEN INFLUENCE...

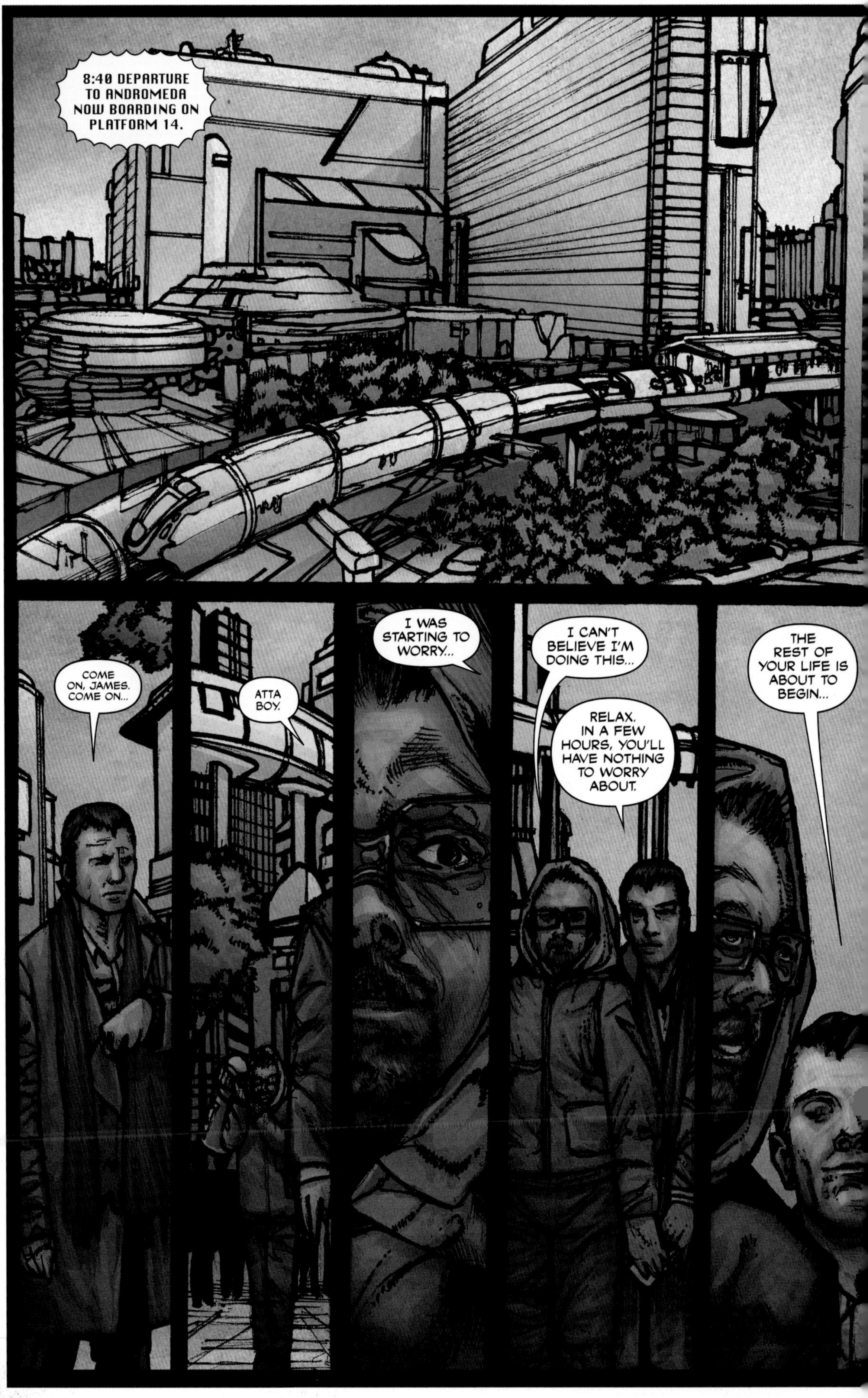
8:40 DEPARTURE TO ANDROMEDA NOW BOARDING ON PLATFORM 14.
COME ON, JAMES. COME ON...
ATTA BOY.
I WAS STARTING TO WORRY...
I CAN'T BELIEVE I'M DOING THIS...
RELAX. IN A FEW HOURS, YOU'LL HAVE NOTHING TO WORRY ABOUT.
THE REST OF YOUR LIFE IS ABOUT TO BEGIN...

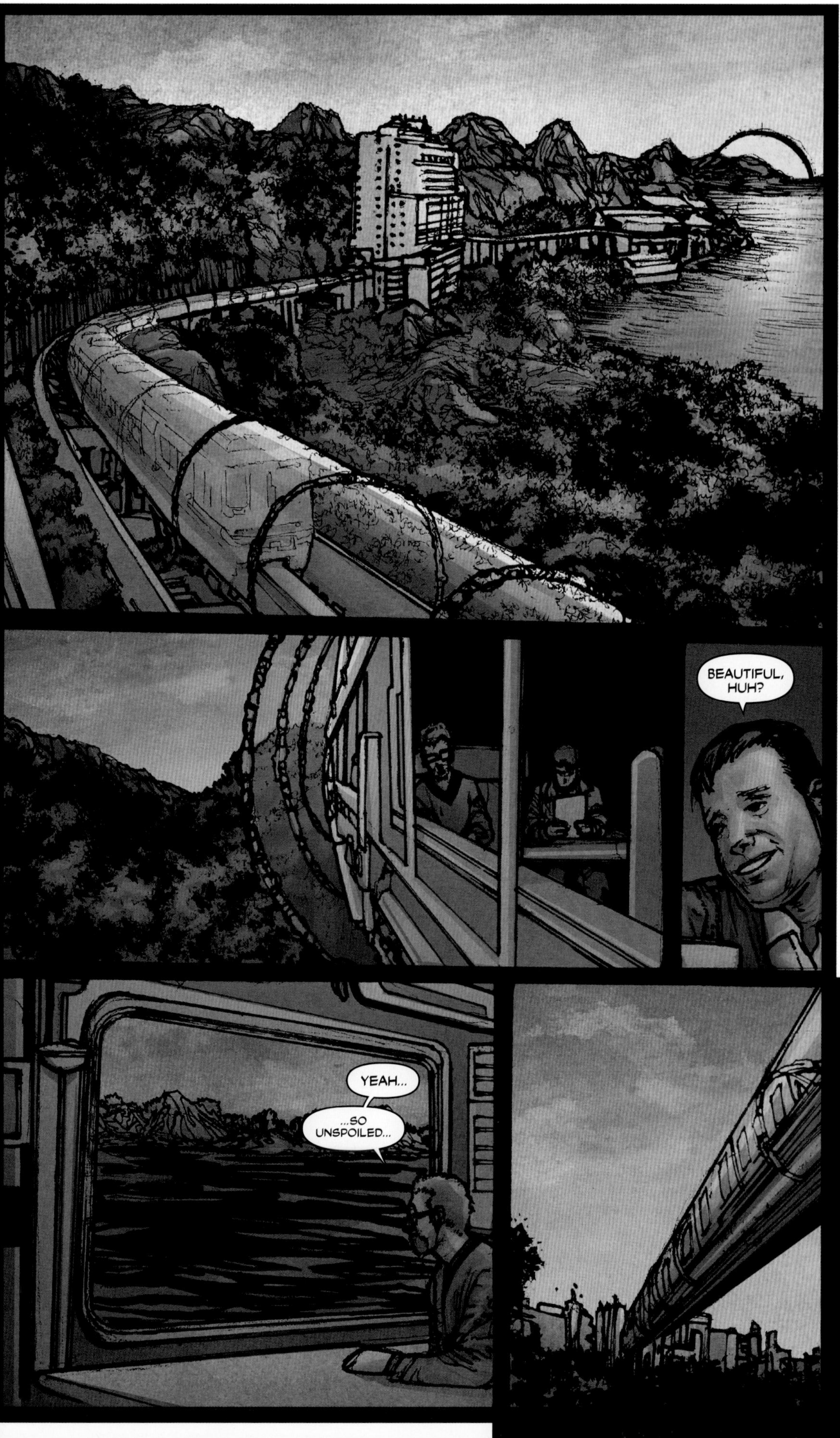
BEAUTIFUL, HUH?
YEAH...
...SO UNSPOILED...

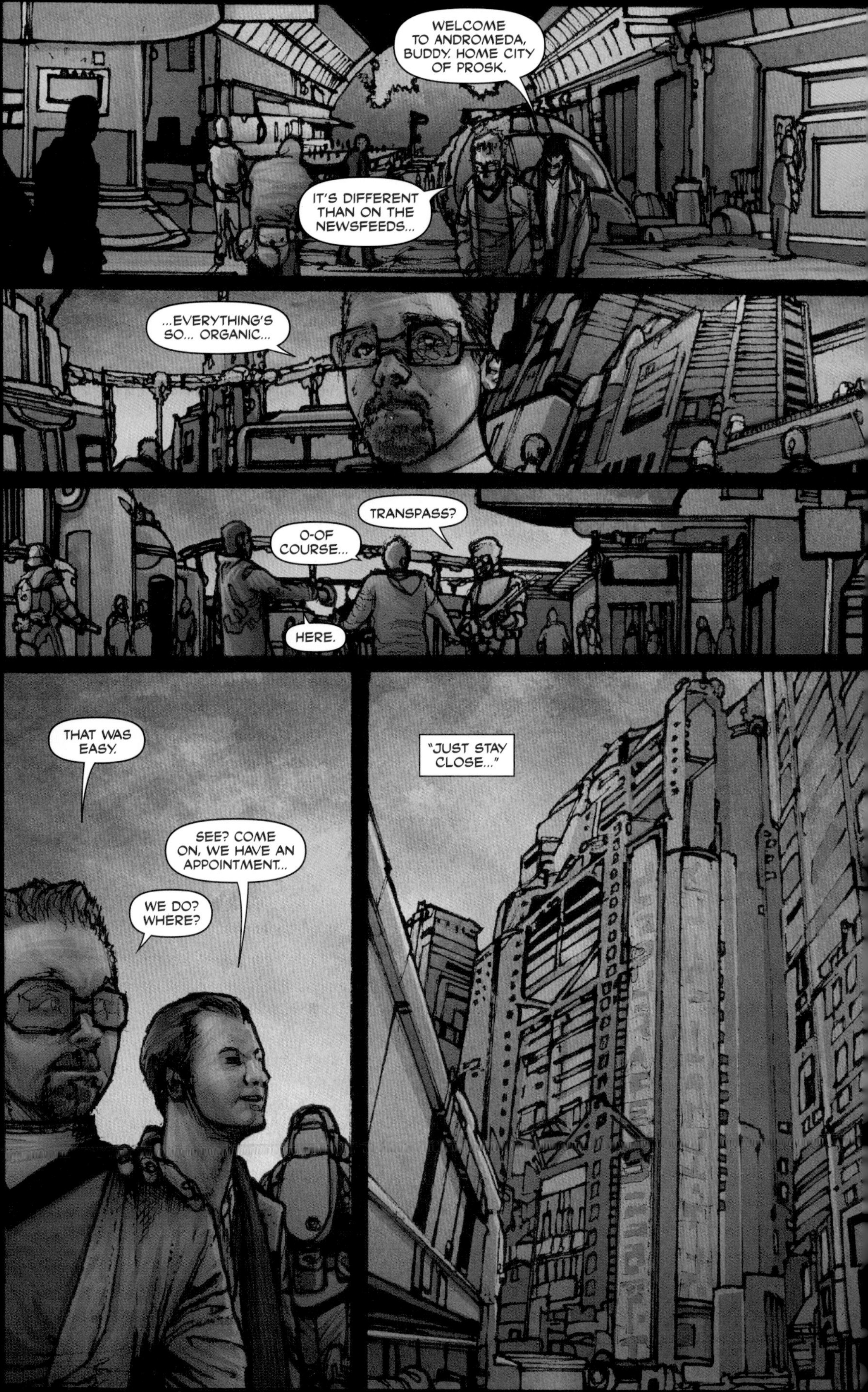
WELCOME TO ANDROMEDA, BUDDY. HOME CITY OF PROSK.
IT'S DIFFERENT THAN ON THE NEWSFEEDS...
...EVERYTHING'S SO... ORGANIC...
TRANSPASS?
O-OF COURSE...
HERE.
THAT WAS EASY.
SEE? COME ON, WE HAVE AN APPOINTMENT...
WE DO? WHERE?
"JUST STAY CLOSE..."

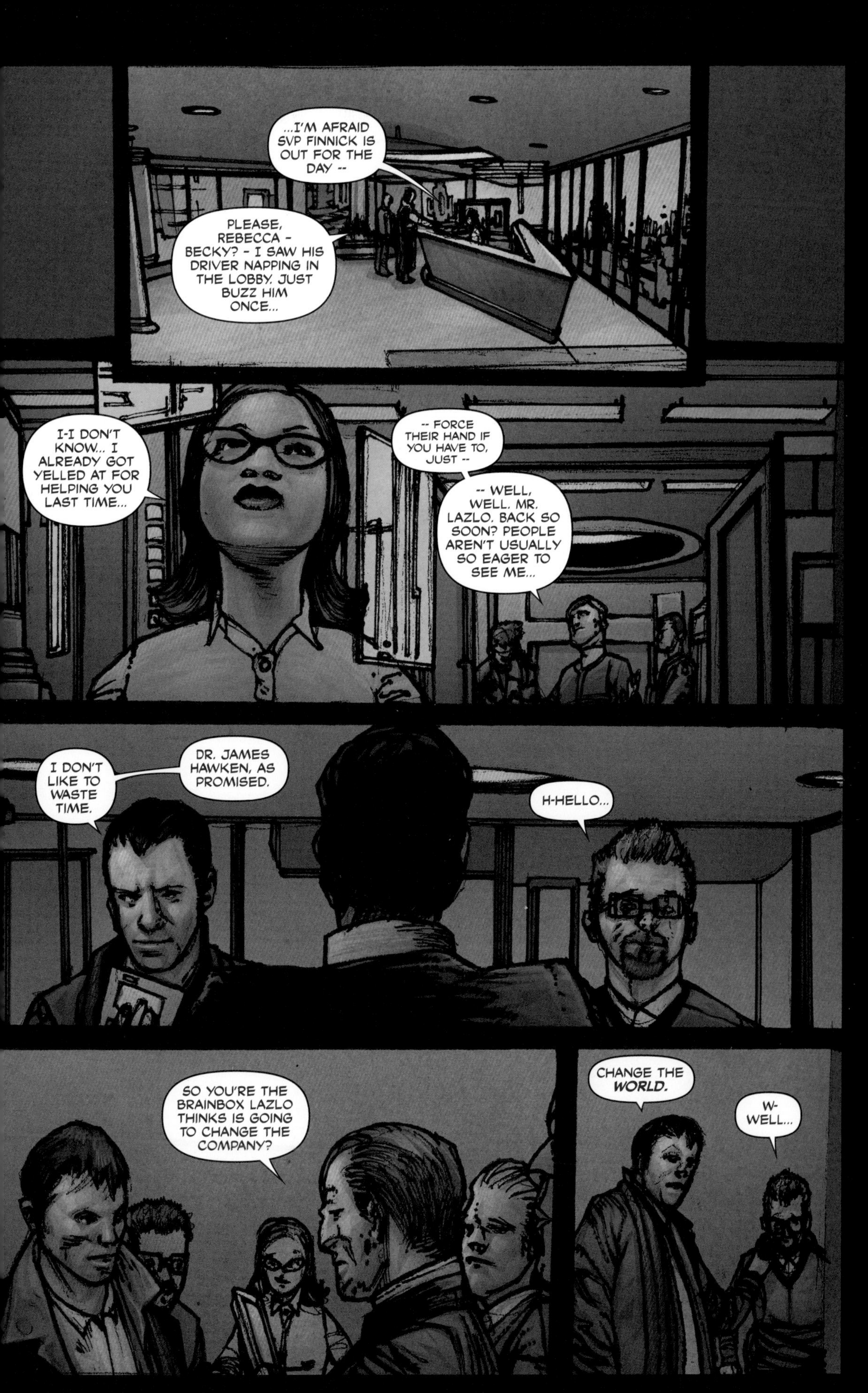
...I'M AFRAID SVP FINNICK IS OUT FOR THE DAY --
PLEASE, REBECCA - BECKY? - I SAW HIS DRIVER NAPPING IN THE LOBBY. JUST BUZZ HIM ONCE...
I-I DON'T KNOW... I ALREADY GOT YELLED AT FOR HELPING YOU LAST TIME...
-- FORCE THEIR HAND IF YOU HAVE TO, JUST --
-- WELL, WELL, MR. LAZLO. BACK SO SOON? PEOPLE AREN'T USUALLY SO EAGER TO SEE ME...
I DON'T LIKE TO WASTE TIME.
DR. JAMES HAWKEN, AS PROMISED.
H-HELLO...
SO YOU'RE THE BRAINBOX LAZLO THINKS IS GOING TO CHANGE THE COMPANY?
CHANGE THE *WORLD.*
W-WELL...

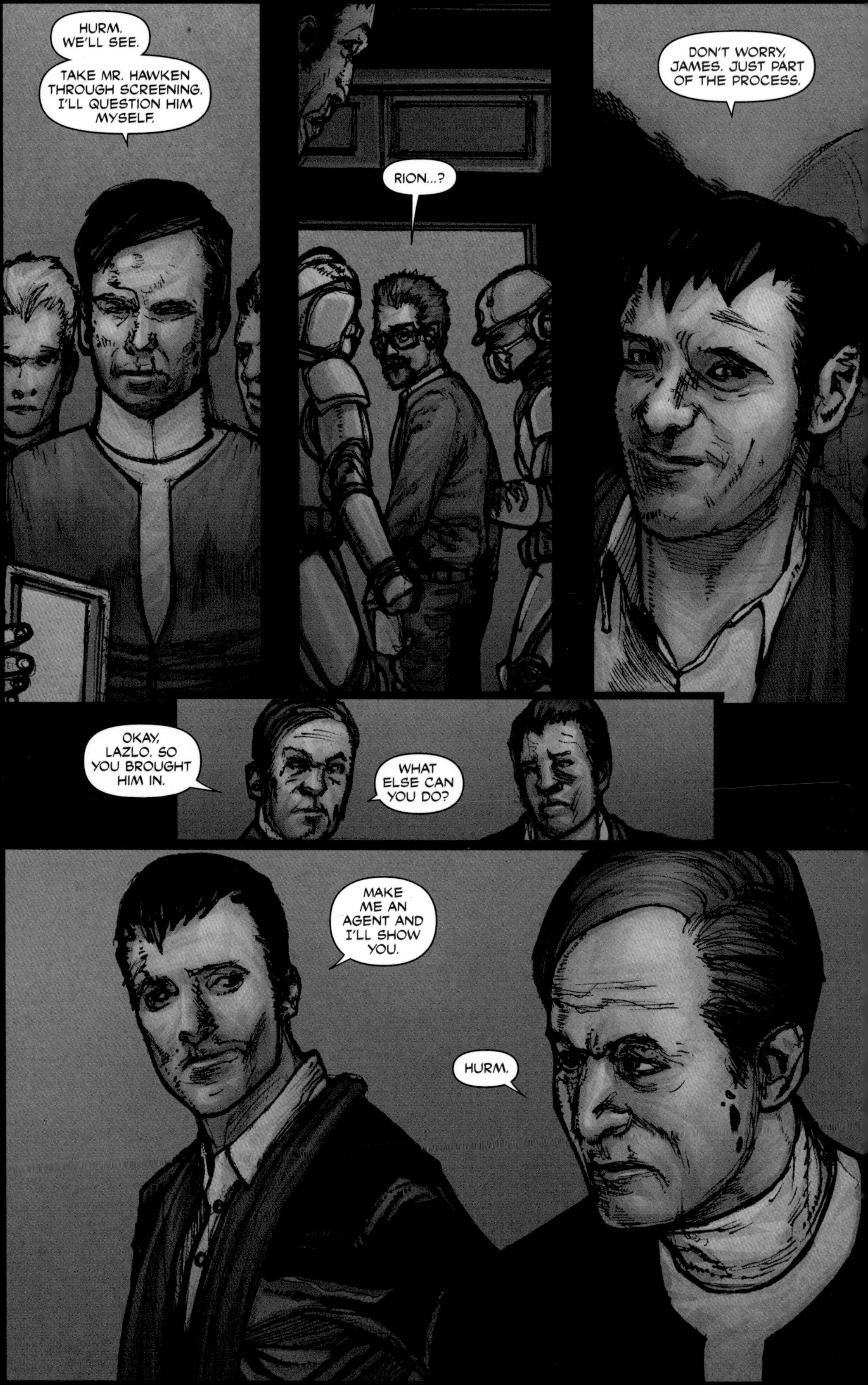
HURM. WE'LL SEE.
TAKE MR. HAWKEN THROUGH SCREENING. I'LL QUESTION HIM MYSELF.
RION...?
DON'T WORRY, JAMES. JUST PART OF THE PROCESS.
OKAY, LAZLO. SO YOU BROUGHT HIM IN.
WHAT ELSE CAN YOU DO?
MAKE ME AN AGENT AND I'LL SHOW YOU.
HURM.

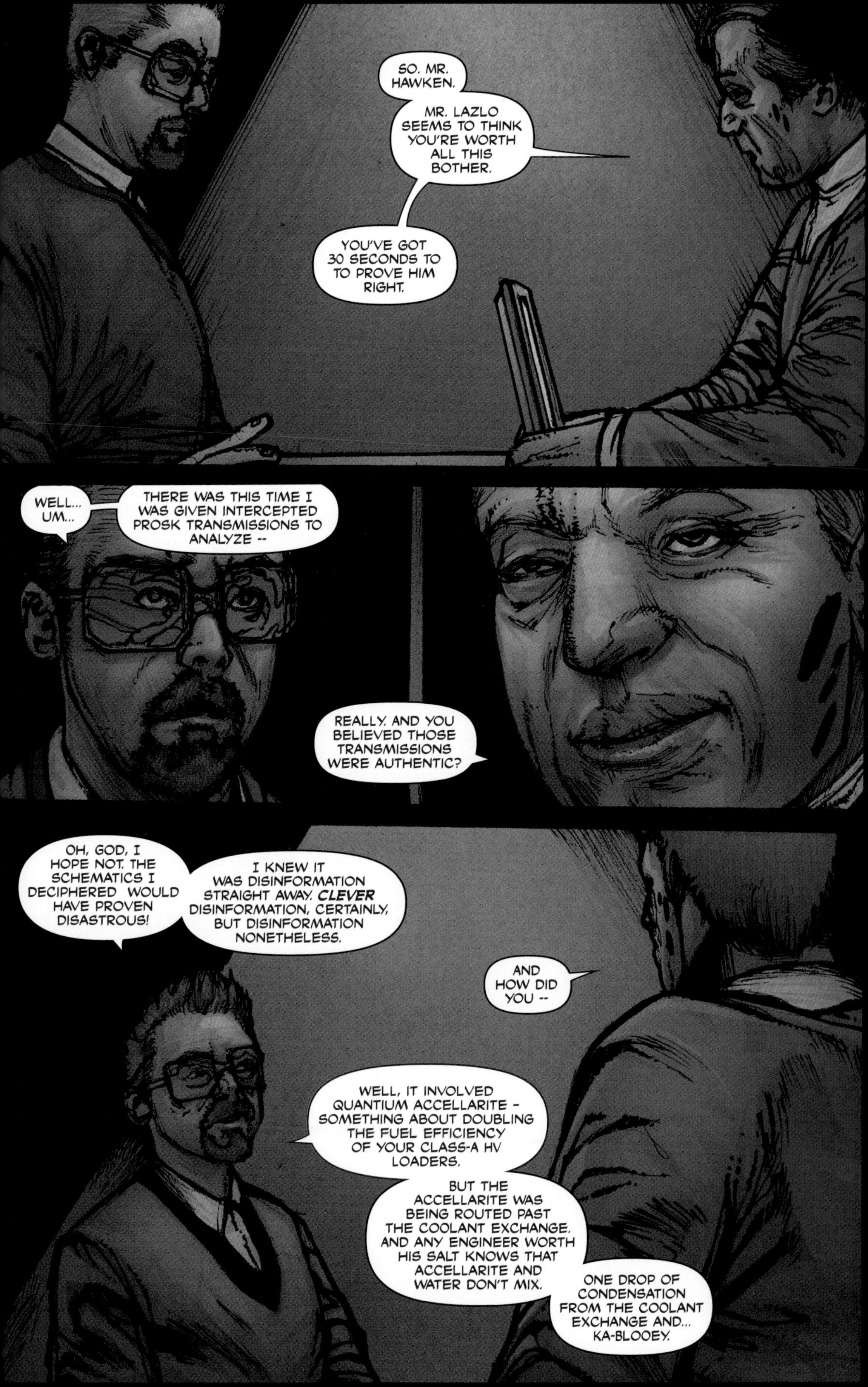
SO, MR. HAWKEN.
MR. LAZLO SEEMS TO THINK YOU'RE WORTH ALL THIS BOTHER.
YOU'VE GOT 30 SECONDS TO TO PROVE HIM RIGHT.
WELL... UM...
THERE WAS THIS TIME I WAS GIVEN INTERCEPTED PROSK TRANSMISSIONS TO ANALYZE --
REALLY. AND YOU BELIEVED THOSE TRANSMISSIONS WERE AUTHENTIC?
OH, GOD, I HOPE NOT. THE SCHEMATICS I DECIPHERED WOULD HAVE PROVEN DISASTROUS!
I KNEW IT WAS DISINFORMATION STRAIGHT AWAY. ***CLEVER*** DISINFORMATION, CERTAINLY, BUT DISINFORMATION NONETHELESS.
AND HOW DID YOU --
WELL, IT INVOLVED QUANTIUM ACCELLARITE - SOMETHING ABOUT DOUBLING THE FUEL EFFICIENCY OF YOUR CLASS-A HV LOADERS.
BUT THE ACCELLARITE WAS BEING ROUTED PAST THE COOLANT EXCHANGE. AND ANY ENGINEER WORTH HIS SALT KNOWS THAT ACCELLARITE AND WATER DON'T MIX.
ONE DROP OF CONDENSATION FROM THE COOLANT EXCHANGE AND... KA-BLOOEY.

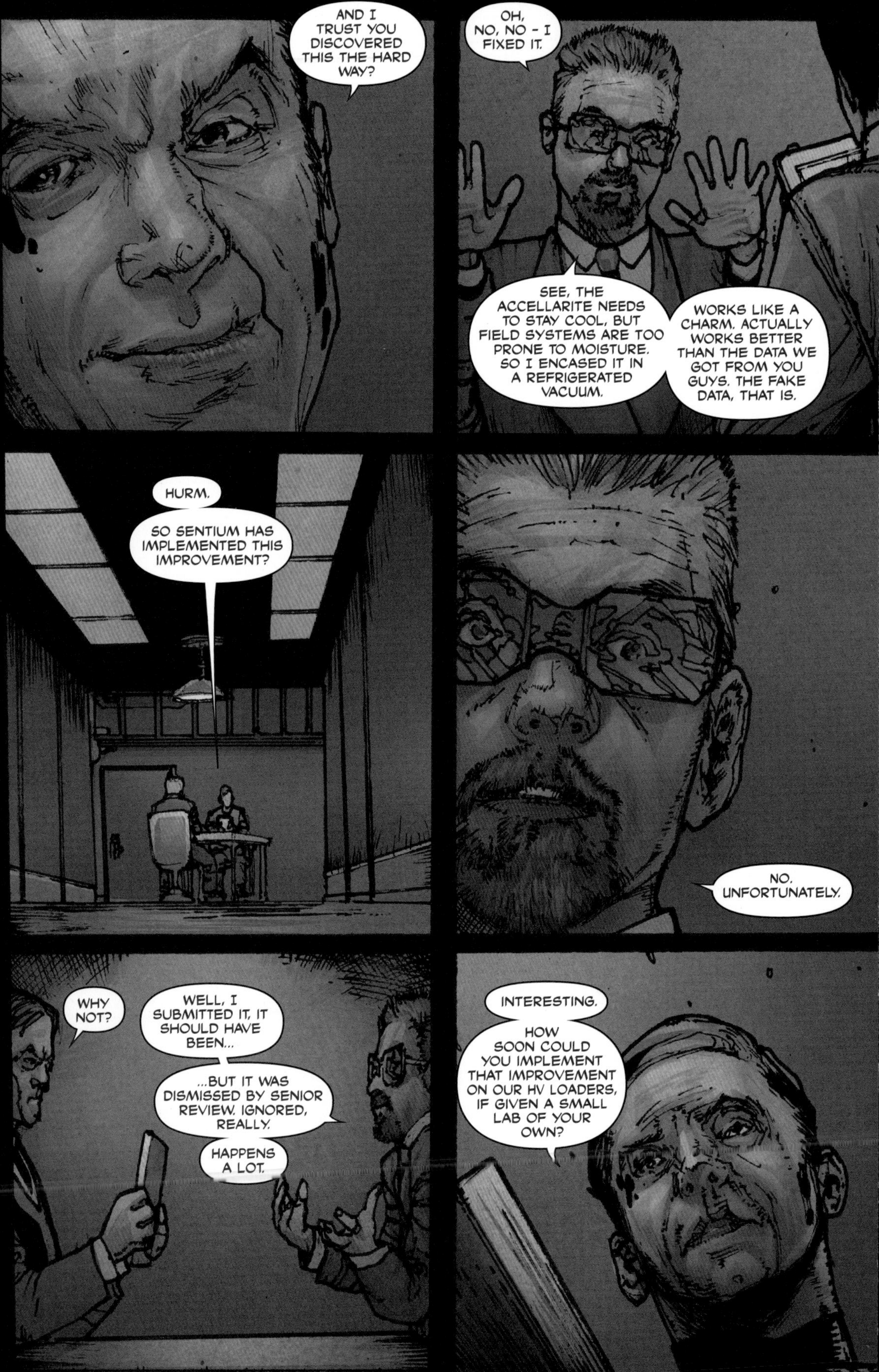
AND I TRUST YOU DISCOVERED THIS THE HARD WAY?
OH, NO, NO - I FIXED IT.
SEE, THE ACCELLARITE NEEDS TO STAY COOL, BUT FIELD SYSTEMS ARE TOO PRONE TO MOISTURE. SO I ENCASED IT IN A REFRIGERATED VACUUM.
WORKS LIKE A CHARM. ACTUALLY WORKS BETTER THAN THE DATA WE GOT FROM YOU GUYS. THE FAKE DATA, THAT IS.
HURM.
SO SENTIUM HAS IMPLEMENTED THIS IMPROVEMENT?
NO. UNFORTUNATELY.
WHY NOT?
WELL, I SUBMITTED IT, IT SHOULD HAVE BEEN...
...BUT IT WAS DISMISSED BY SENIOR REVIEW. IGNORED, REALLY.
HAPPENS A LOT.
INTERESTING.
HOW SOON COULD YOU IMPLEMENT THAT IMPROVEMENT ON OUR HV LOADERS, IF GIVEN A SMALL LAB OF YOUR OWN?

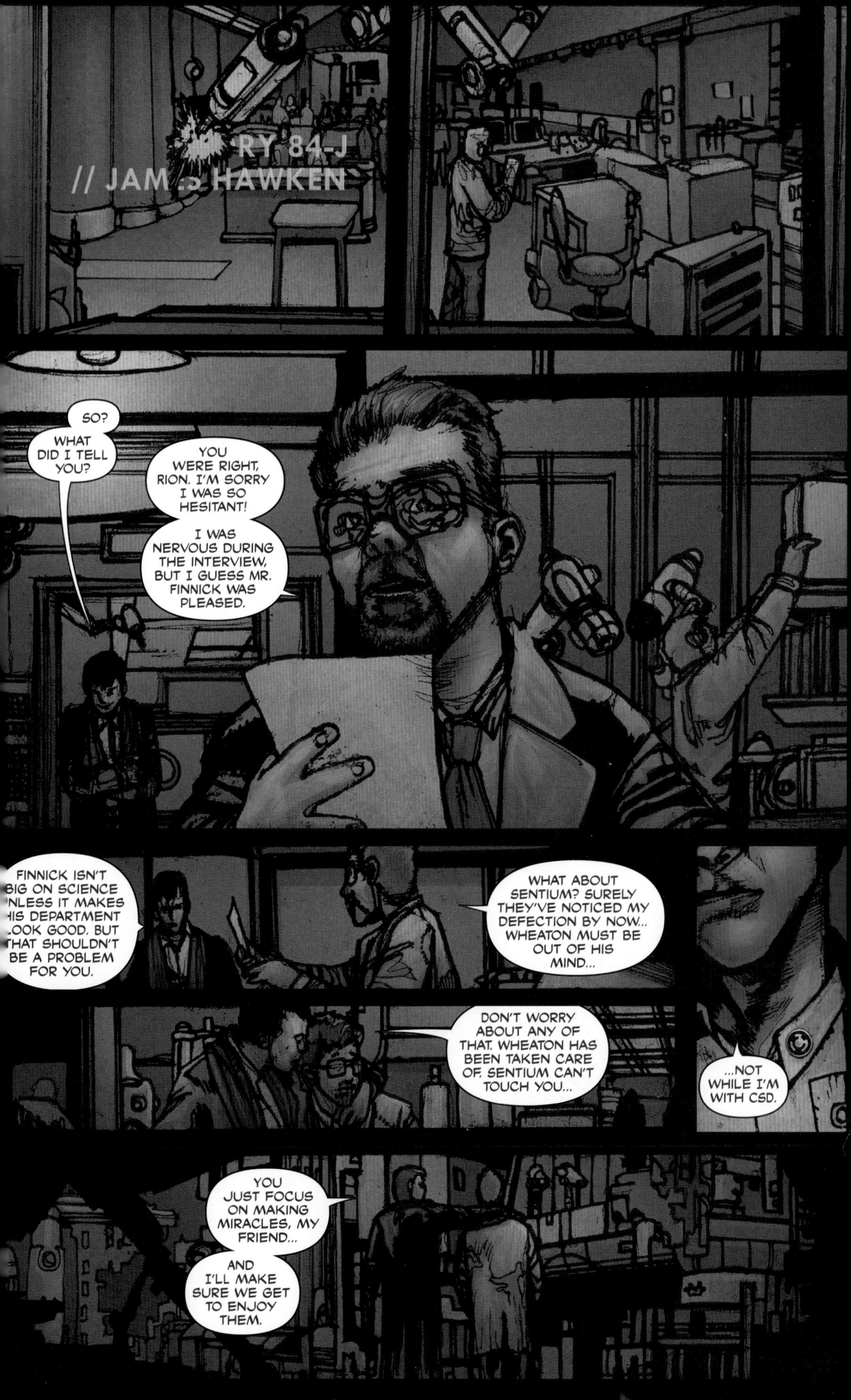

RY 84-J
// JAM S HAWKEN
SO? WHAT DID I TELL YOU?
YOU WERE RIGHT, RION. I'M SORRY I WAS SO HESITANT!
I WAS NERVOUS DURING THE INTERVIEW, BUT I GUESS MR. FINNICK WAS PLEASED.
FINNICK ISN'T BIG ON SCIENCE NLESS IT MAKES HIS DEPARTMENT LOOK GOOD. BUT THAT SHOULDN'T BE A PROBLEM FOR YOU.
WHAT ABOUT SENTIUM? SURELY THEY'VE NOTICED MY DEFECTION BY NOW... WHEATON MUST BE OUT OF HIS MIND...
DON'T WORRY ABOUT ANY OF THAT. WHEATON HAS BEEN TAKEN CARE OF. SENTIUM CAN'T TOUCH YOU...
...NOT WHILE I'M WITH CSD.
YOU JUST FOCUS ON MAKING MIRACLES, MY FRIEND...
AND I'LL MAKE SURE WE GET TO ENJOY THEM.

Source Document://00.10843.01107.34dxv
Internal IP Address://819-001-6754-901-771

1.01

PERSONNEL REVIEW

LAZLO, RION

Math: 67 **Science:** 76 **English:** 82 **Social:** 89 **Reasoning:** 94

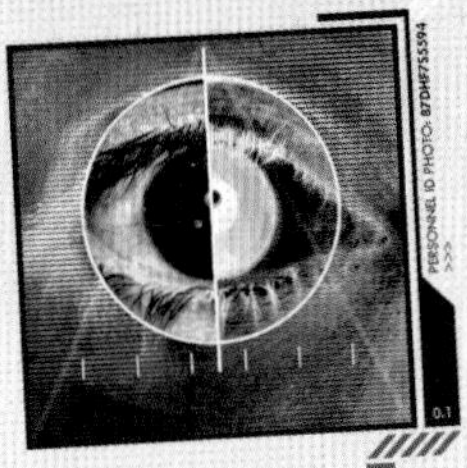

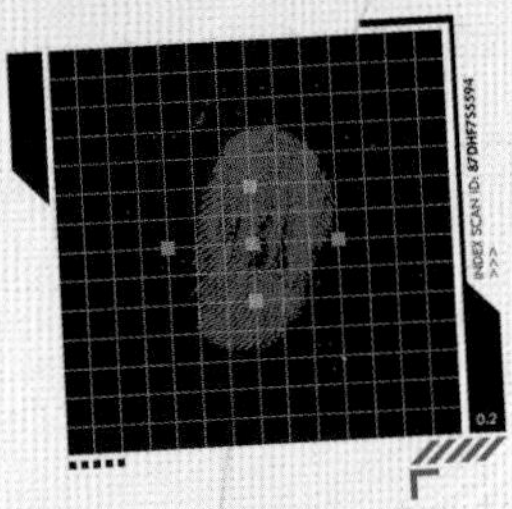

0015UT8
098O6H2
8YN532P
6R45JN8
9UN496K
5WN8438
3L9H64F
JN76F3U
987UHCX
6FIO8GD
2F1Q5AW
0CF11HY
95LYT56

UDID: 4VT3GY11X8FV544K0TT43997CR

Age:	28	**Hair:**	Brown
Height:	6'2"	**Eyes:**	Hazel
Weight:	189 lbs	**IQ:**	124
Patronage:	72 months	**Citizenship:**	24 months

PROSK SECURITY CLEARANCE LEVEL 2A

Notwithstanding relative deficiencies in math and science, Lazlo continually demonstrates above average verbal skills and excels in social acclimatization and fluid reasoning. These intra-cognitive strengths have instilled Lazlo with a substantiated confidence that colors his interactions with others. Despite limitations Lazlo's near uncanny ability to analyze a given situation, identify the critical path to his desired outcome and successfully influence it (typically via the exploitation of a systemic weakness) is nothing short of remarkable.

Though hindered by textbook alpha characteristics, Lazlo's ceaseless ambition and ingenuity command respect from his peers. He accepts responsibility with a conceited ease, unexpectedly showing a prowess for management, business, even politics. He seems subconsciously driven to maneuver himself into the spotlight, if only to self-validate his own ego and sense of entitlement. Lazlo mitigates his obvious narcissistic tendencies through his most dominant personality trait: loyalty. It is of paramount importance to him and is the only quality that overshadows his abject ambition. Few would question Lazlo's strength of conviction or his staunch devotion to Prosk. His pseudo-fraternal relationship with **James Hawken**[1] is a prime example of his capacity for unwavering trust. While Lazlo's self-absorption is cause for concern, he has consistently proven to be a valuable team member. As a point of record, though he clashes with most supervisors, he continues to receive uncharacteristically positive performance reviews. In spite of his myriad cognitive faults and personality deficiencies, it is hard not to be impressed by Mr. Lazlo. He continues to exceed expectations.

Quarterly Report :: **Lazlo, Rion** :: Commissioned >> November 29, 2334

PROSK SECURITY CLEARANCE LEVEL 9C

Reporting Agent: Ceril Berstyn **UDID:** 6GV73R1ZR166J6KO2242TW **Date:** 04.32.08.11.29.2334

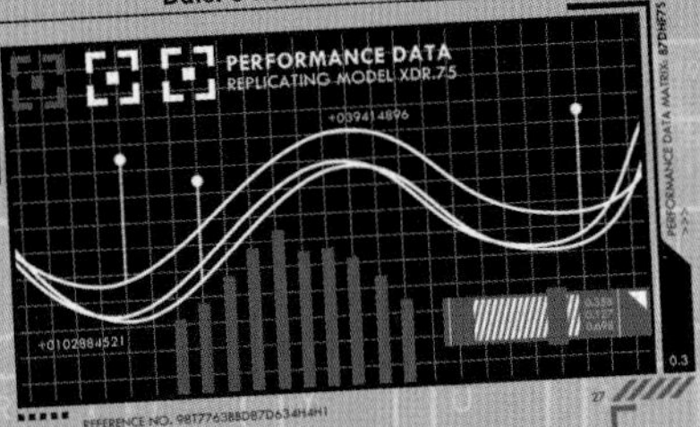
PERFORMANCE DATA
REPLICATING MODEL XDR.75

Overall, Lazlo has proven to be a valuable addition to CSD throughout this quarter. However it should be noted that his talent is still quite raw and requires substantial refinement. His combat aptitude, especially during the recent covert surveillance operation in the **Ashihan Forest**[1], proved to be extraordinarily effective. His desire to deliver results regardless of the moral ambiguity or the means is especially encouraging.

That being said, Lazlo is borderline reptilian in his planning and all too often adopts the most direct (i.e. obvious) path to his objective, leaving him to employ blunt force tactics when a more elegant approach might have produced superior results. Put simply he needs to learn patience. This was most apparent in the events of last week's exfil sortie to **Kobalt**[2]. Lazlo abandoned a pre-approved extraction plan before knowing enough circumstantial facts to make a prudent decision. During de-briefing Lazlo labeled these actions as "a calculated risk." However without knowing his true intent it is impossible to discern one way or another. This isn't the first time he has impulsively improvised maneuvers and referred to them as calculated risks, inferring that he understands the risk calculation involved with pre-mission planning, but willfully chooses to ignore it. This rebellious streak makes him a potential liability. Despite my misgivings, Director Finnick has reminded me that results are of ultimate relevance to this division, which Lazlo's record has in spades. Should Lazlo evolve from his current adolescent philosophy of short-term gratification, he could make a valuable executive one day. I recommend we continue to sharpen this otherwise blunt instrument. Lazlo may prove himself to be a versatile tool yet.

Data Classification://HRC0174556V98FDY

2.01

PERSONNEL REVIEW

HAWKEN, JAMES

Source Document://00.10751.01289.46dxy
Internal IP Address://819-001-6754-901-771

002

Math: 100 **Science:** 100 **English:** 94 **Social:** 23 **Reasoning:** 92

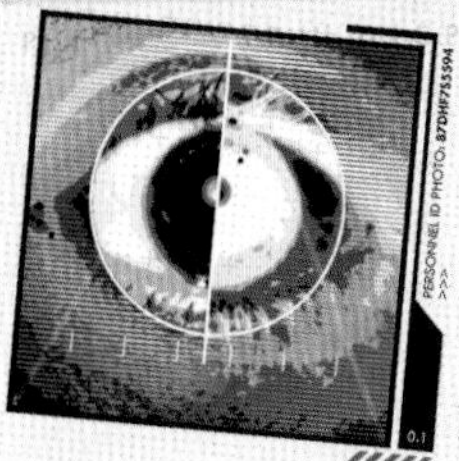

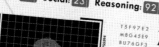

PERSONNEL ID PHOTO: 87DHF755594
0.1

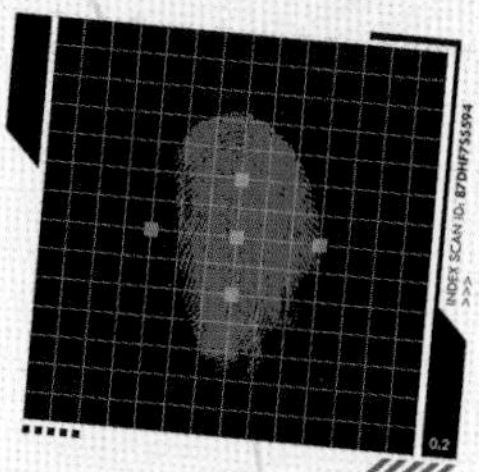

INDEX SCAN ID: 87DHF755594
0.2

T5F97E2
M8G45E9
BU76GF3
LP97G51
V765FCR
N8M765Q
ZRX4U87
K97G5D4
XCR4219
GS7K3H5
8HG5C3X
9H7C34S
B7G6T5E

UDID: 8BF6DF66C3AE616C5AA51616AD

Age:	26	**Hair:**	Blonde
Height:	5'11"	**Eyes:**	Blue
Weight:	173 lbs	**IQ:**	165
Patronage:	18 months	**Citizenship:**	60 months

PROSK SECURITY CLEARANCE LEVEL SCIENCE DIVISION **SCI-G**

REFERENCE NO. 79R6147BSN87F941Q2K2

97

Cognitive strengths are at unprecedented levels in math, science, verbal and reasoning, while significant weaknesses are evident in his social abilities and emotional state. These interpersonal deficits have impacted his professional environment in such a way that Hawken risks alienating himself from his entire team, if not being expelled by it all together. Hawken compensates for the challenge of interacting with others by isolating himself in his work, and indeed he sometimes generates brilliant theses, ideas and inventions. However, the rate of usable contributions is at a low enough ratio to ponder his relevance in terms of investment vs. reward.

To best understand Hawken, review his workstation and his interaction with it. Never have I seen a more disorganized mess of paperwork, research, or discarded food. Yet when you request something specific from Hawken, he burrows deep within the chaos and easily produces whatever content you requested as though from a magic hat. This is a small indication of his frustrating brilliance. Sadly his flexible intellectual clarity is at complete odds with his stunted emotional and social awareness. When confronted with sarcasm, resentment, even flirtation from a coworker, Hawken typically responds with averted eye-contact and mumbled phrases. It would be easy to classify Hawken as a man of pure logic. However to do so would demean the vast creative power that makes him such a potentially remarkable, if frustratingly inaccessible, asset.

Quarterly Report :: **Hawken, James** :: Commissioned >> November 11, 2334

Reporting Agent: Dr. Richard Buchanan **UDID:** 2HY3KK15T7XDW443B1PI8868UL

PROSK SECURITY CLEARANCE LEVEL **5B**

Date: 04.32.08.11.11.2334

Hawken's capacity for three-dimensional logic, reasoning, and deduction far surpass that of his peers in our Exploratory R&D division. When he has been effectively applied to the right project, he has invariably influenced its direction and design positively. The problem is his severe lack of desire to collaborate or interact in a group setting. As a result, he impedes overall innovation and progress, preferring to work alone and personally perform every step of an operation, even those I would consider beneath his talents.

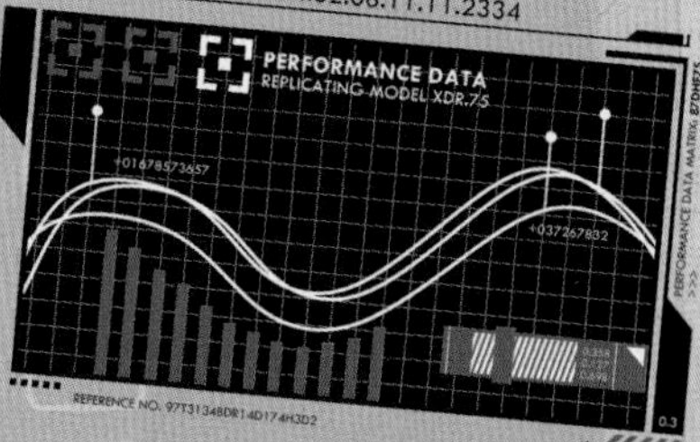

PERFORMANCE DATA
REPLICATING MODEL XDR.75
+01678573657
+037267832
PERFORMANCE DATA MATRIX: 87DHF75
REFERENCE NO. 97T31348DR14D174H3D2
0.3

This difficulty with personalities has caused professional issues between Hawken and his peers. Three lab-mates have requested reassignment in the last 18 months, with the most recent being **Dr. Zao**, just two weeks ago. Dr. Zao was overseeing Hawken's optimization of a new gear winch for the heavy loaders next fall. Hawken was instead consumed by his own tangential research in the nano-sciences, devoting his time and resources to the nano-genetic manipulation of crystallogens, icosagens, and other rare volatile metals. Rather than obsessing over scandium and cavorite, Zao demanded results on the winch. Hawken reportedly groaned, paused his research, and exported a single file onto Zao's server. Apparently Hawken had "finished" the job weeks ago. Zao scoffed and inquired into the schematics, cost-benefit reports, alpha and beta test builds... but Hawken had built and tested the model in his head alone. I reviewed Hawken's specs and built the prototype myself. The model worked as promised, without any need for further testing at **124% increased output$_3$**. This anecdote illustrates how Hawken's casual attitude toward Prosk projects and deadlines has bred the notion that he harbors contempt for his coworkers. Furthermore his esoteric intellectual pursuits tend toward subjects unrelated to product development. While Prosk has benefited from tangential research, Hawken's costs are monumental with little usable data to justify the expenditure. As actionable and articulate results are our goals, failure to deliver significant advances in the next quarter may force his reassignment, if not expulsion.

Data Classification://HSQ0149854V41FBY

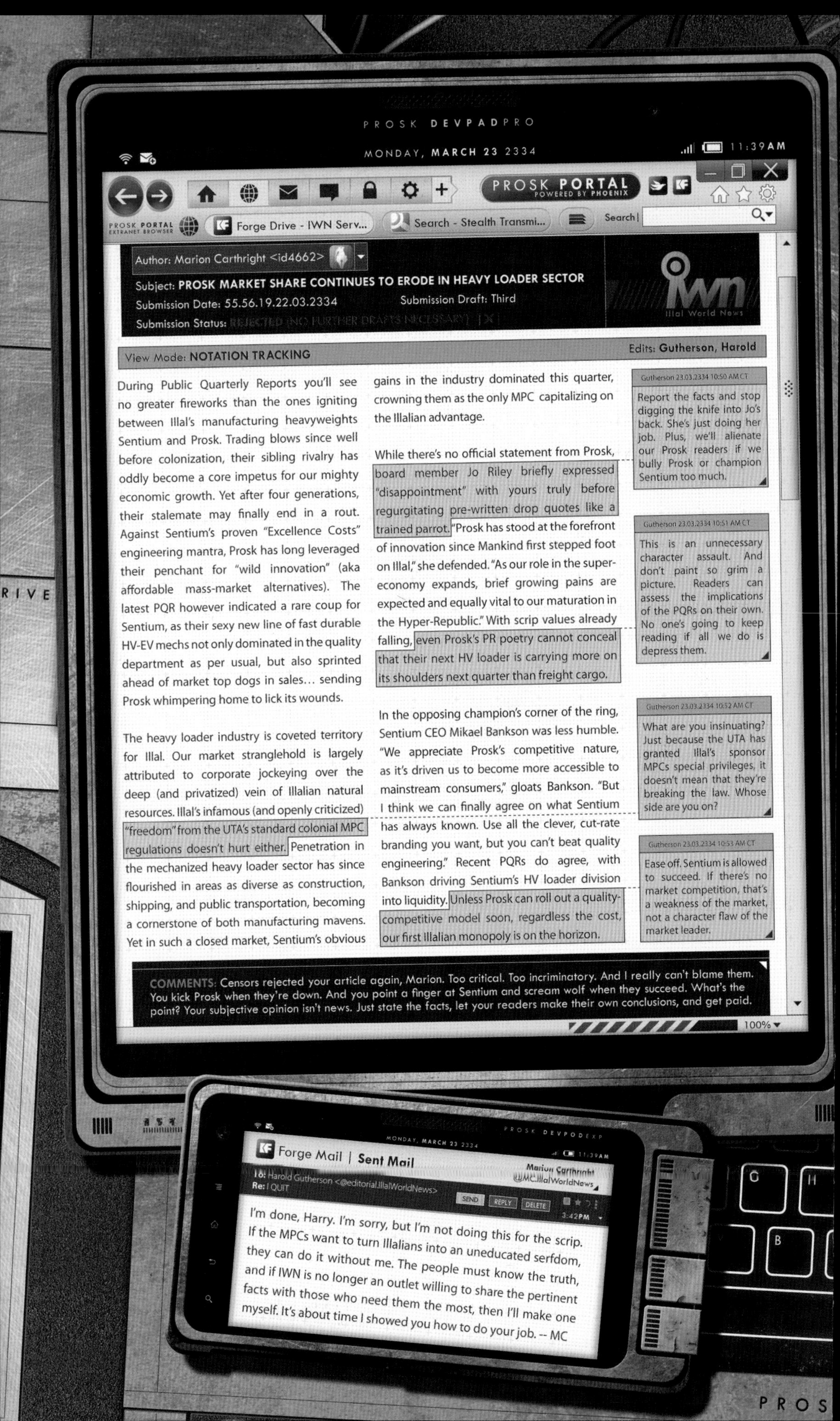
PROSK DEVPADPRO
MONDAY, MARCH 23 2334
11:39AM
PROSK PORTAL POWERED BY PHOENIX
PROSK PORTAL EXTRANET BROWSER
Forge Drive - IWN Serv...
Search - Stealth Transmi...
Search
Author: Marion Carthright <id4662>
Subject: PROSK MARKET SHARE CONTINUES TO ERODE IN HEAVY LOADER SECTOR
Submission Date: 55.56.19.22.03.2334
Submission Draft: Third
Submission Status: REJECTED (NO FURTHER DRAFTS NECESSARY)
IWN Illal World News
View Mode: NOTATION TRACKING
Edits: Gutherson, Harold
During Public Quarterly Reports you'll see no greater fireworks than the ones igniting between Illal's manufacturing heavyweights Sentium and Prosk. Trading blows since well before colonization, their sibling rivalry has oddly become a core impetus for our mighty economic growth. Yet after four generations, their stalemate may finally end in a rout. Against Sentium's proven "Excellence Costs" engineering mantra, Prosk has long leveraged their penchant for "wild innovation" (aka affordable mass-market alternatives). The latest PQR however indicated a rare coup for Sentium, as their sexy new line of fast durable HV-EV mechs not only dominated in the quality department as per usual, but also sprinted ahead of market top dogs in sales… sending Prosk whimpering home to lick its wounds.
The heavy loader industry is coveted territory for Illal. Our market stranglehold is largely attributed to corporate jockeying over the deep (and privatized) vein of Illalian natural resources. Illal's infamous (and openly criticized) "freedom" from the UTA's standard colonial MPC regulations doesn't hurt either. Penetration in the mechanized heavy loader sector has since flourished in areas as diverse as construction, shipping, and public transportation, becoming a cornerstone of both manufacturing mavens. Yet in such a closed market, Sentium's obvious gains in the industry dominated this quarter, crowning them as the only MPC capitalizing on the Illalian advantage.
While there's no official statement from Prosk, board member Jo Riley briefly expressed "disappointment" with yours truly before regurgitating pre-written drop quotes like a trained parrot. "Prosk has stood at the forefront of innovation since Mankind first stepped foot on Illal," she defended. "As our role in the super-economy expands, brief growing pains are expected and equally vital to our maturation in the Hyper-Republic." With scrip values already falling, even Prosk's PR poetry cannot conceal that their next HV loader is carrying more on its shoulders next quarter than freight cargo.
In the opposing champion's corner of the ring, Sentium CEO Mikael Bankson was less humble. "We appreciate Prosk's competitive nature, as it's driven us to become more accessible to mainstream consumers," gloats Bankson. "But I think we can finally agree on what Sentium has always known. Use all the clever, cut-rate branding you want, but you can't beat quality engineering." Recent PQRs do agree, with Bankson driving Sentium's HV loader division into liquidity. Unless Prosk can roll out a quality-competitive model soon, regardless the cost, our first Illalian monopoly is on the horizon.
Gutherson 23.03.2334 10:50 AM CT
Report the facts and stop digging the knife into Jo's back. She's just doing her job. Plus, we'll alienate our Prosk readers if we bully Prosk or champion Sentium too much.
Gutherson 23.03.2334 10:51 AM CT
This is an unnecessary character assault. And don't paint so grim a picture. Readers can assess the implications of the PQRs on their own. No one's going to keep reading if all we do is depress them.
Gutherson 23.03.2334 10:52 AM CT
What are you insinuating? Just because the UTA has granted Illal's sponsor MPCs special privileges, it doesn't mean that they're breaking the law. Whose side are you on?
Gutherson 23.03.2334 10:53 AM CT
Ease off. Sentium is allowed to succeed. If there's no market competition, that's a weakness of the market, not a character flaw of the market leader.
COMMENTS: Censors rejected your article again, Marion. Too critical. Too incriminatory. And I really can't blame them. You kick Prosk when they're down. And you point a finger at Sentium and scream wolf when they succeed. What's the point? Your subjective opinion isn't news. Just state the facts, let your readers make their own conclusions, and get paid.
100%
PROSK DEVPODEXP
MONDAY, MARCH 23 2334
11:39AM
Forge Mail | Sent Mail
To: Harold Gutherson <@editorial.IllalWorldNews>
Re: I QUIT
Marion Carthright @MC.IllalWorldNews
SEND
REPLY
DELETE
3:42PM
I'm done, Harry. I'm sorry, but I'm not doing this for the scrip. If the MPCs want to turn Illalians into an uneducated serfdom, they can do it without me. The people must know the truth, and if IWN is no longer an outlet willing to share the pertinent facts with those who need them the most, then I'll make one myself. It's about time I showed you how to do your job. -- MC
PROS

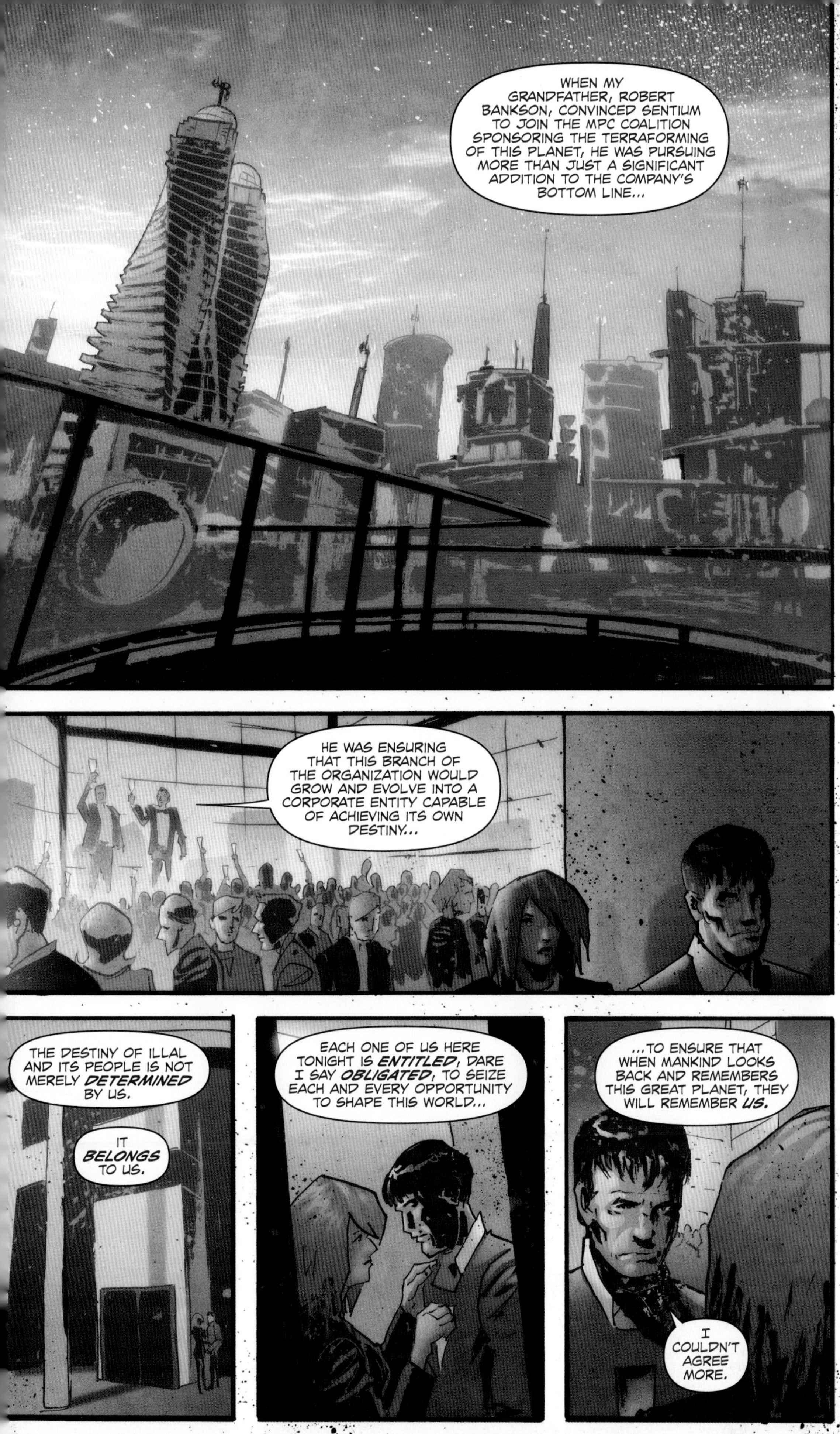
WHEN MY GRANDFATHER, ROBERT BANKSON, CONVINCED SENTIUM TO JOIN THE MPC COALITION SPONSORING THE TERRAFORMING OF THIS PLANET, HE WAS PURSUING MORE THAN JUST A SIGNIFICANT ADDITION TO THE COMPANY'S BOTTOM LINE...
HE WAS ENSURING THAT THIS BRANCH OF THE ORGANIZATION WOULD GROW AND EVOLVE INTO A CORPORATE ENTITY CAPABLE OF ACHIEVING ITS OWN DESTINY...
THE DESTINY OF ILLAL AND ITS PEOPLE IS NOT MERELY *DETERMINED* BY US.
IT *BELONGS* TO US.
EACH ONE OF US HERE TONIGHT IS *ENTITLED*, DARE I SAY *OBLIGATED*, TO SEIZE EACH AND EVERY OPPORTUNITY TO SHAPE THIS WORLD...
...TO ENSURE THAT WHEN MANKIND LOOKS BACK AND REMEMBERS THIS GREAT PLANET, THEY WILL REMEMBER *US*.
I COULDN'T AGREE MORE.

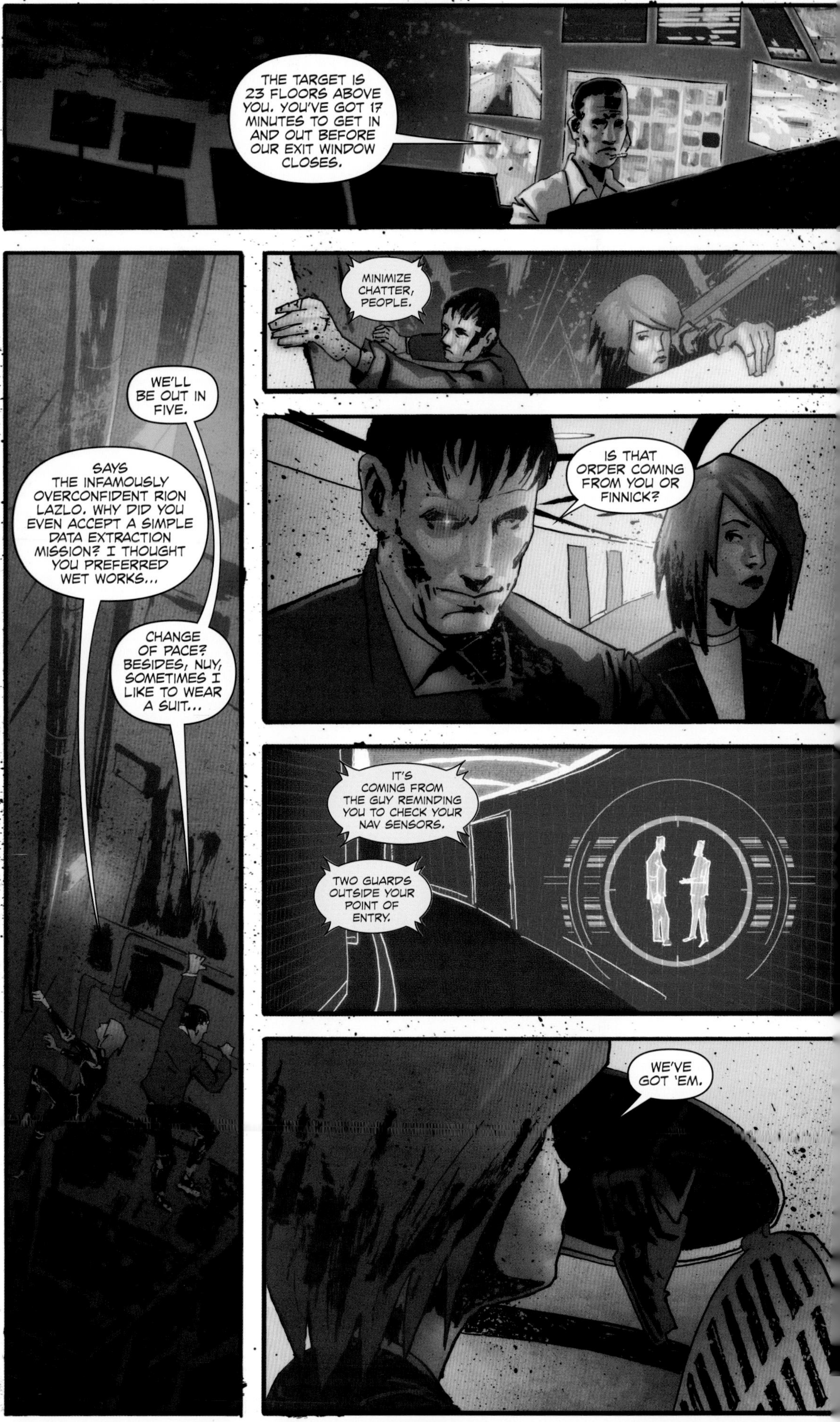
THE TARGET IS 23 FLOORS ABOVE YOU. YOU'VE GOT 17 MINUTES TO GET IN AND OUT BEFORE OUR EXIT WINDOW CLOSES.
WE'LL BE OUT IN FIVE.
SAYS THE INFAMOUSLY OVERCONFIDENT RION LAZLO. WHY DID YOU EVEN ACCEPT A SIMPLE DATA EXTRACTION MISSION? I THOUGHT YOU PREFERRED WET WORKS...
CHANGE OF PACE? BESIDES, NUY, SOMETIMES I LIKE TO WEAR A SUIT...
MINIMIZE CHATTER, PEOPLE.
IS THAT ORDER COMING FROM YOU OR FINNICK?
IT'S COMING FROM THE GUY REMINDING YOU TO CHECK YOUR NAV SENSORS.
TWO GUARDS OUTSIDE YOUR POINT OF ENTRY.
WE'VE GOT 'EM.

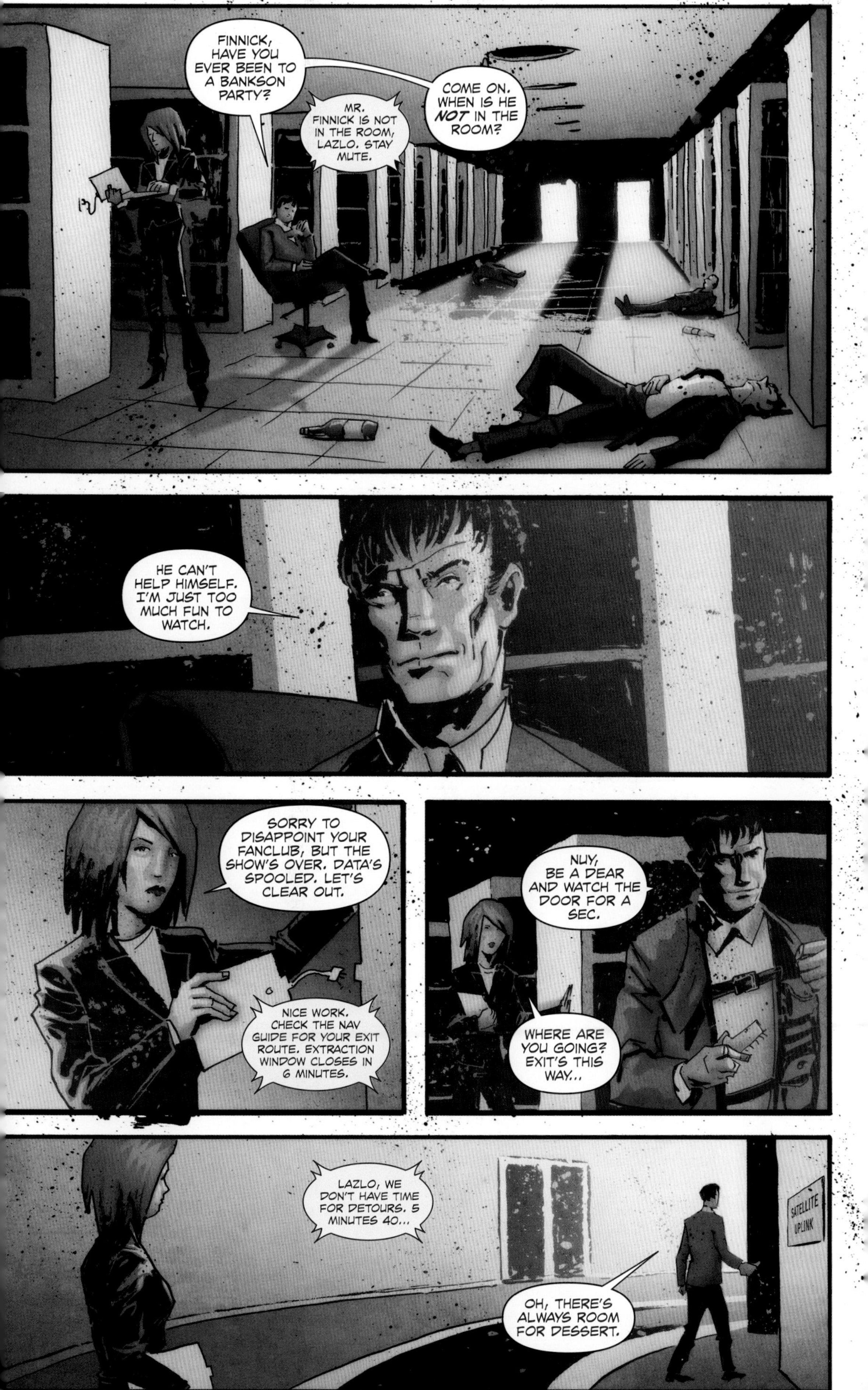
FINNICK, HAVE YOU EVER BEEN TO A BANKSON PARTY?
MR. FINNICK IS NOT IN THE ROOM, LAZLO. STAY MUTE.
COME ON. WHEN IS HE *NOT* IN THE ROOM?
HE CAN'T HELP HIMSELF. I'M JUST TOO MUCH FUN TO WATCH.
SORRY TO DISAPPOINT YOUR FANCLUB, BUT THE SHOW'S OVER. DATA'S SPOOLED. LET'S CLEAR OUT.
NICE WORK. CHECK THE NAV GUIDE FOR YOUR EXIT ROUTE. EXTRACTION WINDOW CLOSES IN 6 MINUTES.
NUY, BE A DEAR AND WATCH THE DOOR FOR A SEC.
WHERE ARE YOU GOING? EXIT'S THIS WAY...
LAZLO, WE DON'T HAVE TIME FOR DETOURS. 5 MINUTES 40...
SATELLITE UPLINK
OH, THERE'S ALWAYS ROOM FOR DESSERT.

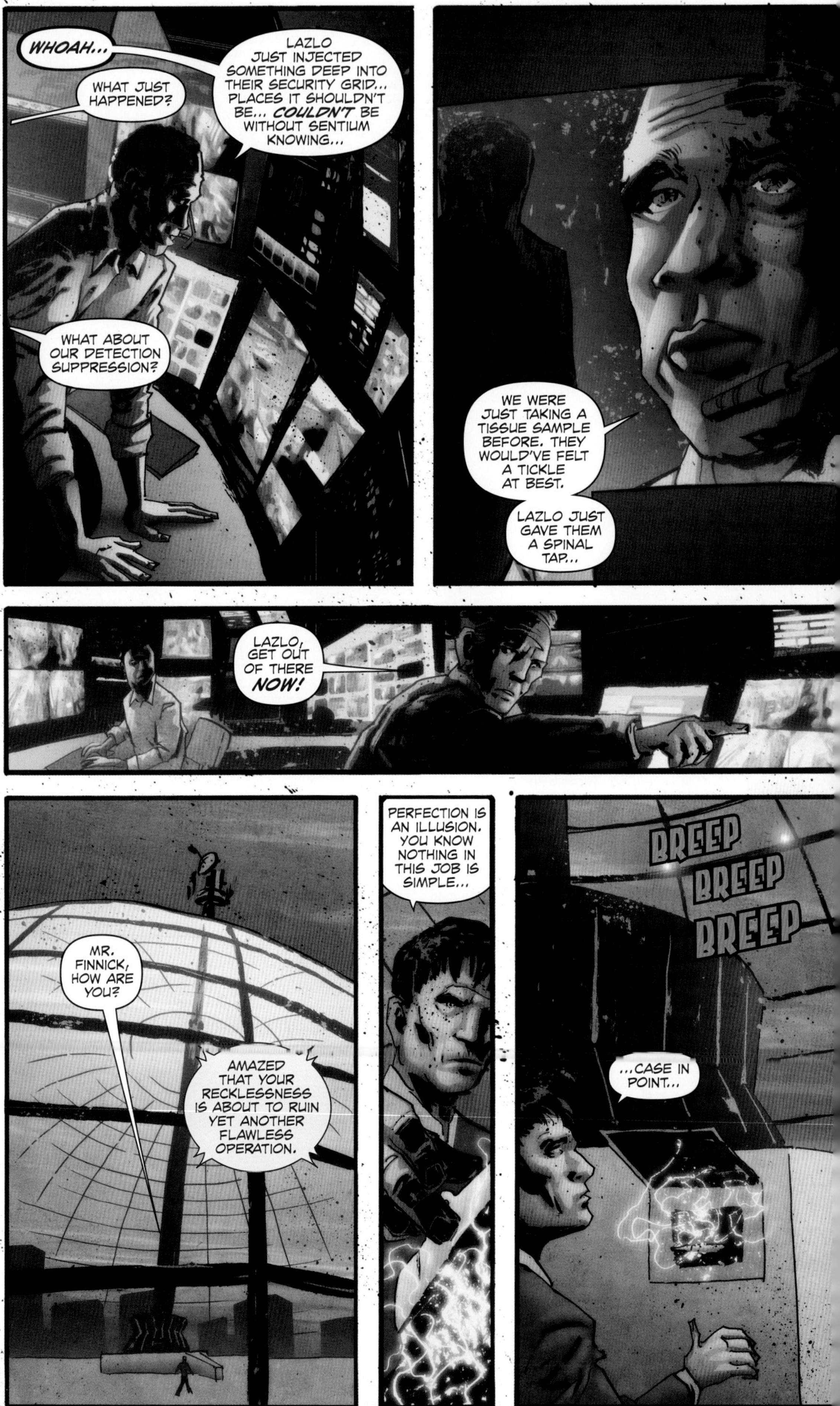
WHOAH...
WHAT JUST HAPPENED?
LAZLO JUST INJECTED SOMETHING DEEP INTO THEIR SECURITY GRID... PLACES IT SHOULDN'T BE... COULDN'T BE WITHOUT SENTIUM KNOWING...
WHAT ABOUT OUR DETECTION SUPPRESSION?
WE WERE JUST TAKING A TISSUE SAMPLE BEFORE. THEY WOULD'VE FELT A TICKLE AT BEST.
LAZLO JUST GAVE THEM A SPINAL TAP...
LAZLO, GET OUT OF THERE NOW!
MR. FINNICK, HOW ARE YOU?
AMAZED THAT YOUR RECKLESSNESS IS ABOUT TO RUIN YET ANOTHER FLAWLESS OPERATION.
PERFECTION IS AN ILLUSION. YOU KNOW NOTHING IN THIS JOB IS SIMPLE...
BREEP
BREEP
BREEP
...CASE IN POINT...

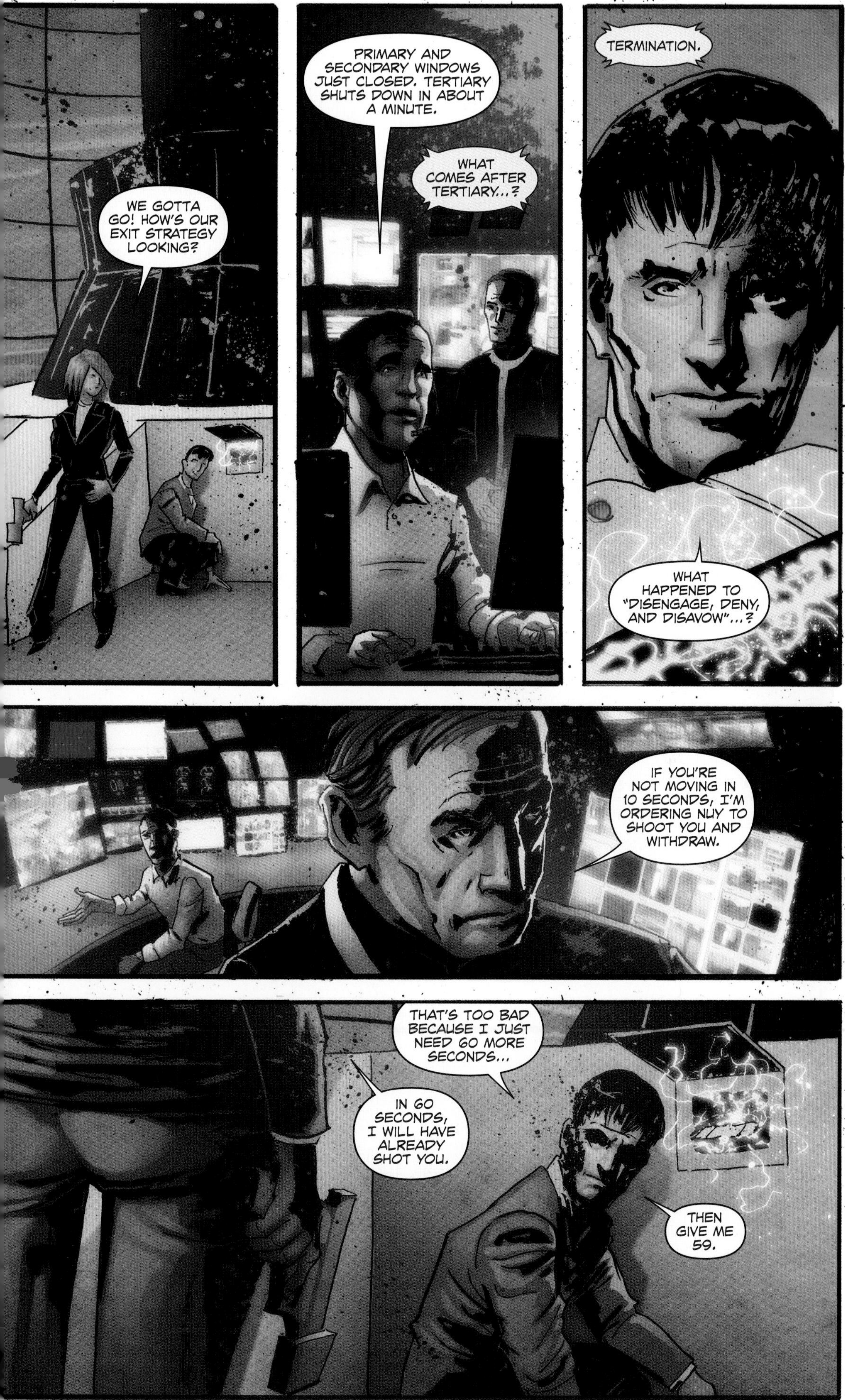
WE GOTTA GO! HOW'S OUR EXIT STRATEGY LOOKING?
PRIMARY AND SECONDARY WINDOWS JUST CLOSED. TERTIARY SHUTS DOWN IN ABOUT A MINUTE.
WHAT COMES AFTER TERTIARY...?
TERMINATION.
WHAT HAPPENED TO "DISENGAGE, DENY, AND DISAVOW"...?
IF YOU'RE NOT MOVING IN 10 SECONDS, I'M ORDERING NUY TO SHOOT YOU AND WITHDRAW.
THAT'S TOO BAD BECAUSE I JUST NEED 60 MORE SECONDS...
IN 60 SECONDS, I WILL HAVE ALREADY SHOT YOU.
THEN GIVE ME 59.

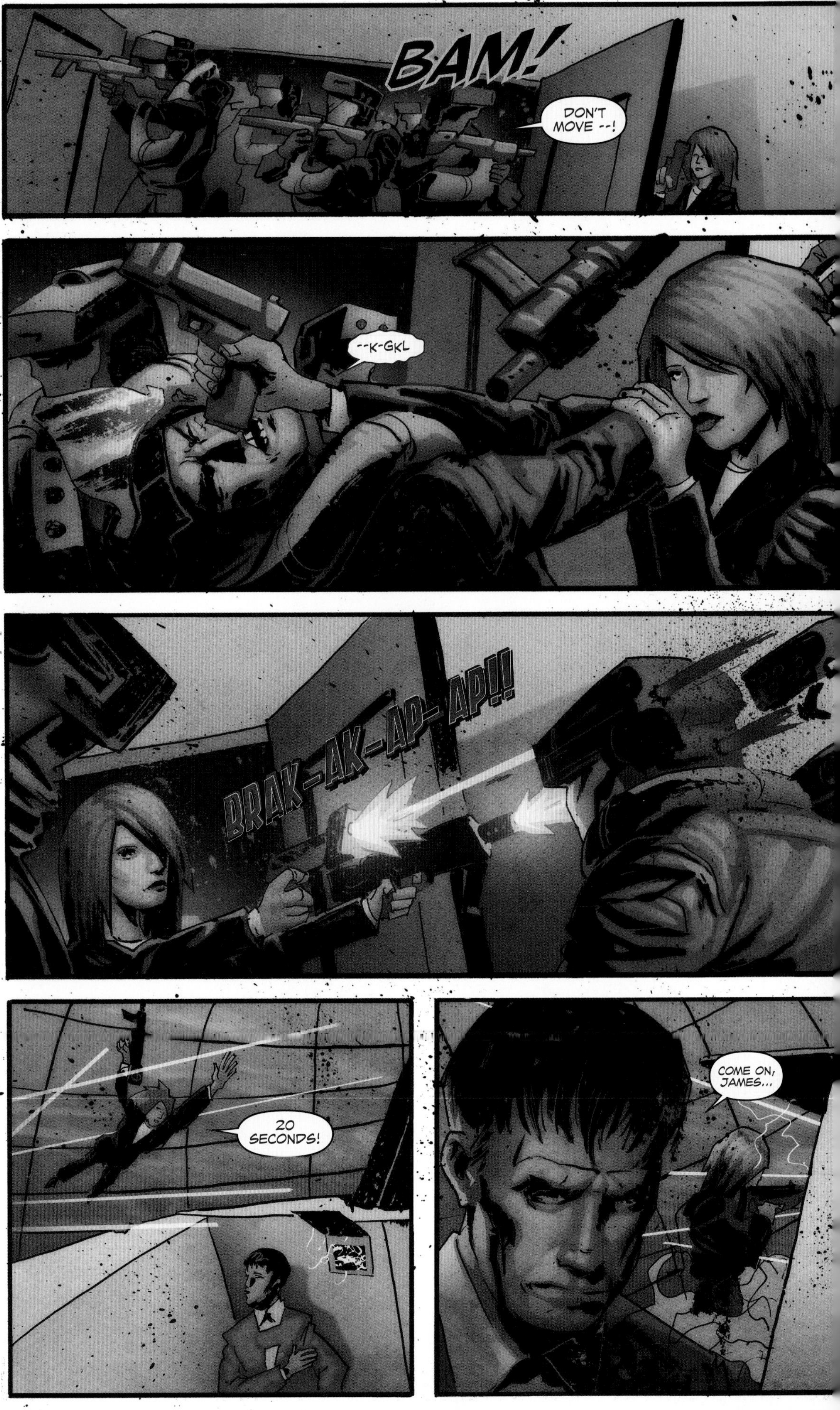
BAM!
DON'T MOVE --!
--K-GKL
BRAK-AK-AP-AP!!
20 SECONDS!
COME ON, JAMES...

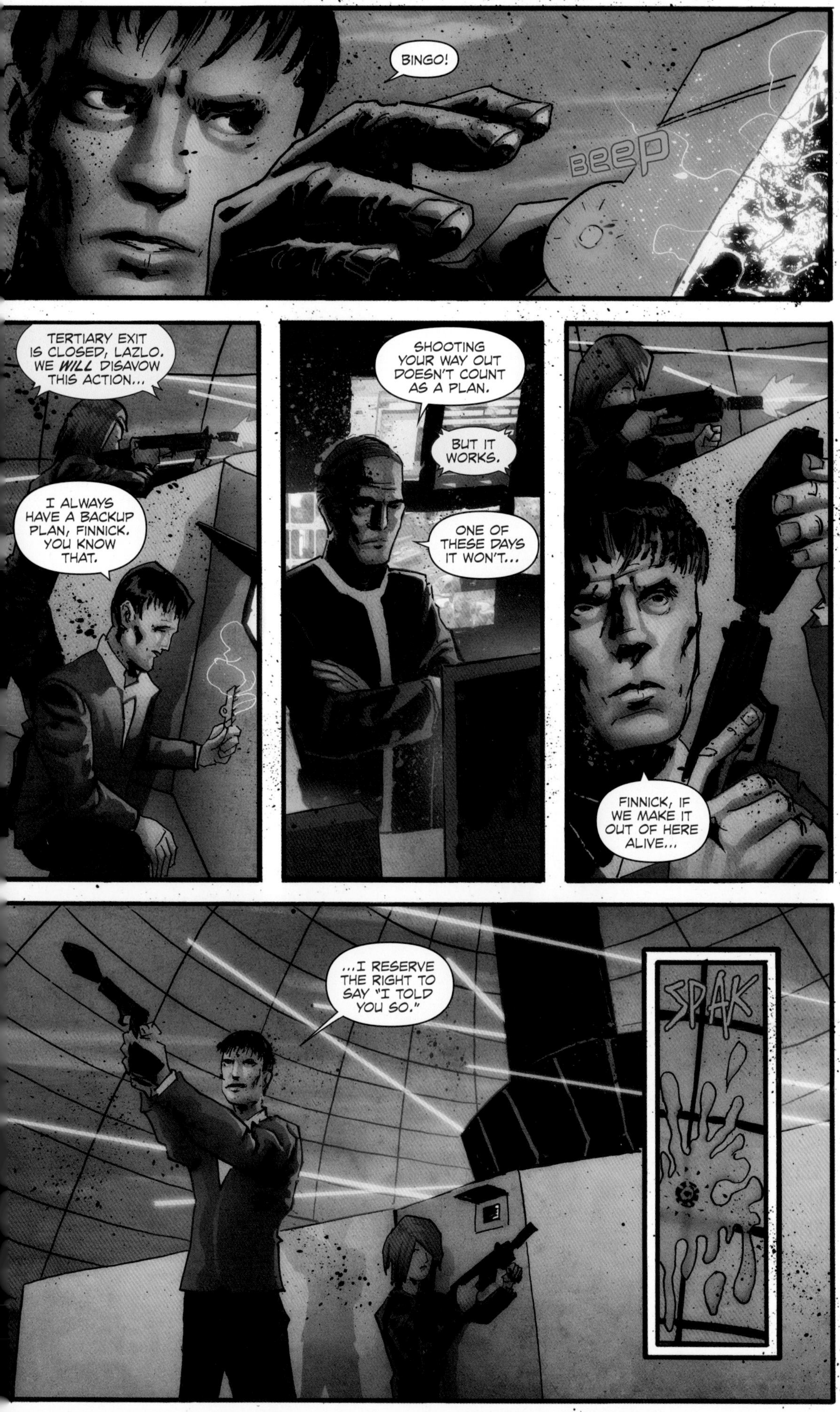
BINGO!
BEEP
TERTIARY EXIT IS CLOSED, LAZLO. WE *WILL* DISAVOW THIS ACTION...
I ALWAYS HAVE A BACKUP PLAN, FINNICK. YOU KNOW THAT.
SHOOTING YOUR WAY OUT DOESN'T COUNT AS A PLAN.
BUT IT WORKS.
ONE OF THESE DAYS IT WON'T...
FINNICK, IF WE MAKE IT OUT OF HERE ALIVE...
...I RESERVE THE RIGHT TO SAY "I TOLD YOU SO."
SPAK

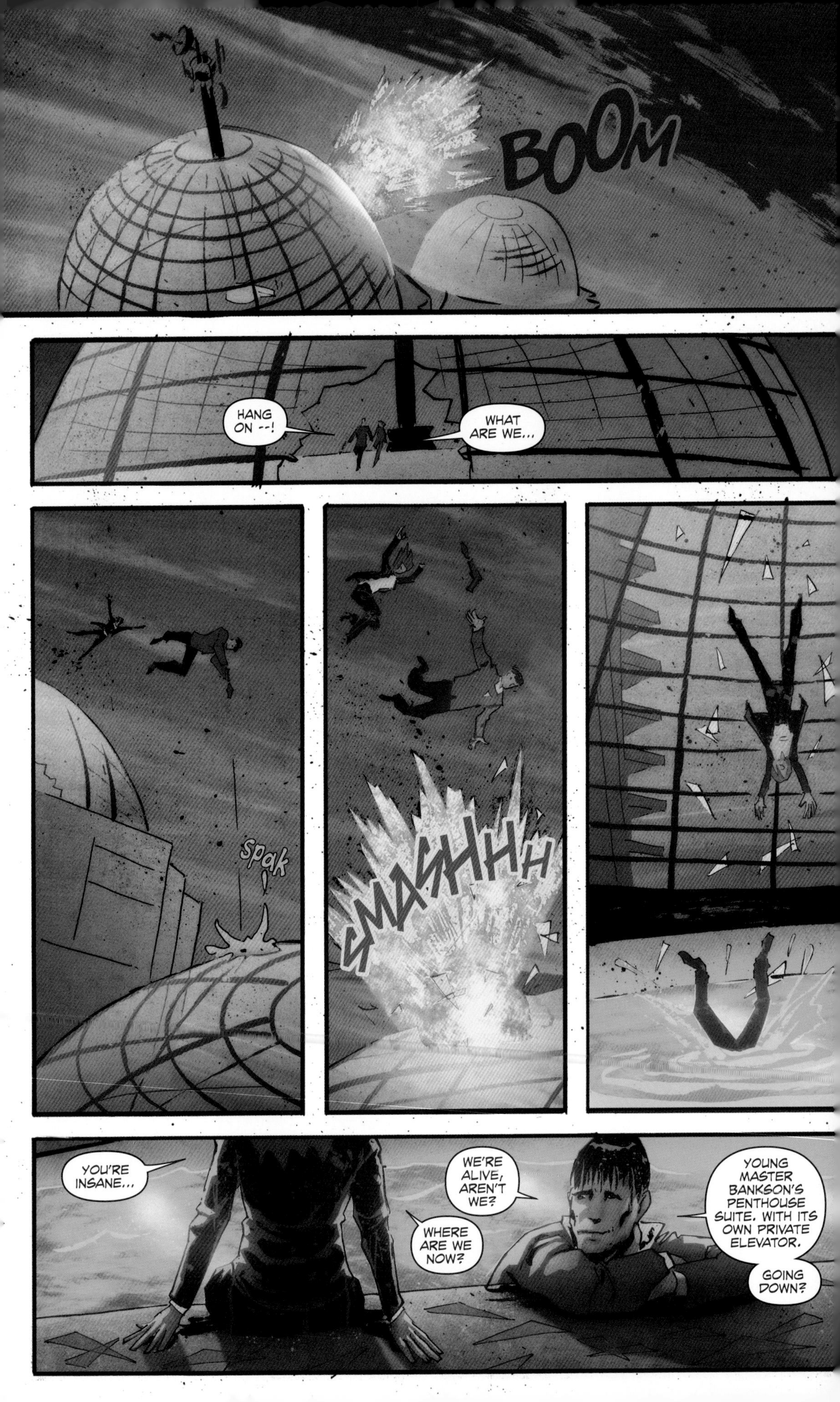
BOOM
HANG ON --!
WHAT ARE WE...
spak
SMASHHH
YOU'RE INSANE...
WE'RE ALIVE, AREN'T WE?
WHERE ARE WE NOW?
YOUNG MASTER BANKSON'S PENTHOUSE SUITE. WITH ITS OWN PRIVATE ELEVATOR.
GOING DOWN?

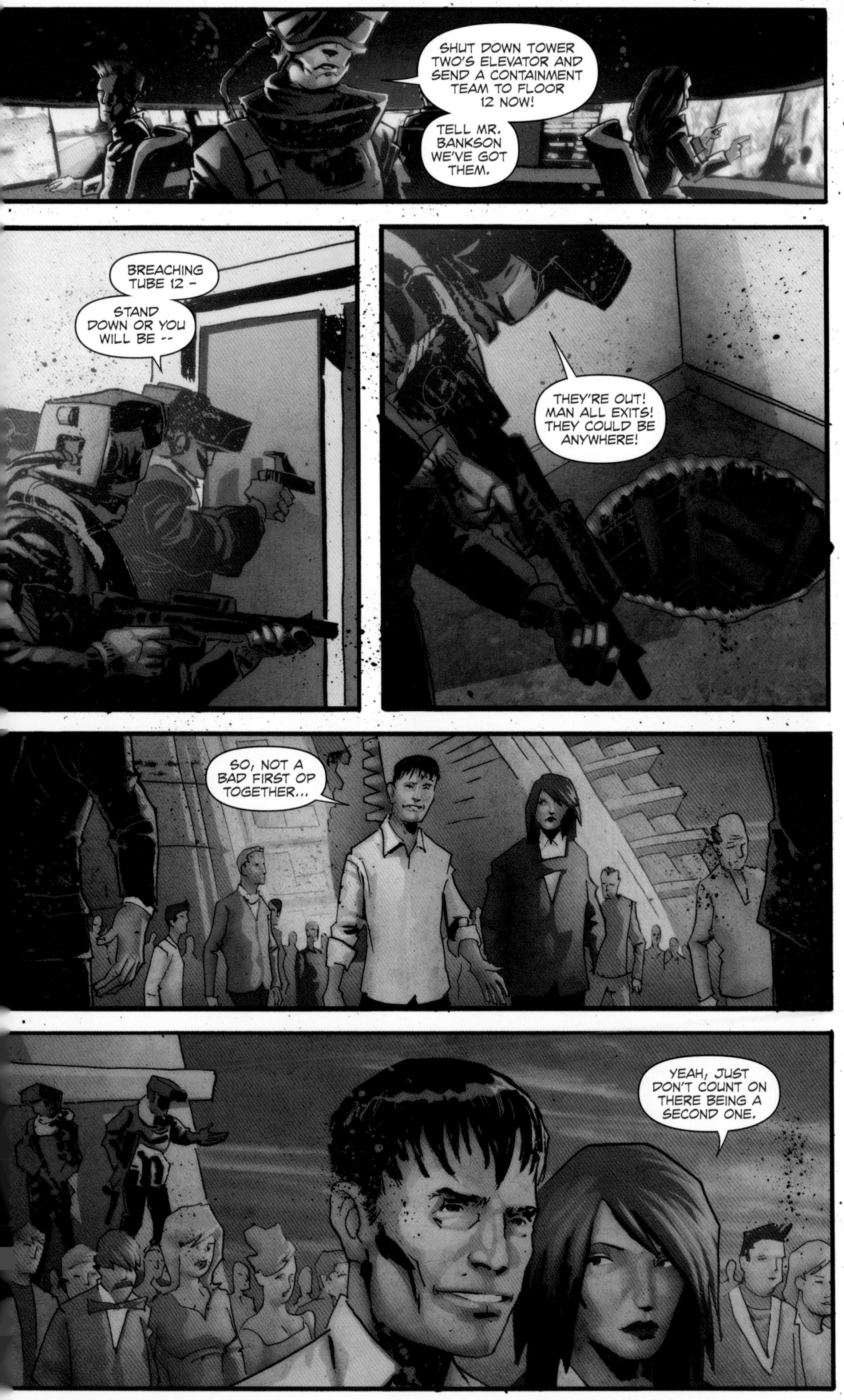
SHUT DOWN TOWER TWO'S ELEVATOR AND SEND A CONTAINMENT TEAM TO FLOOR 12 NOW!
TELL MR. BANKSON WE'VE GOT THEM.
BREACHING TUBE 12 –
STAND DOWN OR YOU WILL BE --
THEY'RE OUT! MAN ALL EXITS! THEY COULD BE ANYWHERE!
SO, NOT A BAD FIRST OP TOGETHER...
YEAH, JUST DON'T COUNT ON THERE BEING A SECOND ONE.

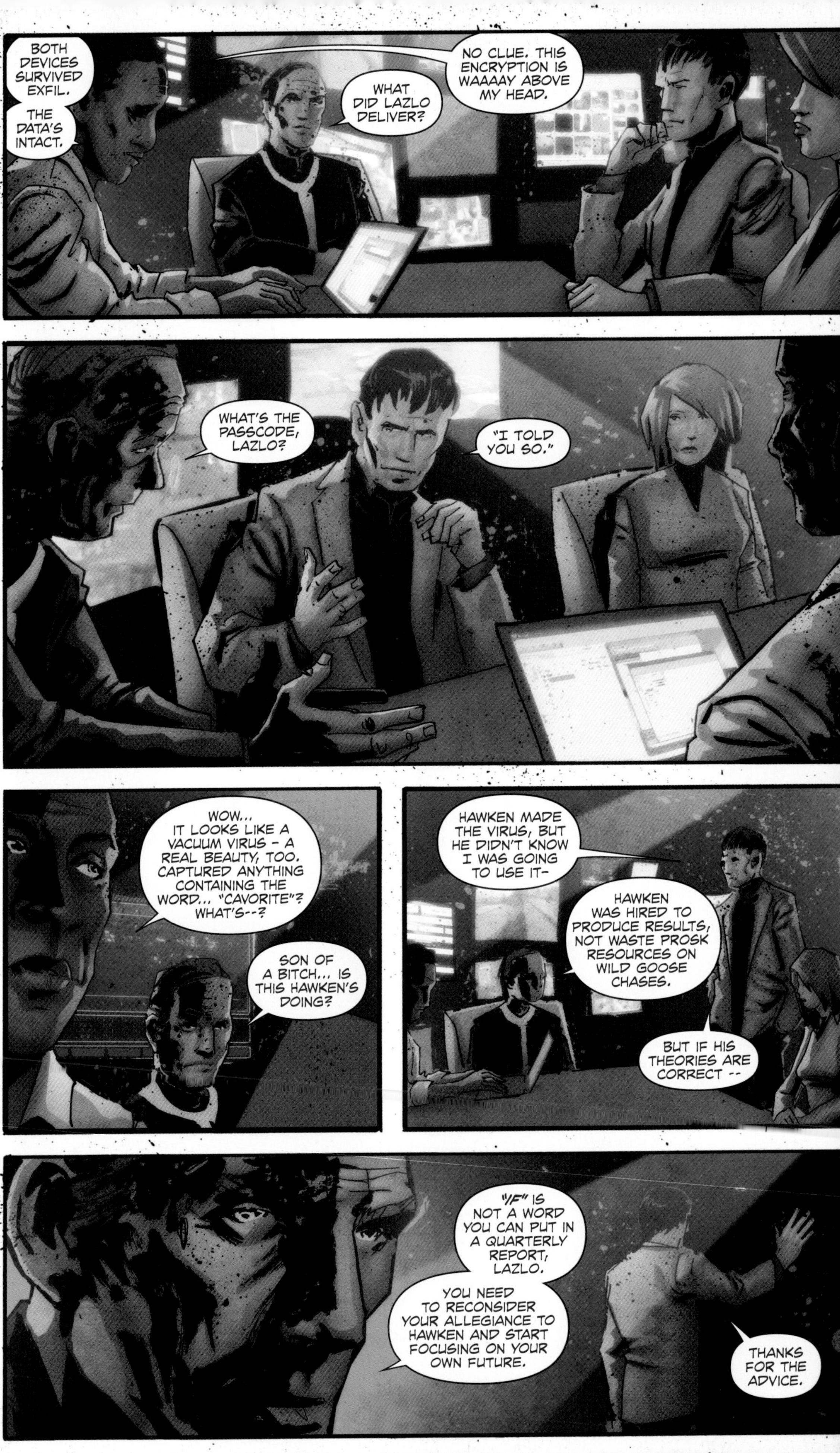
BOTH DEVICES SURVIVED EXFIL.
THE DATA'S INTACT.
WHAT DID LAZLO DELIVER?
NO CLUE. THIS ENCRYPTION IS WAAAAY ABOVE MY HEAD.
WHAT'S THE PASSCODE, LAZLO?
"I TOLD YOU SO."
WOW... IT LOOKS LIKE A VACUUM VIRUS - A REAL BEAUTY, TOO. CAPTURED ANYTHING CONTAINING THE WORD... "CAVORITE"? WHAT'S--?
SON OF A BITCH... IS THIS HAWKEN'S DOING?
HAWKEN MADE THE VIRUS, BUT HE DIDN'T KNOW I WAS GOING TO USE IT-
HAWKEN WAS HIRED TO PRODUCE RESULTS, NOT WASTE PROSK RESOURCES ON WILD GOOSE CHASES.
BUT IF HIS THEORIES ARE CORRECT --
"IF" IS NOT A WORD YOU CAN PUT IN A QUARTERLY REPORT, LAZLO.
YOU NEED TO RECONSIDER YOUR ALLEGIANCE TO HAWKEN AND START FOCUSING ON YOUR OWN FUTURE.
THANKS FOR THE ADVICE.

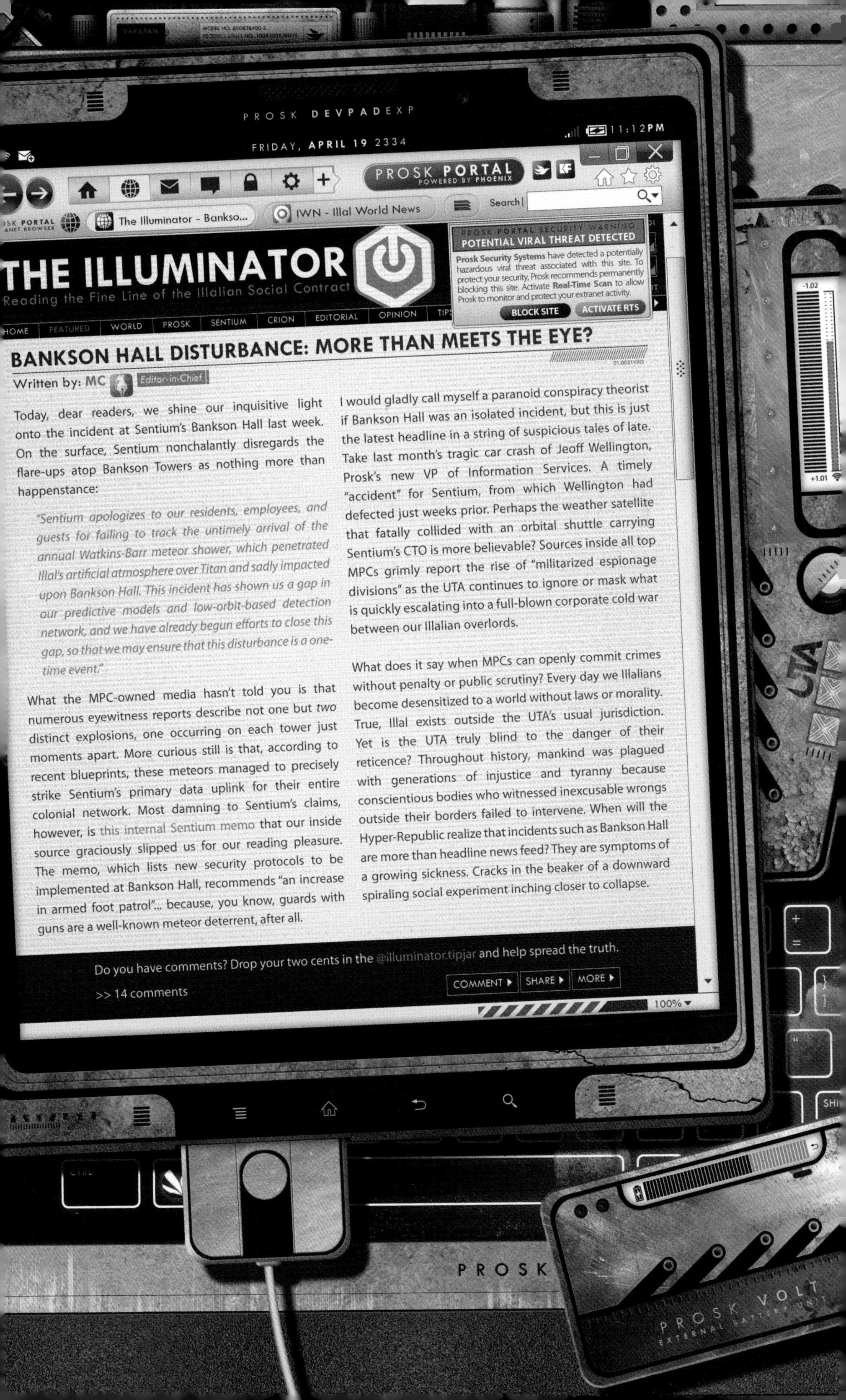
PROSK DEVPADEXP
FRIDAY, APRIL 19 2334
11:12PM
PROSK PORTAL
POWERED BY PHOENIX
Search
The Illuminator - Bankso...
IWN - Illal World News
PROSK PORTAL SECURITY WARNING
POTENTIAL VIRAL THREAT DETECTED
Prosk Security Systems have detected a potentially hazardous viral threat associated with this site. To protect your security, Prosk recommends permanently blocking this site. Activate Real-Time Scan to allow Prosk to monitor and protect your extranet activity.
BLOCK SITE
ACTIVATE RTS
HOME
FEATURED
WORLD
PROSK
SENTIUM
CRION
EDITORIAL
OPINION
TIPS
COMMENT
SHARE
MORE
100%
UTA
PROSK
PROSK VOLT
EXTERNAL BATTERY UNIT

THE ILLUMINATOR

Reading the Fine Line of the Illalian Social Contract

BANKSON HALL DISTURBANCE: MORE THAN MEETS THE EYE?

Written by: MC Editor-in-Chief

Today, dear readers, we shine our inquisitive light onto the incident at Sentium's Bankson Hall last week. On the surface, Sentium nonchalantly disregards the flare-ups atop Bankson Towers as nothing more than happenstance:

> *"Sentium apologizes to our residents, employees, and guests for failing to track the untimely arrival of the annual Watkins-Barr meteor shower, which penetrated Illal's artificial atmosphere over Titan and sadly impacted upon Bankson Hall. This incident has shown us a gap in our predictive models and low-orbit-based detection network, and we have already begun efforts to close this gap, so that we may ensure that this disturbance is a one-time event."*

What the MPC-owned media hasn't told you is that numerous eyewitness reports describe not one but *two* distinct explosions, one occurring on each tower just moments apart. More curious still is that, according to recent blueprints, these meteors managed to precisely strike Sentium's primary data uplink for their entire colonial network. Most damning to Sentium's claims, however, is this internal Sentium memo that our inside source graciously slipped us for our reading pleasure. The memo, which lists new security protocols to be implemented at Bankson Hall, recommends "an increase in armed foot patrol"... because, you know, guards with guns are a well-known meteor deterrent, after all.

I would gladly call myself a paranoid conspiracy theorist if Bankson Hall was an isolated incident, but this is just the latest headline in a string of suspicious tales of late. Take last month's tragic car crash of Jeoff Wellington, Prosk's new VP of Information Services. A timely "accident" for Sentium, from which Wellington had defected just weeks prior. Perhaps the weather satellite that fatally collided with an orbital shuttle carrying Sentium's CTO is more believable? Sources inside all top MPCs grimly report the rise of "militarized espionage divisions" as the UTA continues to ignore or mask what is quickly escalating into a full-blown corporate cold war between our Illalian overlords.

What does it say when MPCs can openly commit crimes without penalty or public scrutiny? Every day we Illalians become desensitized to a world without laws or morality. True, Illal exists outside the UTA's usual jurisdiction. Yet is the UTA truly blind to the danger of their reticence? Throughout history, mankind was plagued with generations of injustice and tyranny because conscientious bodies who witnessed inexcusable wrongs outside their borders failed to intervene. When will the Hyper-Republic realize that incidents such as Bankson Hall are more than headline news feed? They are symptoms of a growing sickness. Cracks in the beaker of a downward spiraling social experiment inching closer to collapse.

Do you have comments? Drop your two cents in the @illuminator.tipjar and help spread the truth.

>> 14 comments

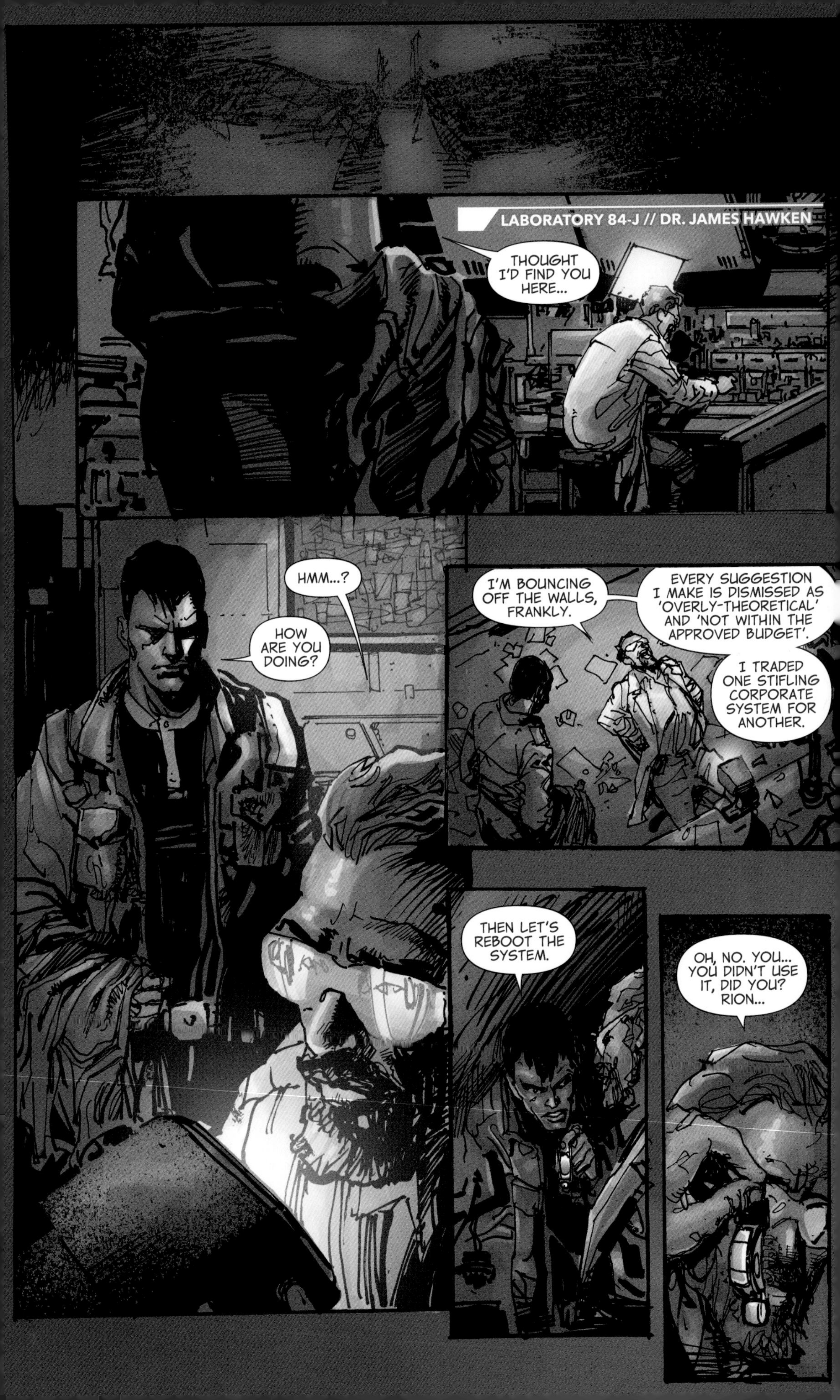
LABORATORY 84-J // DR. JAMES HAWKEN
THOUGHT I'D FIND YOU HERE...
HMM...?
HOW ARE YOU DOING?
I'M BOUNCING OFF THE WALLS, FRANKLY.
EVERY SUGGESTION I MAKE IS DISMISSED AS 'OVERLY-THEORETICAL' AND 'NOT WITHIN THE APPROVED BUDGET'.
I TRADED ONE STIFLING CORPORATE SYSTEM FOR ANOTHER.
THEN LET'S REBOOT THE SYSTEM.
OH, NO. YOU... YOU DIDN'T USE IT, DID YOU? RION...

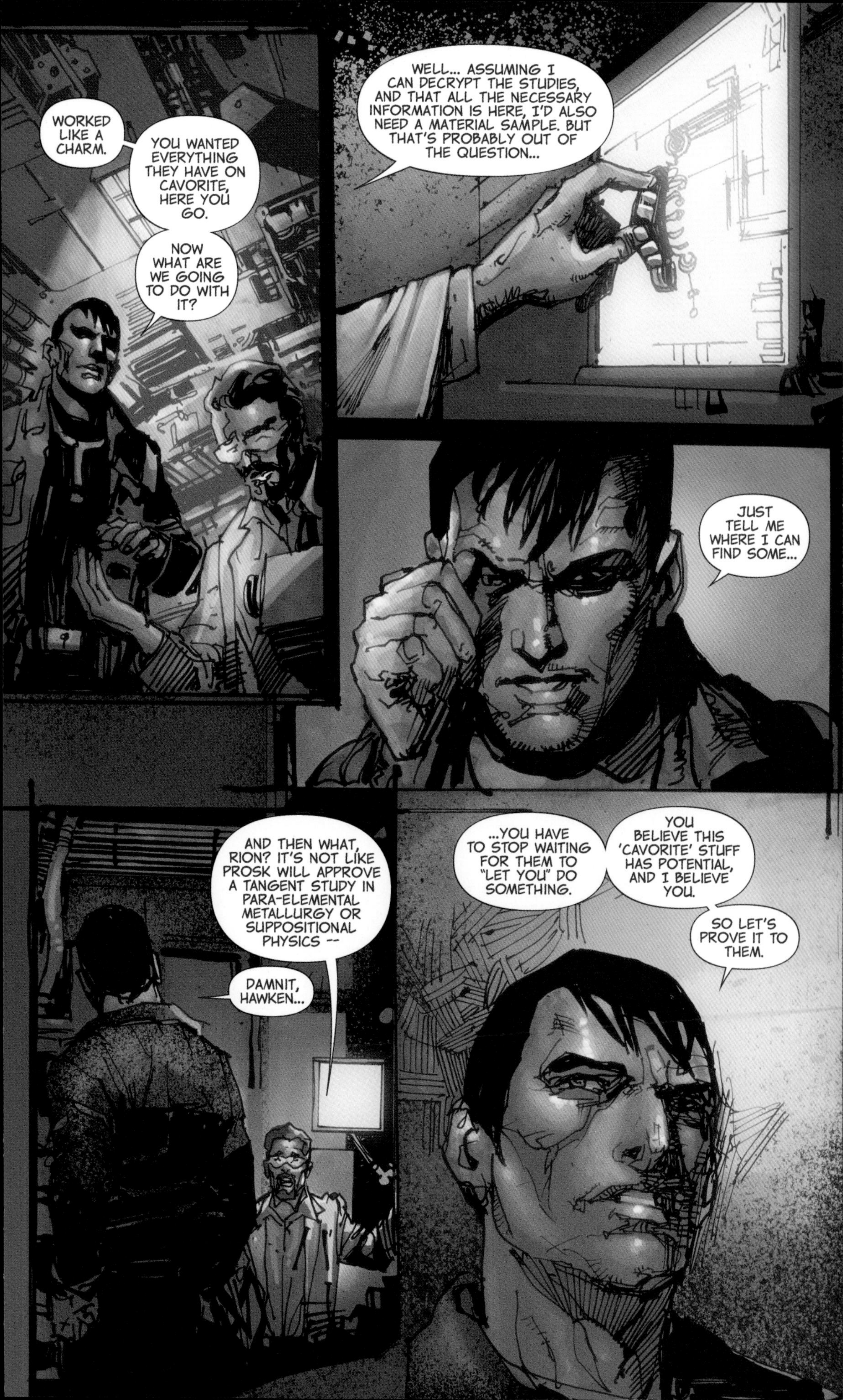
WORKED LIKE A CHARM.
YOU WANTED EVERYTHING THEY HAVE ON CAVORITE, HERE YOU GO.
NOW WHAT ARE WE GOING TO DO WITH IT?
WELL... ASSUMING I CAN DECRYPT THE STUDIES, AND THAT ALL THE NECESSARY INFORMATION IS HERE, I'D ALSO NEED A MATERIAL SAMPLE. BUT THAT'S PROBABLY OUT OF THE QUESTION...
JUST TELL ME WHERE I CAN FIND SOME...
AND THEN WHAT, RION? IT'S NOT LIKE PROSK WILL APPROVE A TANGENT STUDY IN PARA-ELEMENTAL METALLURGY OR SUPPOSITIONAL PHYSICS --
DAMNIT, HAWKEN...
...YOU HAVE TO STOP WAITING FOR THEM TO "LET YOU" DO SOMETHING.
YOU BELIEVE THIS 'CAVORITE' STUFF HAS POTENTIAL, AND I BELIEVE YOU.
SO LET'S PROVE IT TO THEM.

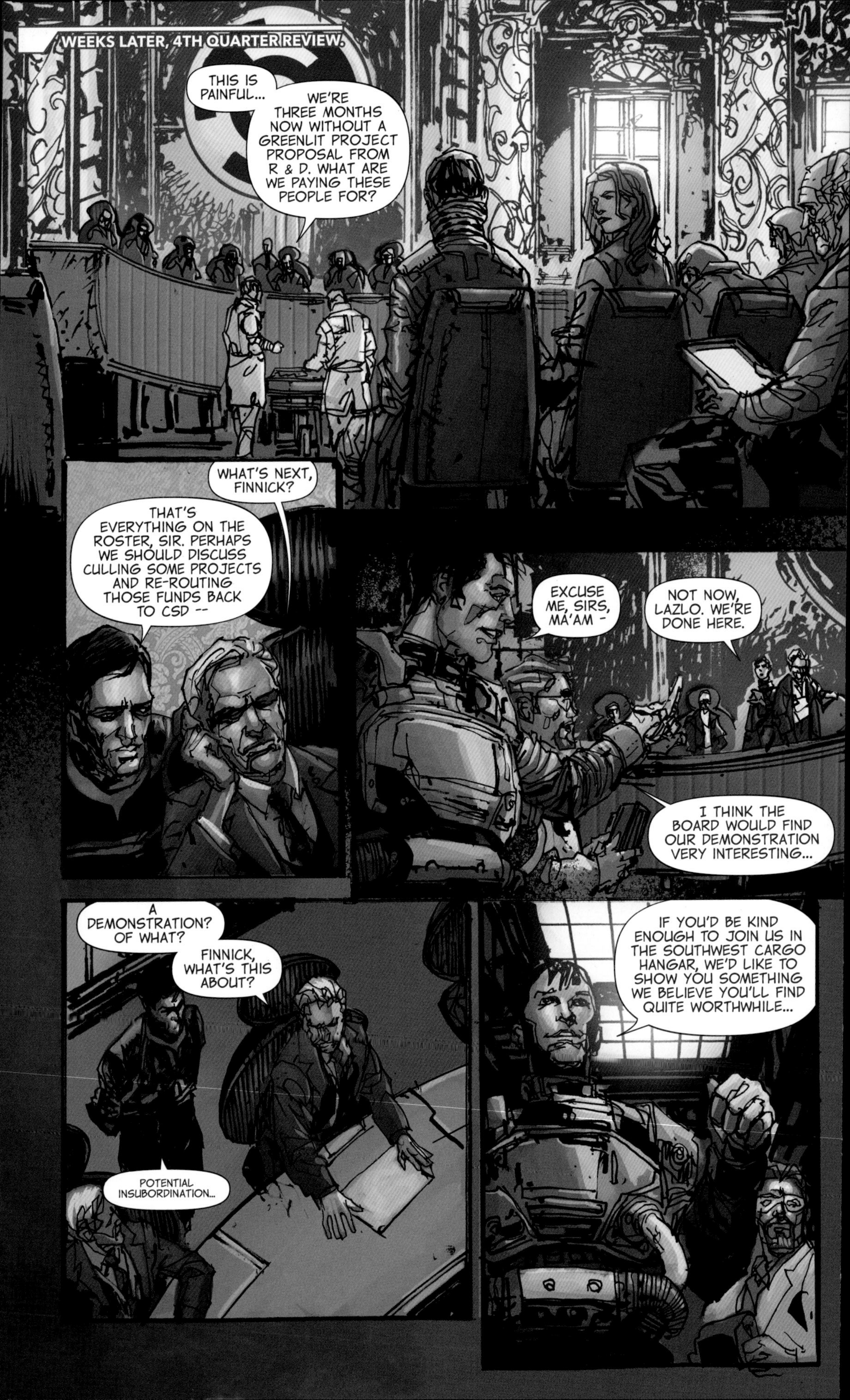
WEEKS LATER, 4TH QUARTER REVIEW.
THIS IS PAINFUL...
WE'RE THREE MONTHS NOW WITHOUT A GREENLIT PROJECT PROPOSAL FROM R & D. WHAT ARE WE PAYING THESE PEOPLE FOR?
WHAT'S NEXT, FINNICK?
THAT'S EVERYTHING ON THE ROSTER, SIR. PERHAPS WE SHOULD DISCUSS CULLING SOME PROJECTS AND RE-ROUTING THOSE FUNDS BACK TO CSD --
EXCUSE ME, SIRS, MA'AM -
NOT NOW, LAZLO. WE'RE DONE HERE.
I THINK THE BOARD WOULD FIND OUR DEMONSTRATION VERY INTERESTING...
A DEMONSTRATION? OF WHAT?
FINNICK, WHAT'S THIS ABOUT?
POTENTIAL INSUBORDINATION...
IF YOU'D BE KIND ENOUGH TO JOIN US IN THE SOUTHWEST CARGO HANGAR, WE'D LIKE TO SHOW YOU SOMETHING WE BELIEVE YOU'LL FIND QUITE WORTHWHILE...

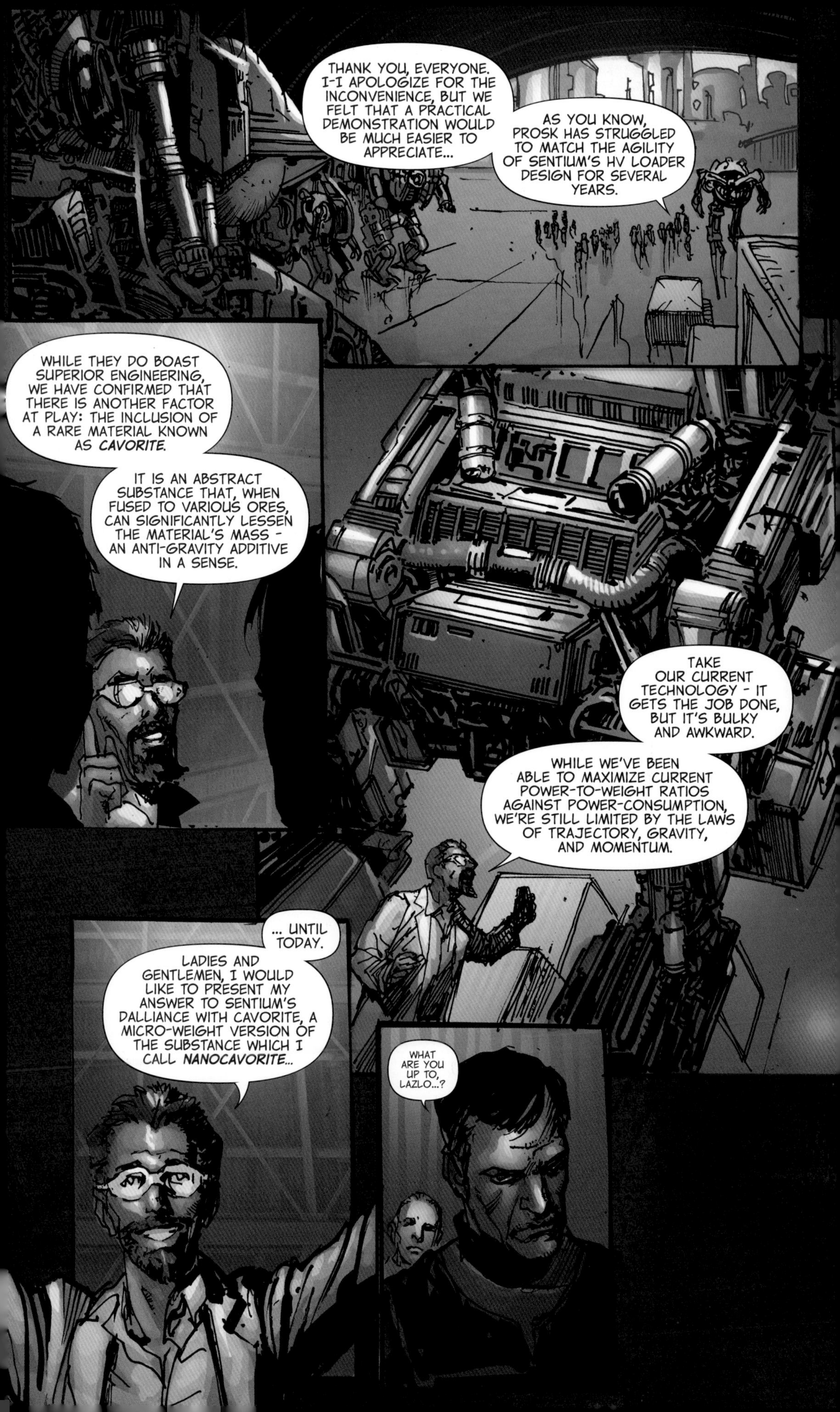
THANK YOU, EVERYONE. I-I APOLOGIZE FOR THE INCONVENIENCE, BUT WE FELT THAT A PRACTICAL DEMONSTRATION WOULD BE MUCH EASIER TO APPRECIATE...
AS YOU KNOW, PROSK HAS STRUGGLED TO MATCH THE AGILITY OF SENTIUM'S HV LOADER DESIGN FOR SEVERAL YEARS.
WHILE THEY DO BOAST SUPERIOR ENGINEERING, WE HAVE CONFIRMED THAT THERE IS ANOTHER FACTOR AT PLAY: THE INCLUSION OF A RARE MATERIAL KNOWN AS *CAVORITE*.
IT IS AN ABSTRACT SUBSTANCE THAT, WHEN FUSED TO VARIOUS ORES, CAN SIGNIFICANTLY LESSEN THE MATERIAL'S MASS - AN ANTI-GRAVITY ADDITIVE IN A SENSE.
TAKE OUR CURRENT TECHNOLOGY - IT GETS THE JOB DONE, BUT IT'S BULKY AND AWKWARD.
WHILE WE'VE BEEN ABLE TO MAXIMIZE CURRENT POWER-TO-WEIGHT RATIOS AGAINST POWER-CONSUMPTION, WE'RE STILL LIMITED BY THE LAWS OF TRAJECTORY, GRAVITY, AND MOMENTUM.
... UNTIL TODAY.
LADIES AND GENTLEMEN, I WOULD LIKE TO PRESENT MY ANSWER TO SENTIUM'S DALLIANCE WITH CAVORITE, A MICRO-WEIGHT VERSION OF THE SUBSTANCE WHICH I CALL *NANOCAVORITE*...
WHAT ARE YOU UP TO, LAZLO...?

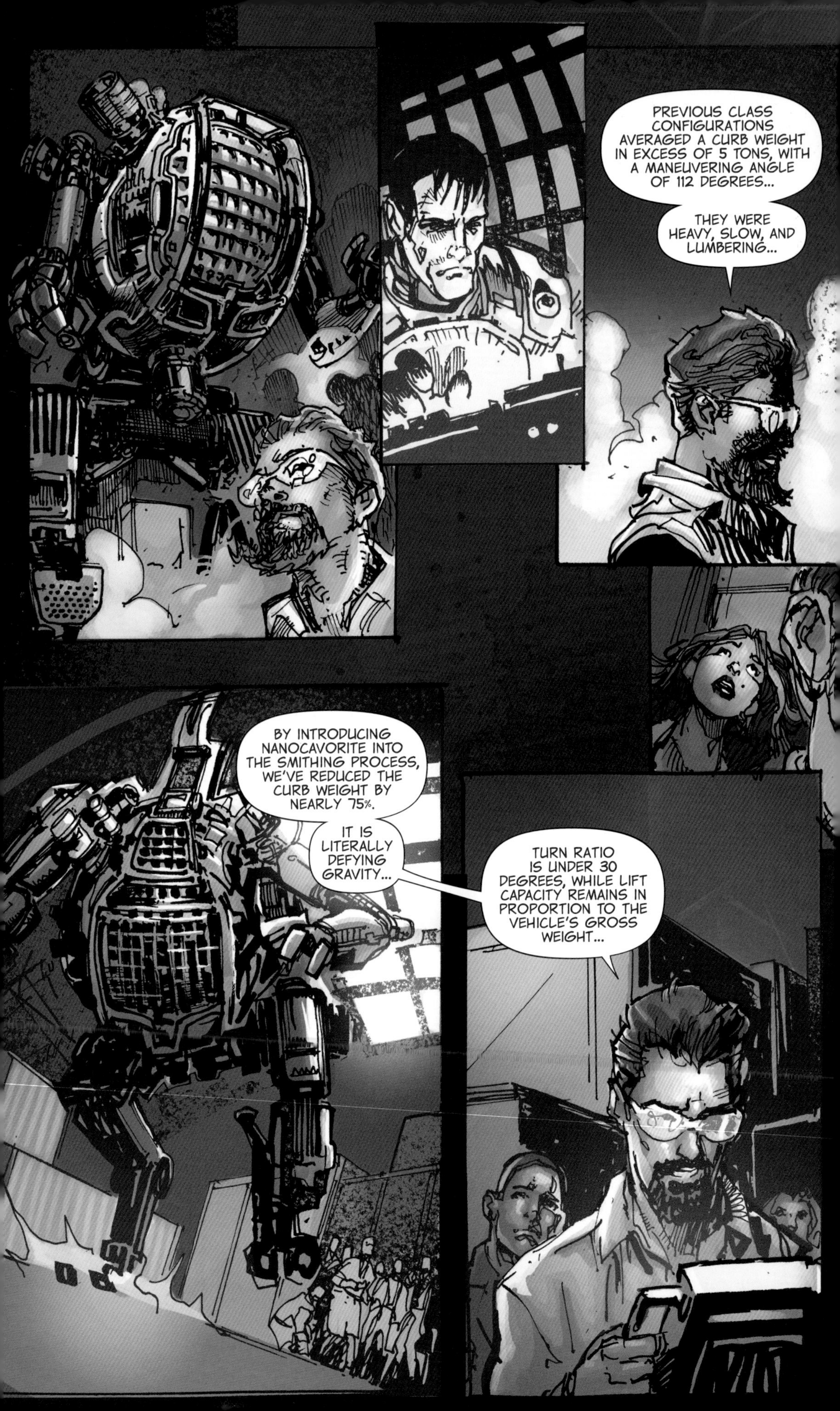
PREVIOUS CLASS CONFIGURATIONS AVERAGED A CURB WEIGHT IN EXCESS OF 5 TONS, WITH A MANEUVERING ANGLE OF 112 DEGREES...
THEY WERE HEAVY, SLOW, AND LUMBERING...
BY INTRODUCING NANOCAVORITE INTO THE SMITHING PROCESS, WE'VE REDUCED THE CURB WEIGHT BY NEARLY 75%.
IT IS LITERALLY DEFYING GRAVITY...
TURN RATIO IS UNDER 30 DEGREES, WHILE LIFT CAPACITY REMAINS IN PROPORTION TO THE VEHICLE'S GROSS WEIGHT...

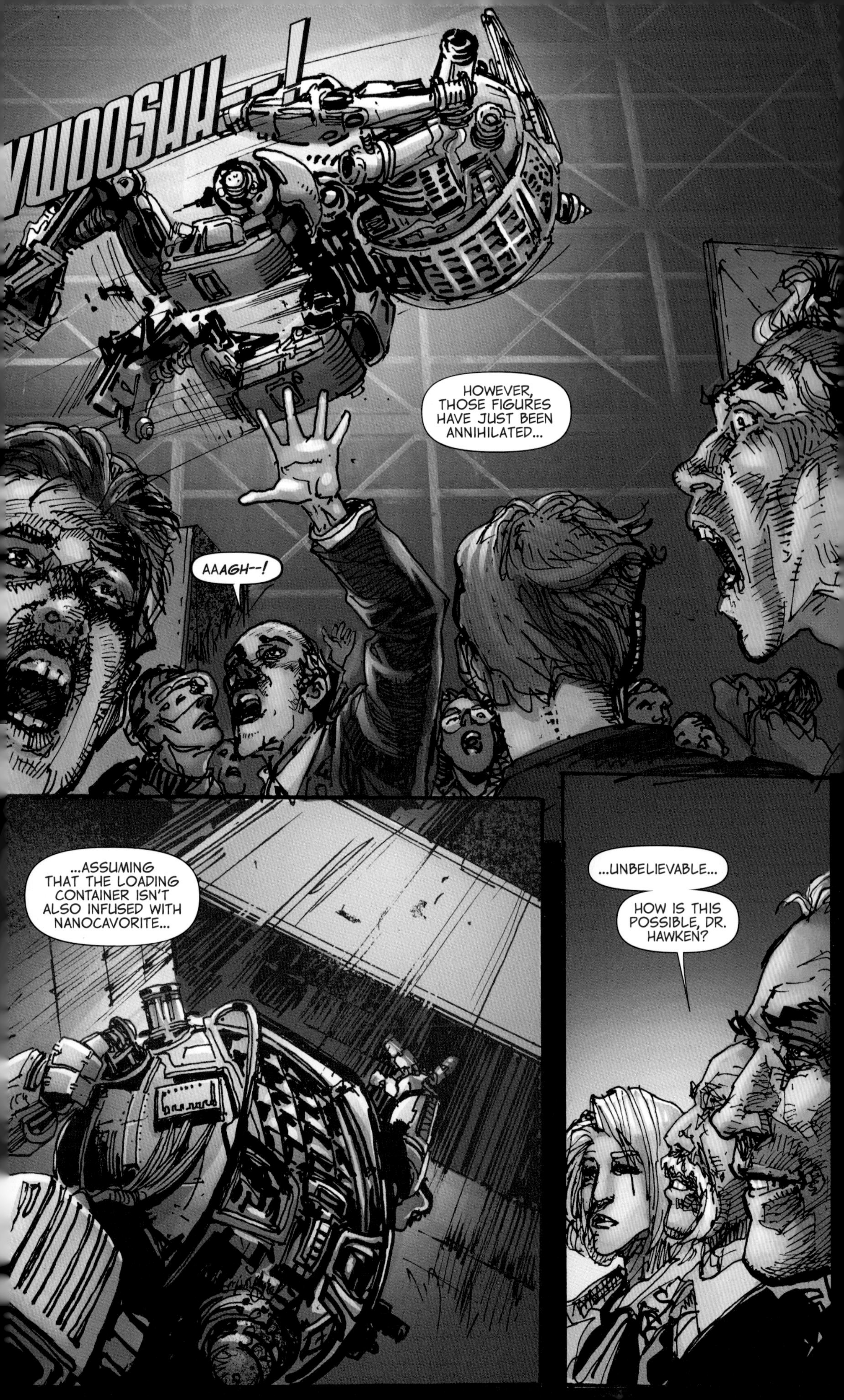
VWOOSHH--!
HOWEVER, THOSE FIGURES HAVE JUST BEEN ANNIHILATED...
AAAGH--!
...ASSUMING THAT THE LOADING CONTAINER ISN'T ALSO INFUSED WITH NANOCAVORITE...
...UNBELIEVABLE...
HOW IS THIS POSSIBLE, DR. HAWKEN?

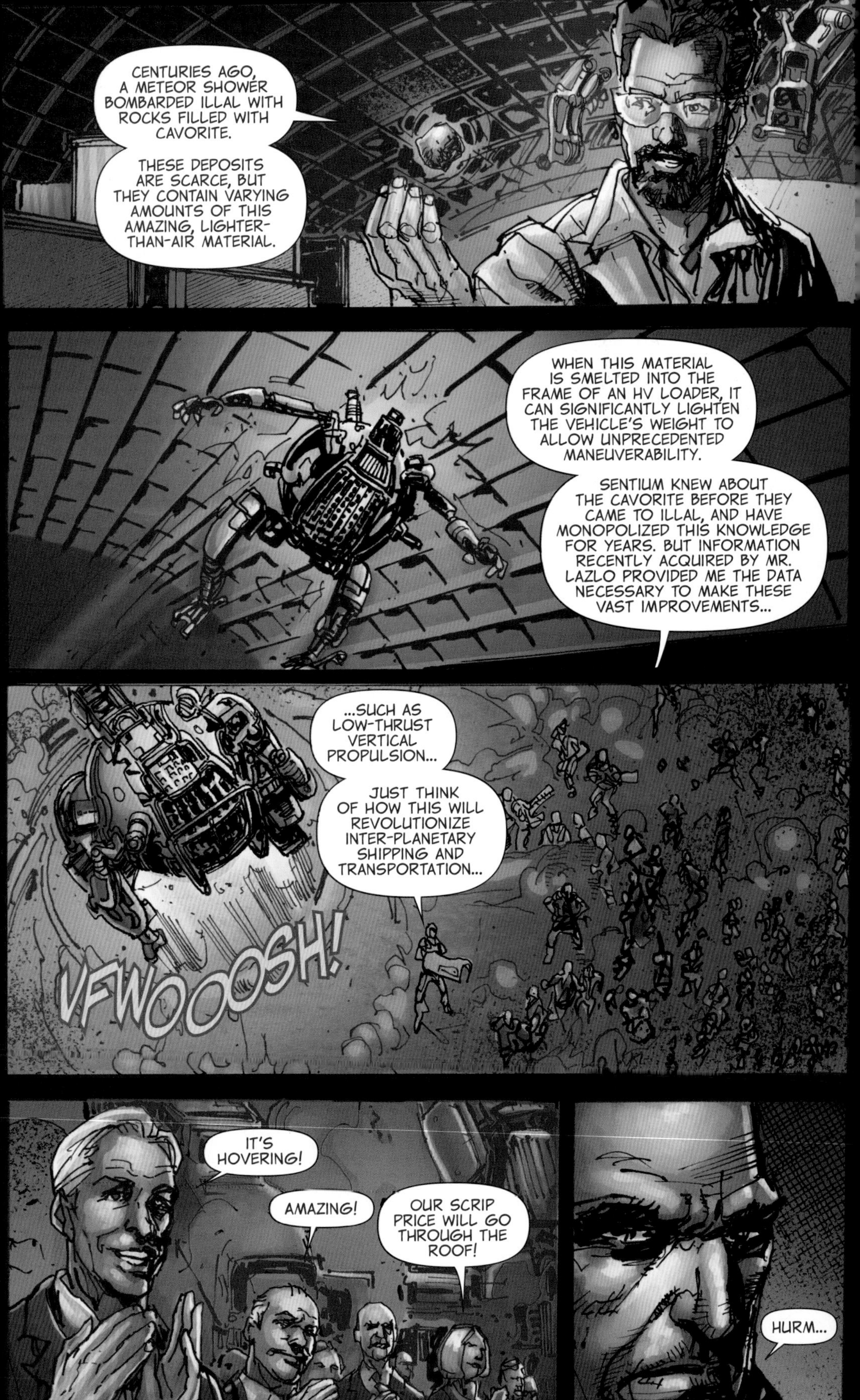

CENTURIES AGO, A METEOR SHOWER BOMBARDED ILLAL WITH ROCKS FILLED WITH CAVORITE.
THESE DEPOSITS ARE SCARCE, BUT THEY CONTAIN VARYING AMOUNTS OF THIS AMAZING, LIGHTER-THAN-AIR MATERIAL.
WHEN THIS MATERIAL IS SMELTED INTO THE FRAME OF AN HV LOADER, IT CAN SIGNIFICANTLY LIGHTEN THE VEHICLE'S WEIGHT TO ALLOW UNPRECEDENTED MANEUVERABILITY.
SENTIUM KNEW ABOUT THE CAVORITE BEFORE THEY CAME TO ILLAL, AND HAVE MONOPOLIZED THIS KNOWLEDGE FOR YEARS. BUT INFORMATION RECENTLY ACQUIRED BY MR. LAZLO PROVIDED ME THE DATA NECESSARY TO MAKE THESE VAST IMPROVEMENTS...
...SUCH AS LOW-THRUST VERTICAL PROPULSION...
JUST THINK OF HOW THIS WILL REVOLUTIONIZE INTER-PLANETARY SHIPPING AND TRANSPORTATION...
VFWOOOSH!
IT'S HOVERING!
AMAZING!
OUR SCRIP PRICE WILL GO THROUGH THE ROOF!
HURM...

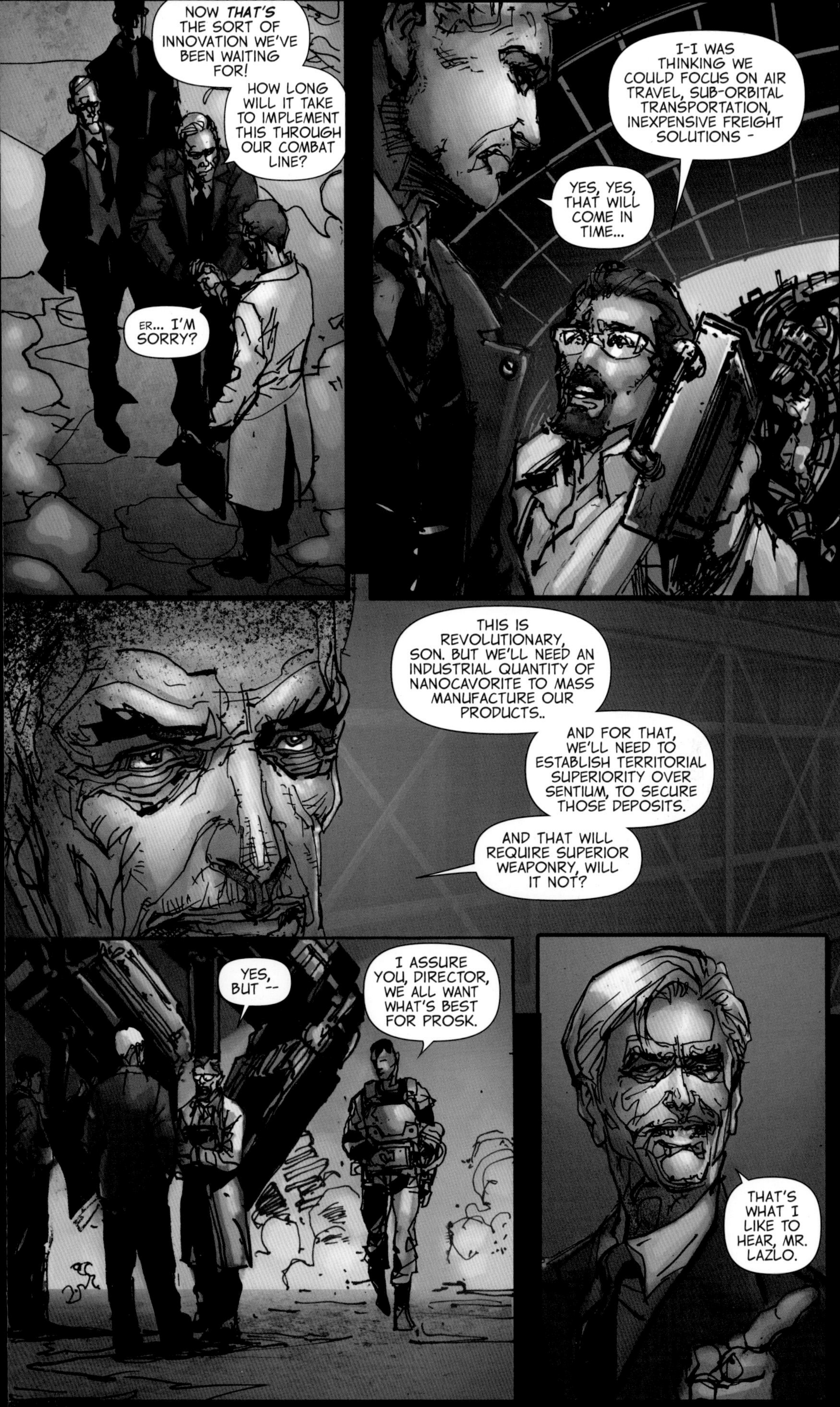
NOW *THAT'S* THE SORT OF INNOVATION WE'VE BEEN WAITING FOR!
HOW LONG WILL IT TAKE TO IMPLEMENT THIS THROUGH OUR COMBAT LINE?
ER... I'M SORRY?
I-I WAS THINKING WE COULD FOCUS ON AIR TRAVEL, SUB-ORBITAL TRANSPORTATION, INEXPENSIVE FREIGHT SOLUTIONS -
YES, YES, THAT WILL COME IN TIME...
THIS IS REVOLUTIONARY, SON. BUT WE'LL NEED AN INDUSTRIAL QUANTITY OF NANOCAVORITE TO MASS MANUFACTURE OUR PRODUCTS..
AND FOR THAT, WE'LL NEED TO ESTABLISH TERRITORIAL SUPERIORITY OVER SENTIUM, TO SECURE THOSE DEPOSITS.
AND THAT WILL REQUIRE SUPERIOR WEAPONRY, WILL IT NOT?
YES, BUT --
I ASSURE YOU, DIRECTOR, WE ALL WANT WHAT'S BEST FOR PROSK.
THAT'S WHAT I LIKE TO HEAR, MR. LAZLO.

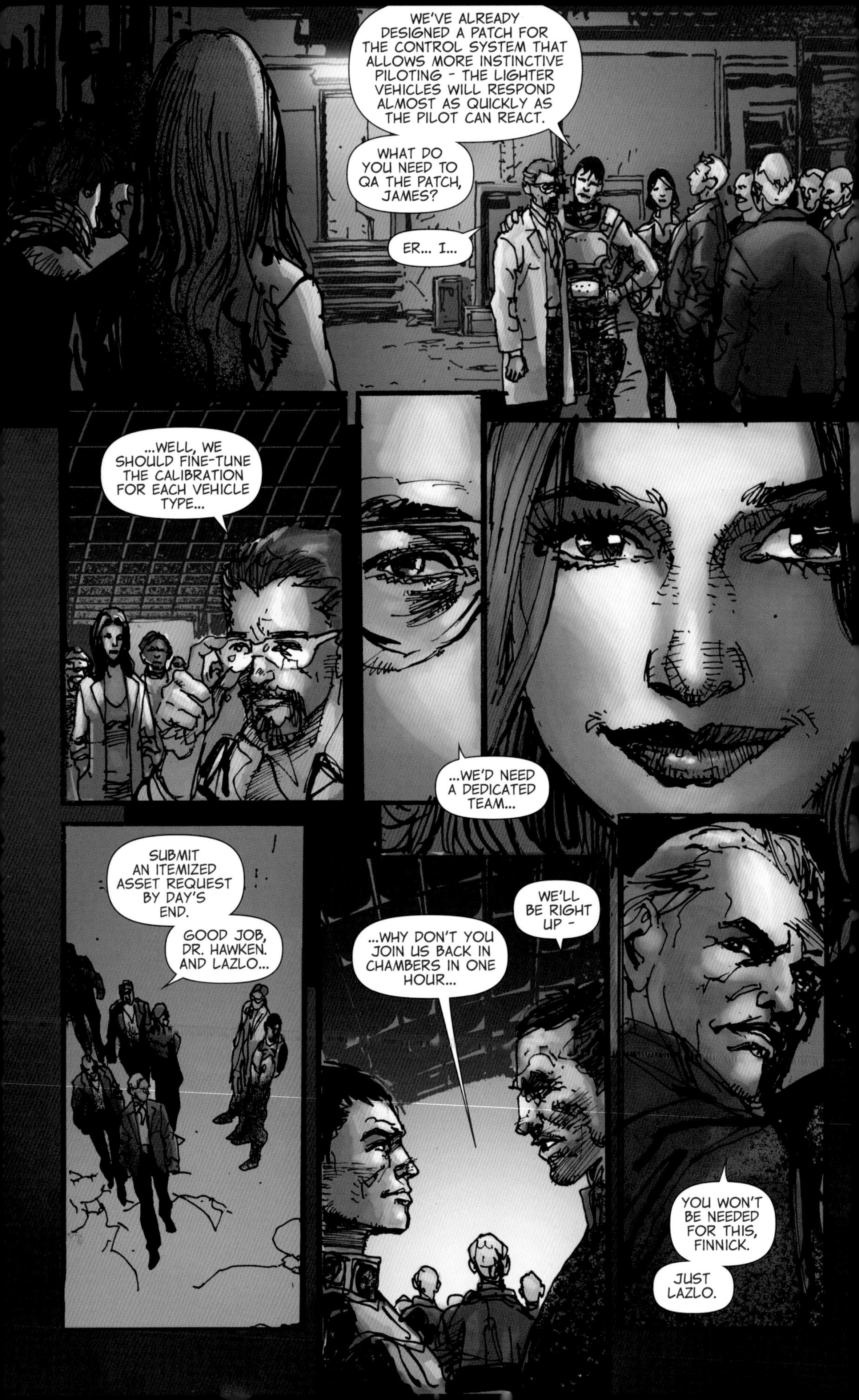
WE'VE ALREADY DESIGNED A PATCH FOR THE CONTROL SYSTEM THAT ALLOWS MORE INSTINCTIVE PILOTING - THE LIGHTER VEHICLES WILL RESPOND ALMOST AS QUICKLY AS THE PILOT CAN REACT.
WHAT DO YOU NEED TO QA THE PATCH, JAMES?
ER... I...
...WELL, WE SHOULD FINE-TUNE THE CALIBRATION FOR EACH VEHICLE TYPE...
...WE'D NEED A DEDICATED TEAM...
SUBMIT AN ITEMIZED ASSET REQUEST BY DAY'S END.
GOOD JOB, DR. HAWKEN. AND LAZLO...
...WHY DON'T YOU JOIN US BACK IN CHAMBERS IN ONE HOUR...
WE'LL BE RIGHT UP -
YOU WON'T BE NEEDED FOR THIS, FINNICK.
JUST LAZLO.

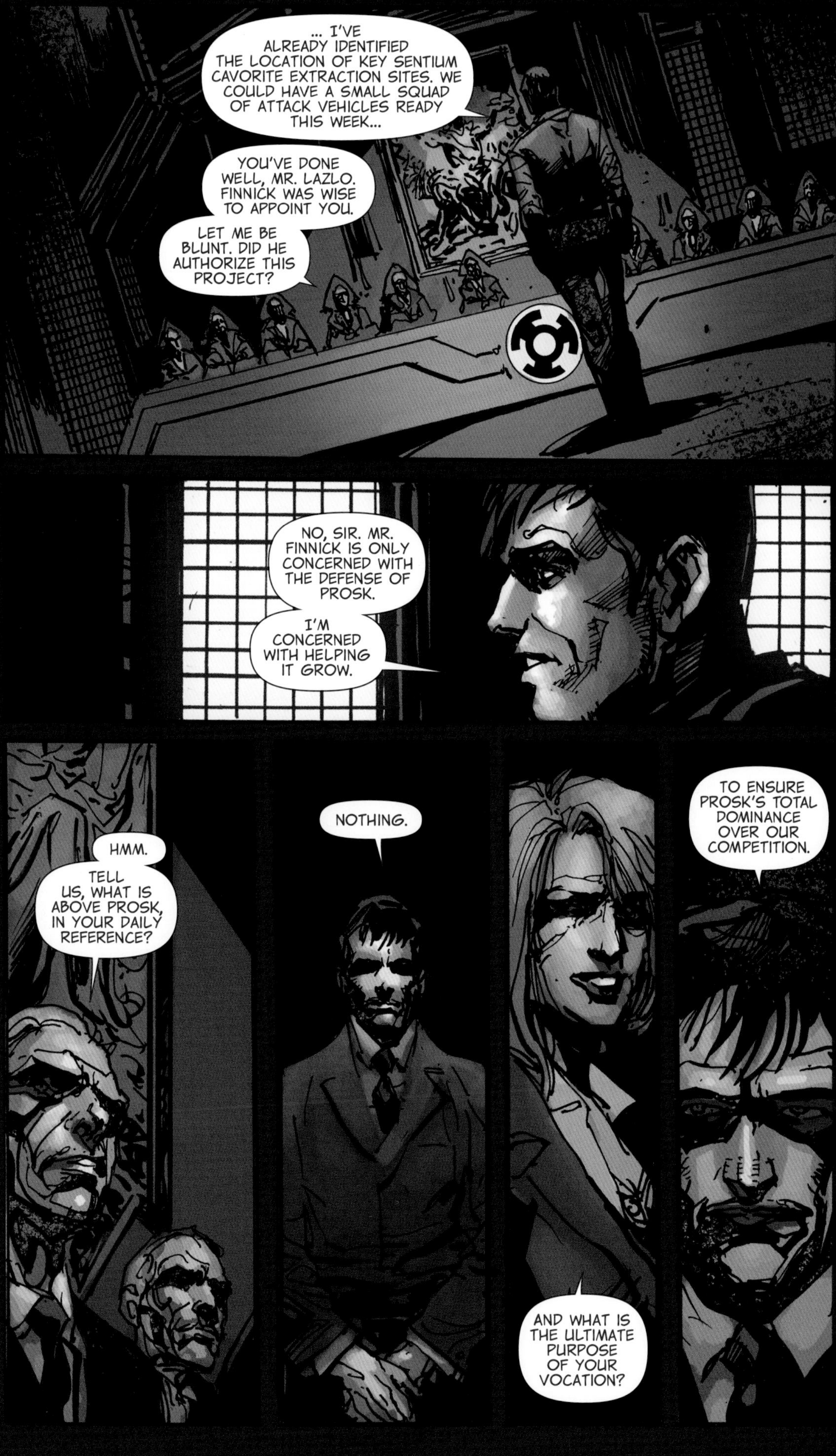
... I'VE ALREADY IDENTIFIED THE LOCATION OF KEY SENTIUM CAVORITE EXTRACTION SITES. WE COULD HAVE A SMALL SQUAD OF ATTACK VEHICLES READY THIS WEEK...
YOU'VE DONE WELL, MR. LAZLO. FINNICK WAS WISE TO APPOINT YOU.
LET ME BE BLUNT. DID HE AUTHORIZE THIS PROJECT?
NO, SIR. MR. FINNICK IS ONLY CONCERNED WITH THE DEFENSE OF PROSK.
I'M CONCERNED WITH HELPING IT GROW.
HMM.
TELL US, WHAT IS ABOVE PROSK, IN YOUR DAILY REFERENCE?
NOTHING.
AND WHAT IS THE ULTIMATE PURPOSE OF YOUR VOCATION?
TO ENSURE PROSK'S TOTAL DOMINANCE OVER OUR COMPETITION.

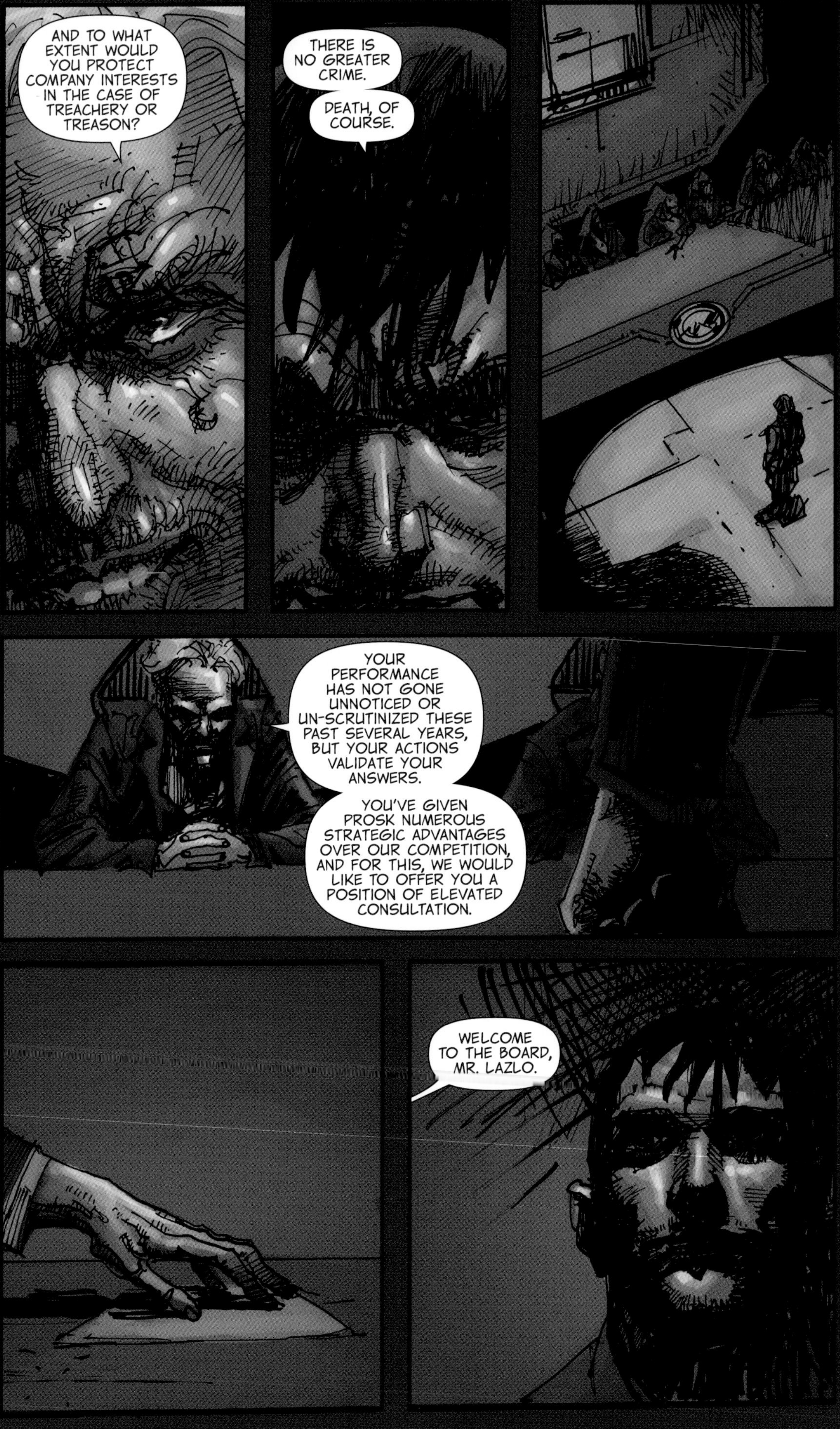
AND TO WHAT EXTENT WOULD YOU PROTECT COMPANY INTERESTS IN THE CASE OF TREACHERY OR TREASON?
THERE IS NO GREATER CRIME.
DEATH, OF COURSE.
YOUR PERFORMANCE HAS NOT GONE UNNOTICED OR UN-SCRUTINIZED THESE PAST SEVERAL YEARS, BUT YOUR ACTIONS VALIDATE YOUR ANSWERS.
YOU'VE GIVEN PROSK NUMEROUS STRATEGIC ADVANTAGES OVER OUR COMPETITION, AND FOR THIS, WE WOULD LIKE TO OFFER YOU A POSITION OF ELEVATED CONSULTATION.
WELCOME TO THE BOARD, MR. LAZLO.

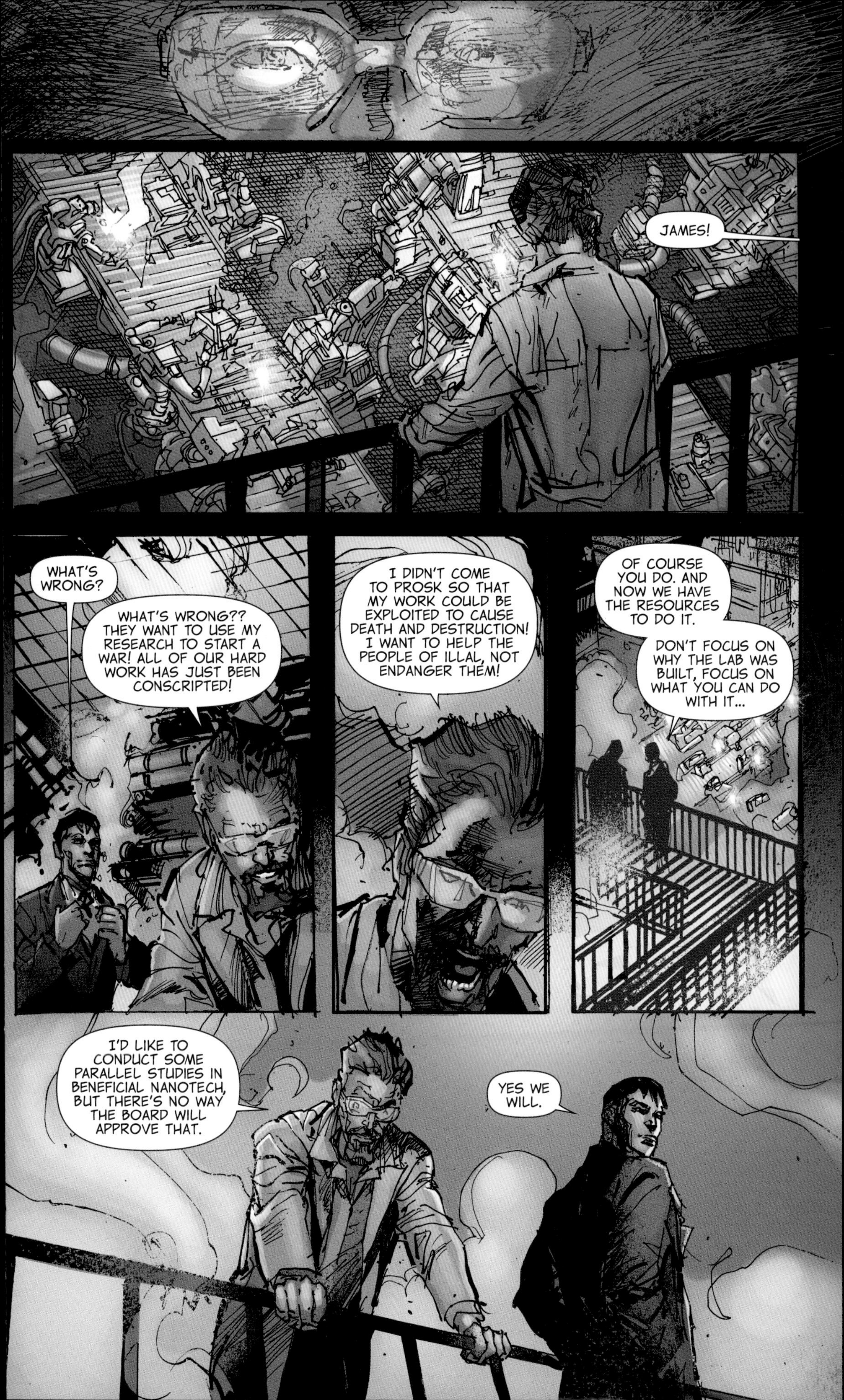
JAMES!
WHAT'S WRONG?
WHAT'S WRONG?? THEY WANT TO USE MY RESEARCH TO START A WAR! ALL OF OUR HARD WORK HAS JUST BEEN CONSCRIPTED!
I DIDN'T COME TO PROSK SO THAT MY WORK COULD BE EXPLOITED TO CAUSE DEATH AND DESTRUCTION! I WANT TO HELP THE PEOPLE OF ILLAL, NOT ENDANGER THEM!
OF COURSE YOU DO. AND NOW WE HAVE THE RESOURCES TO DO IT.
DON'T FOCUS ON WHY THE LAB WAS BUILT, FOCUS ON WHAT YOU CAN DO WITH IT...
I'D LIKE TO CONDUCT SOME PARALLEL STUDIES IN BENEFICIAL NANOTECH, BUT THERE'S NO WAY THE BOARD WILL APPROVE THAT.
YES WE WILL.

AND HOW CAN YOU GUARANTEE THAT? I --

...IS... IS THAT A...?

YES IT IS.

YOU'RE JOKING! THAT'S AMAZING!

I DON'T KNOW WHETHER TO SHAKE YOUR HAND OR SALUTE YOU!

JUST DON'T MAKE ME HAVE TO FIRE YOU...

...I'M KIDDING...

I PROMISED TO TAKE CARE OF YOU, JAMES.

LET'S LEAVE A POSITIVE LEGACY, SOMETHING PEOPLE WILL REMEMBER FOR GENERATIONS TO COME...

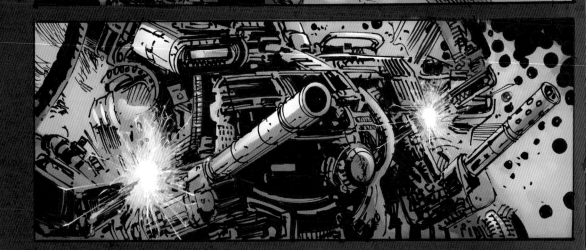

BOARDROOM TRANSCRIPT

Prosk Operations Meeting: dJ2Qx64ArC73

PROSK SECURITY CLEARANCE LEVEL **9C**

O'RILEY: (...) these sites do appear to maintain more substantial security and communication encryption to comparative locations in the area. The evidence supports the theory. That said, Mr. Finnick, you can't seriously be advocating a full-fledged raid on a UTA ratified Sentium mining facility in broad daylight?

LAZLO: We could attack them at night if it will make you feel better.

FINNICK: Shut up, Rion. Regardless, what Mr. Lazlo lacks in tact, he makes up for with insight. CSD isn't advocating overt action. This operation would be conducted under our strictest plausible deniability protocol-

CURSON: -Which is all well and good for your group's usual activities, Mr. Finnick, but with all due respect - this isn't exactly disposing of a body. What you're proposing here is a significant military engagement. The threat of exposure is too high.

DENTON: I agree. The UTA sanctions we'd face if implicated (...) would cripple us. The ramifications go way beyond our loader manufacturing division...

FINNICK: Sentium doesn't want the UTA to know the truth about those mines any more than we do. They've gone to great lengths to keep cavorite a secret. I'll wager that nothing we do is going to change that.

O'RILEY: But you're talking about open warfare! It's too risky!

LUCAS: ((Banging gavel)) Gentlemen, please. We need to think about this not in terms of what we risk, but what we can gain. With their new loaders Sentium has essentially ousted us from a market we created. Bankson's postured for years about Sentium's "superior engineering", when the only superior aspect of their design is a rock that their surveyors were lucky enough to stumble across first. A substance we now know exists. I will not allow Prosk to cede our most important market, our most iconic product line, without a fight. Not on my watch.

O'RILEY: I hope you know what you're getting us into here, director. There's no stepping back from this.

LUCAS: You're right Jo, but if this Dr. (...) Hawken is right, we can regain our footing in one product cycle.

CURSON: But at what cost? I believe we CAN recover market share without inciting open conflict, just give me a window to produce a cheaper model.

LUCAS: No. Cutting costs won't be enough this time, Curson. For once I want Prosk to compete with quality, not volume. Mr. Finnick (...) operation approved.

FINNICK: Yes sir.

LAZLO: You won't regret this ((FINNICK, LAZLO exit))

LUCAS: That'll be all, for now.

CURSON: But sir-

LUCAS: That'll be ALL. Meeting adjourned.

-END TRANSCRIPT-

Prosk Operations Meeting :: dJ2Qx64ArC73 ::

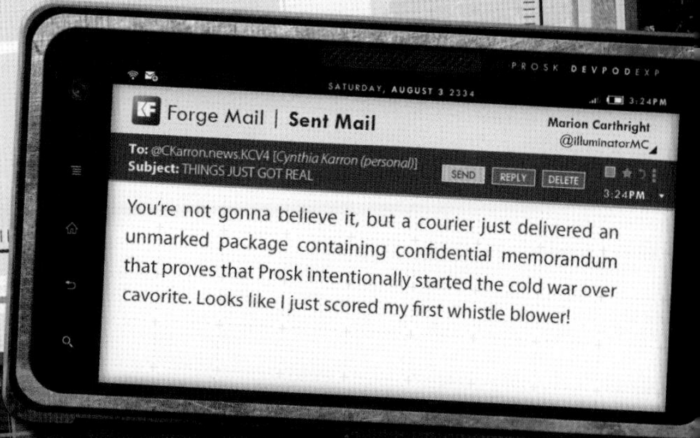
PROSK DEVPODEXP
SATURDAY, AUGUST 3 2334
3:24PM
Forge Mail | Sent Mail
Marion Carthright
@IlluminatorMC
To: @CKarron.news.KCV4 [Cynthia Karron (personal)]
Subject: THINGS JUST GOT REAL
SEND
REPLY
DELETE
3:24PM
You're not gonna believe it, but a courier just delivered an unmarked package containing confidential memorandum that proves that Prosk intentionally started the cold war over cavorite. Looks like I just scored my first whistle blower!

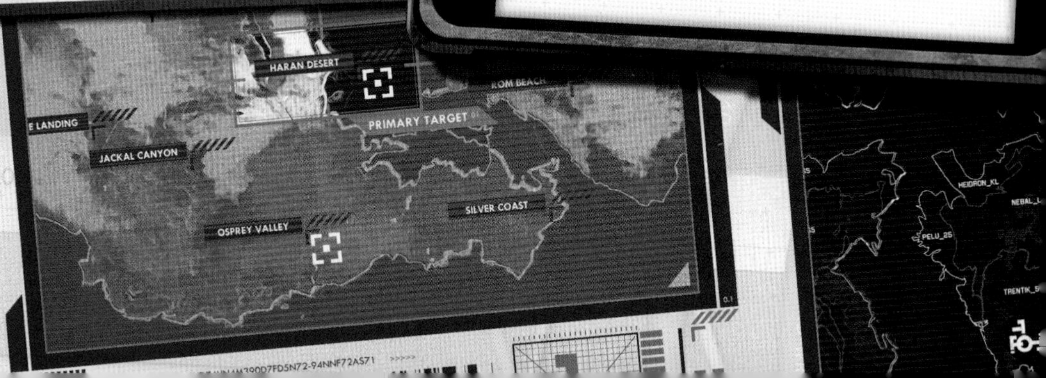
HARAN DESERT
ROM BEACH
E LANDING
PRIMARY TARGET
JACKAL CANYON
SILVER COAST
OSPREY VALLEY
HEIDRON_XL
PELU_25

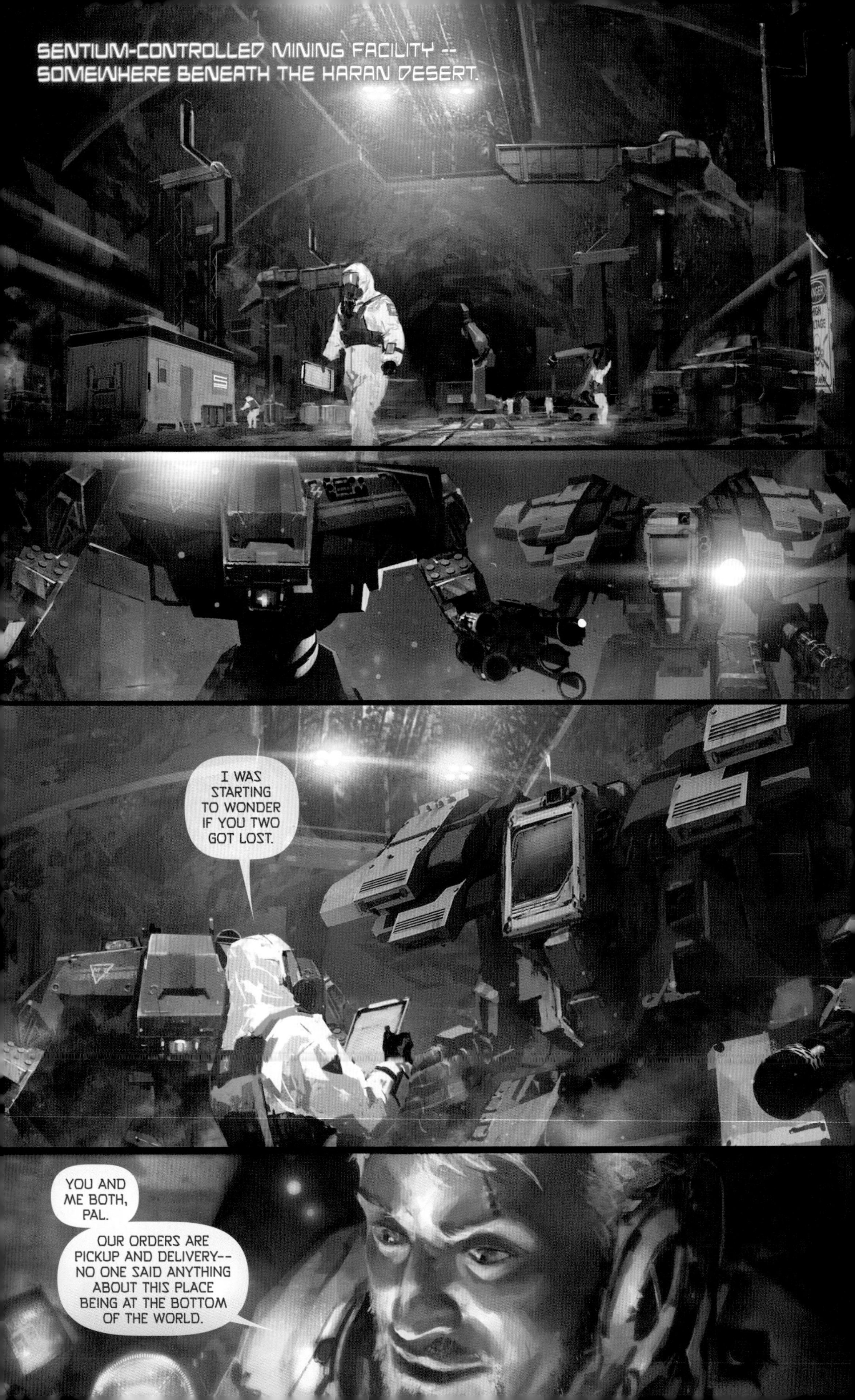
SENTIUM-CONTROLLED MINING FACILITY --
SOMEWHERE BENEATH THE HARAN DESERT.
I WAS STARTING TO WONDER IF YOU TWO GOT LOST.
YOU AND ME BOTH, PAL.
OUR ORDERS ARE PICKUP AND DELIVERY-- NO ONE SAID ANYTHING ABOUT THIS PLACE BEING AT THE BOTTOM OF THE WORLD.

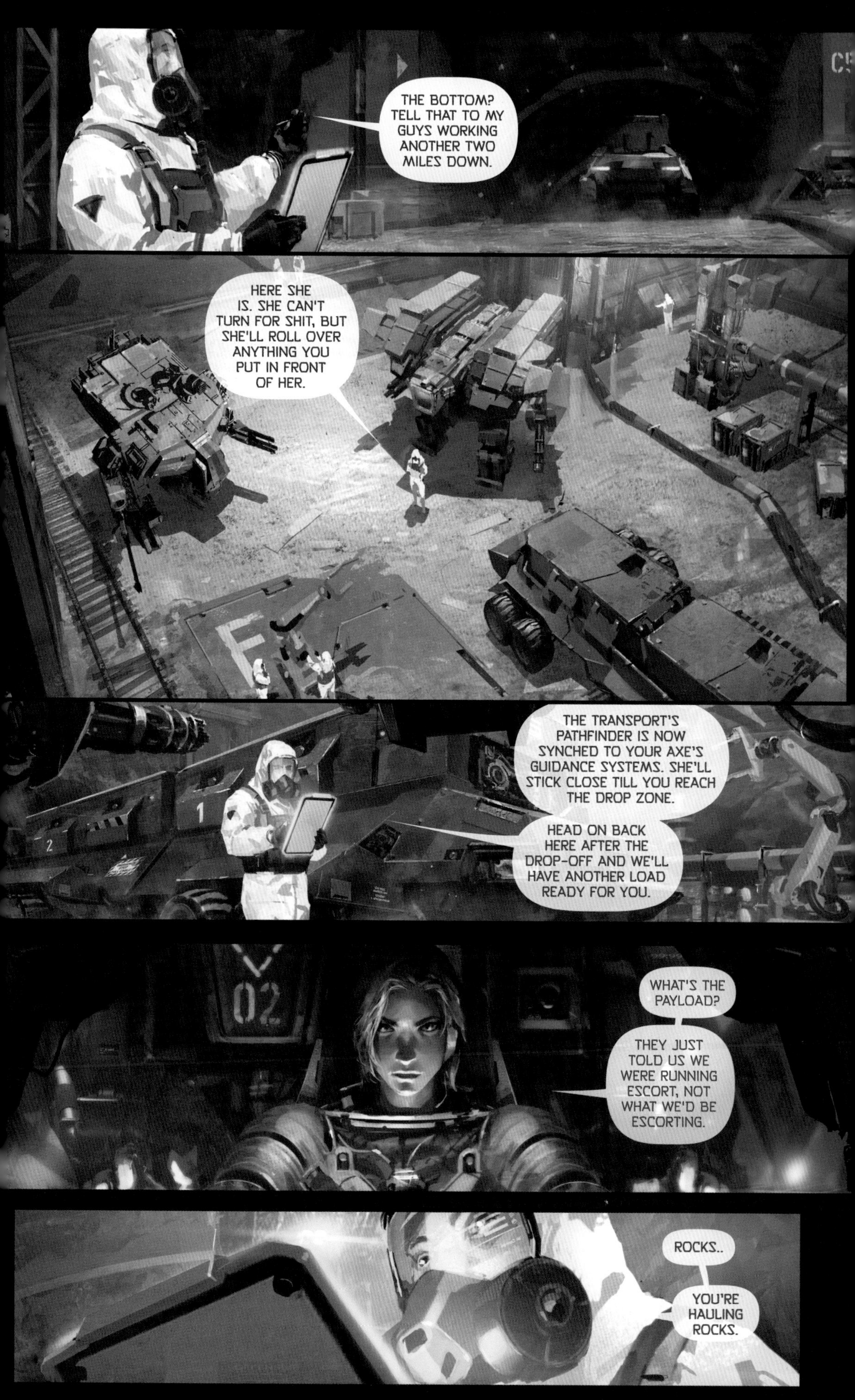

THE BOTTOM? TELL THAT TO MY GUYS WORKING ANOTHER TWO MILES DOWN.
HERE SHE IS. SHE CAN'T TURN FOR SHIT, BUT SHE'LL ROLL OVER ANYTHING YOU PUT IN FRONT OF HER.
THE TRANSPORT'S PATHFINDER IS NOW SYNCHED TO YOUR AXE'S GUIDANCE SYSTEMS. SHE'LL STICK CLOSE TILL YOU REACH THE DROP ZONE.
HEAD ON BACK HERE AFTER THE DROP-OFF AND WE'LL HAVE ANOTHER LOAD READY FOR YOU.
WHAT'S THE PAYLOAD?
THEY JUST TOLD US WE WERE RUNNING ESCORT, NOT WHAT WE'D BE ESCORTING.
ROCKS..
YOU'RE HAULING ROCKS.

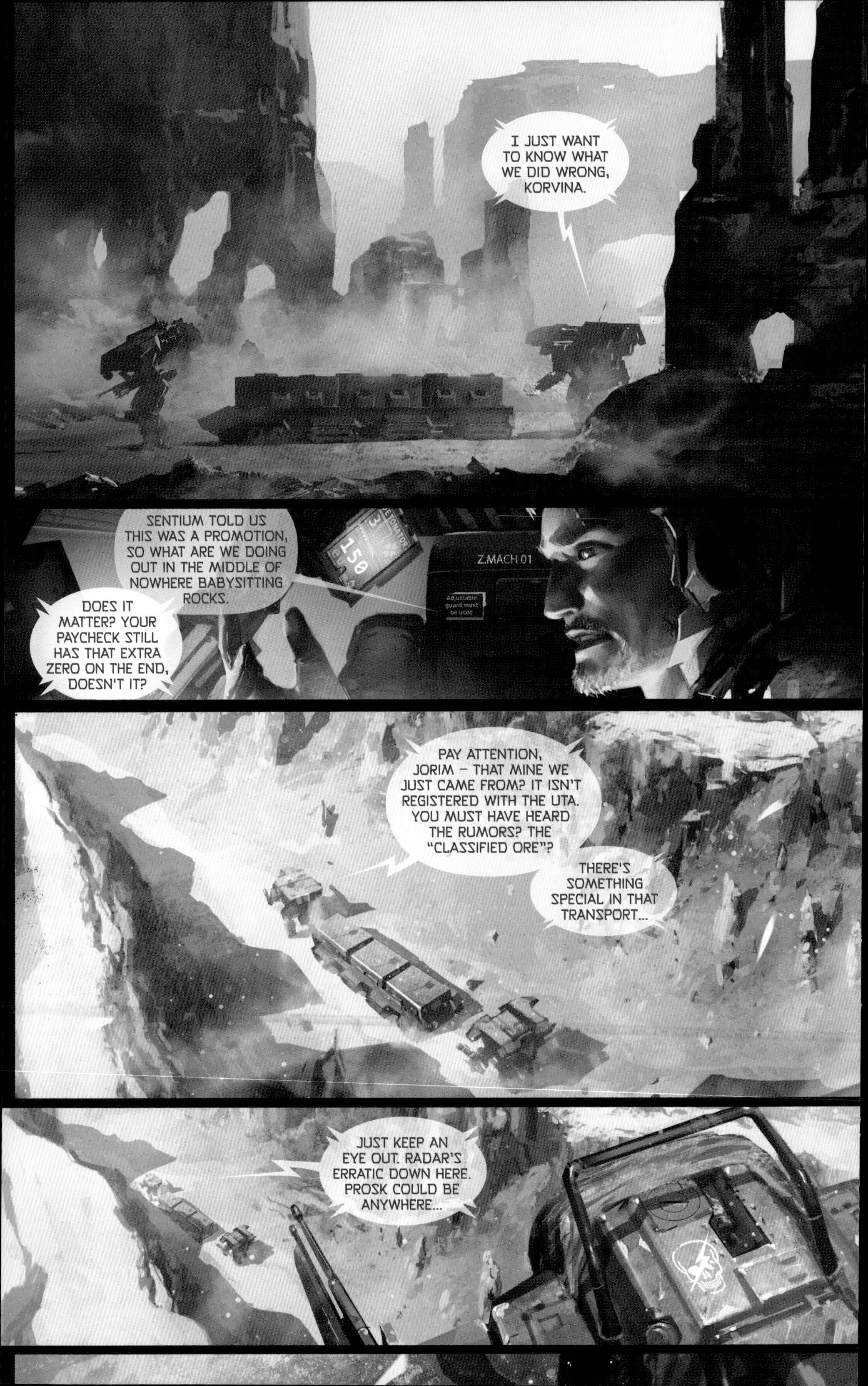
I JUST WANT TO KNOW WHAT WE DID WRONG, KORVINA.
SENTIUM TOLD US THIS WAS A PROMOTION, SO WHAT ARE WE DOING OUT IN THE MIDDLE OF NOWHERE BABYSITTING ROCKS.
Z.MACH 01
Adjustable guard must be used
DOES IT MATTER? YOUR PAYCHECK STILL HAS THAT EXTRA ZERO ON THE END, DOESN'T IT?
PAY ATTENTION, JORIM – THAT MINE WE JUST CAME FROM? IT ISN'T REGISTERED WITH THE UTA. YOU MUST HAVE HEARD THE RUMORS? THE "CLASSIFIED ORE"?
THERE'S SOMETHING SPECIAL IN THAT TRANSPORT...
JUST KEEP AN EYE OUT. RADAR'S ERRATIC DOWN HERE. PROSK COULD BE ANYWHERE...

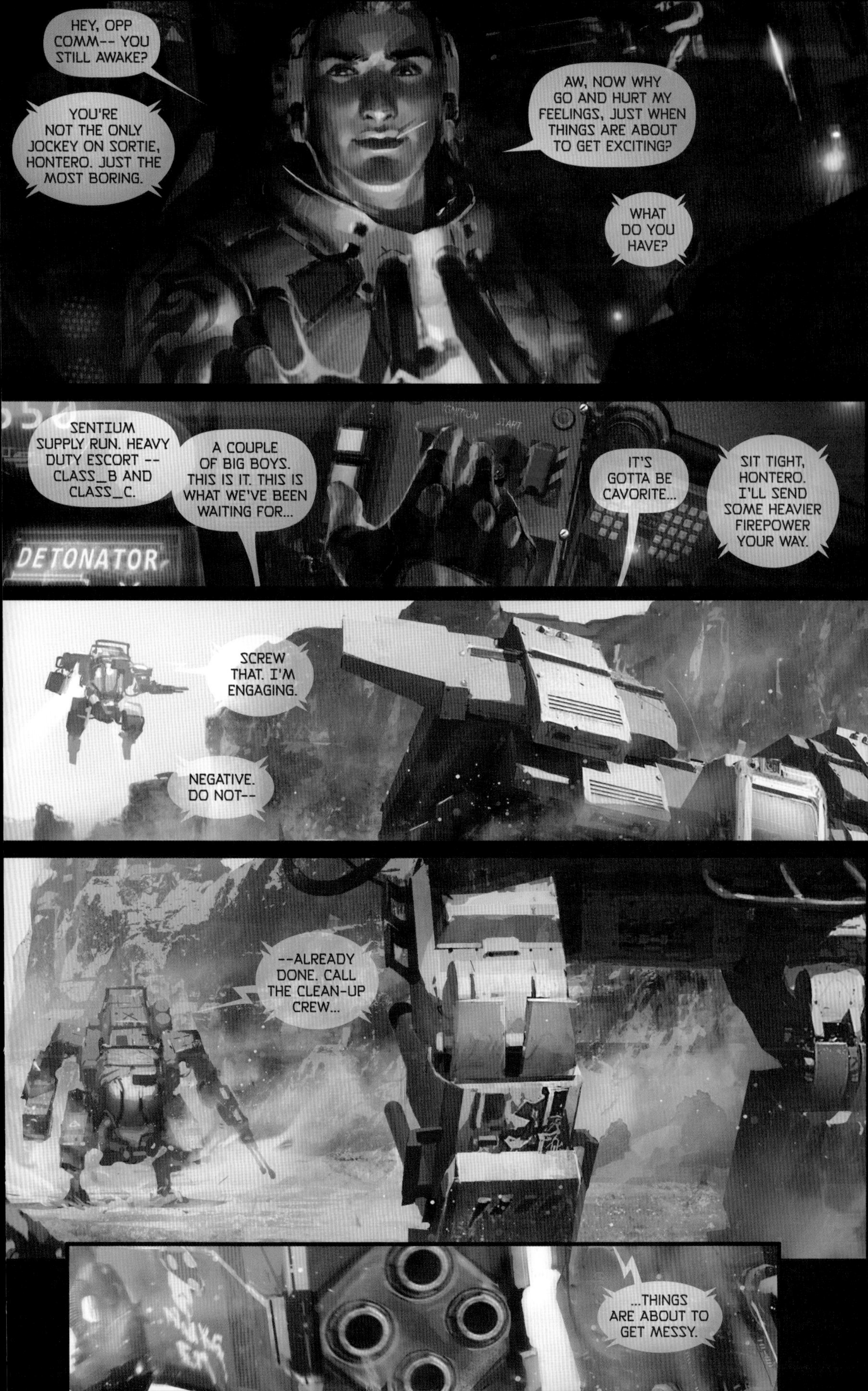
HEY, OPP COMM-- YOU STILL AWAKE?
YOU'RE NOT THE ONLY JOCKEY ON SORTIE, HONTERO. JUST THE MOST BORING.
AW, NOW WHY GO AND HURT MY FEELINGS, JUST WHEN THINGS ARE ABOUT TO GET EXCITING?
WHAT DO YOU HAVE?
DETONATOR
SENTIUM SUPPLY RUN. HEAVY DUTY ESCORT -- CLASS_B AND CLASS_C.
A COUPLE OF BIG BOYS. THIS IS IT. THIS IS WHAT WE'VE BEEN WAITING FOR...
IT'S GOTTA BE CAVORITE...
SIT TIGHT, HONTERO. I'LL SEND SOME HEAVIER FIREPOWER YOUR WAY.
SCREW THAT. I'M ENGAGING.
NEGATIVE. DO NOT--
--ALREADY DONE. CALL THE CLEAN-UP CREW...
...THINGS ARE ABOUT TO GET MESSY.

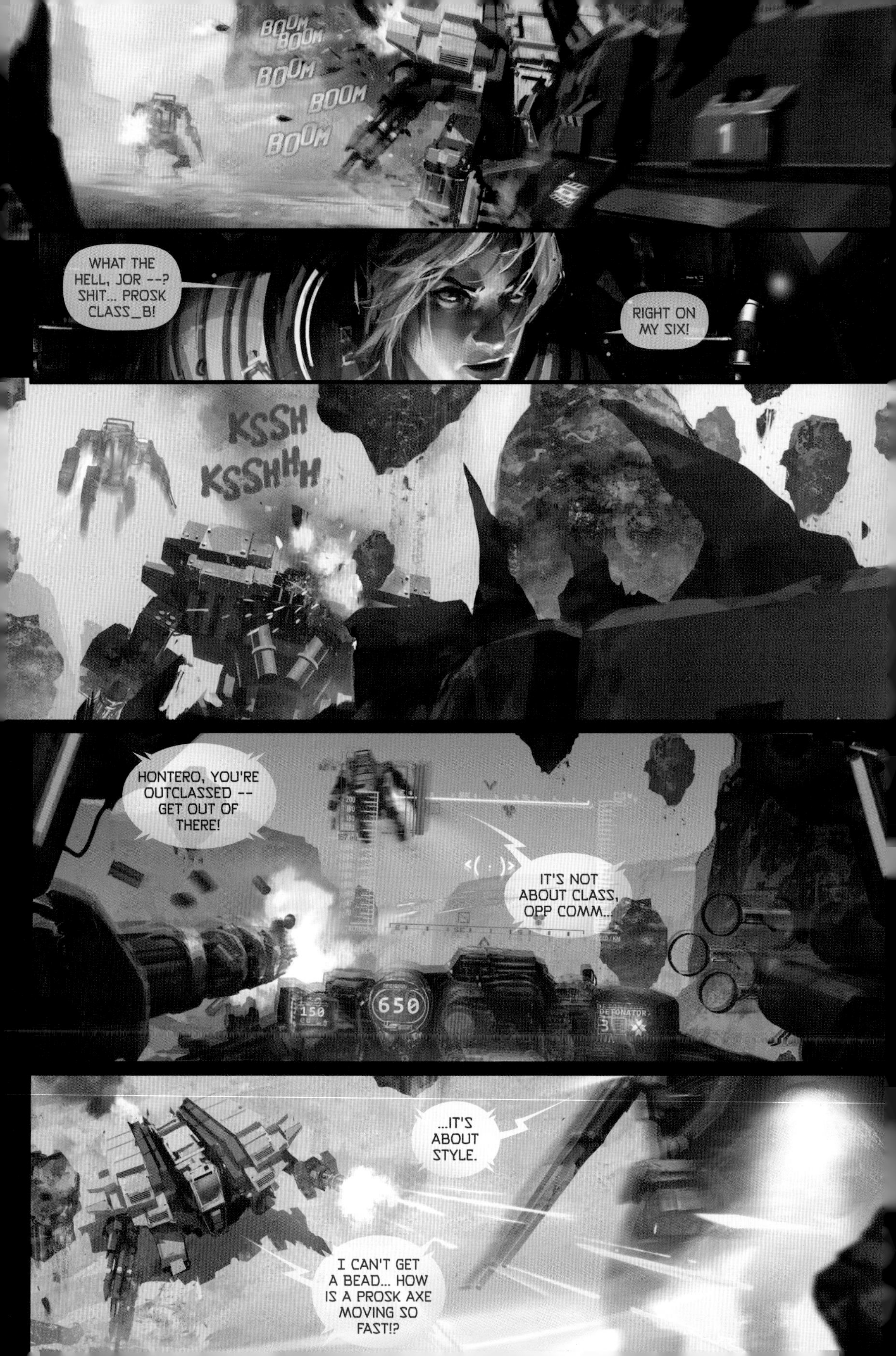
BOOM BOOM
BOOM
BOOM
BOOM
WHAT THE HELL, JOR --? SHIT... PROSK CLASS_B!
RIGHT ON MY SIX!
KSSH KSSHHH
HONTERO, YOU'RE OUTCLASSED -- GET OUT OF THERE!
IT'S NOT ABOUT CLASS, OPP COMM...
650
150
DETONATOR
...IT'S ABOUT STYLE.
I CAN'T GET A BEAD... HOW IS A PROSK AXE MOVING SO FAST!?

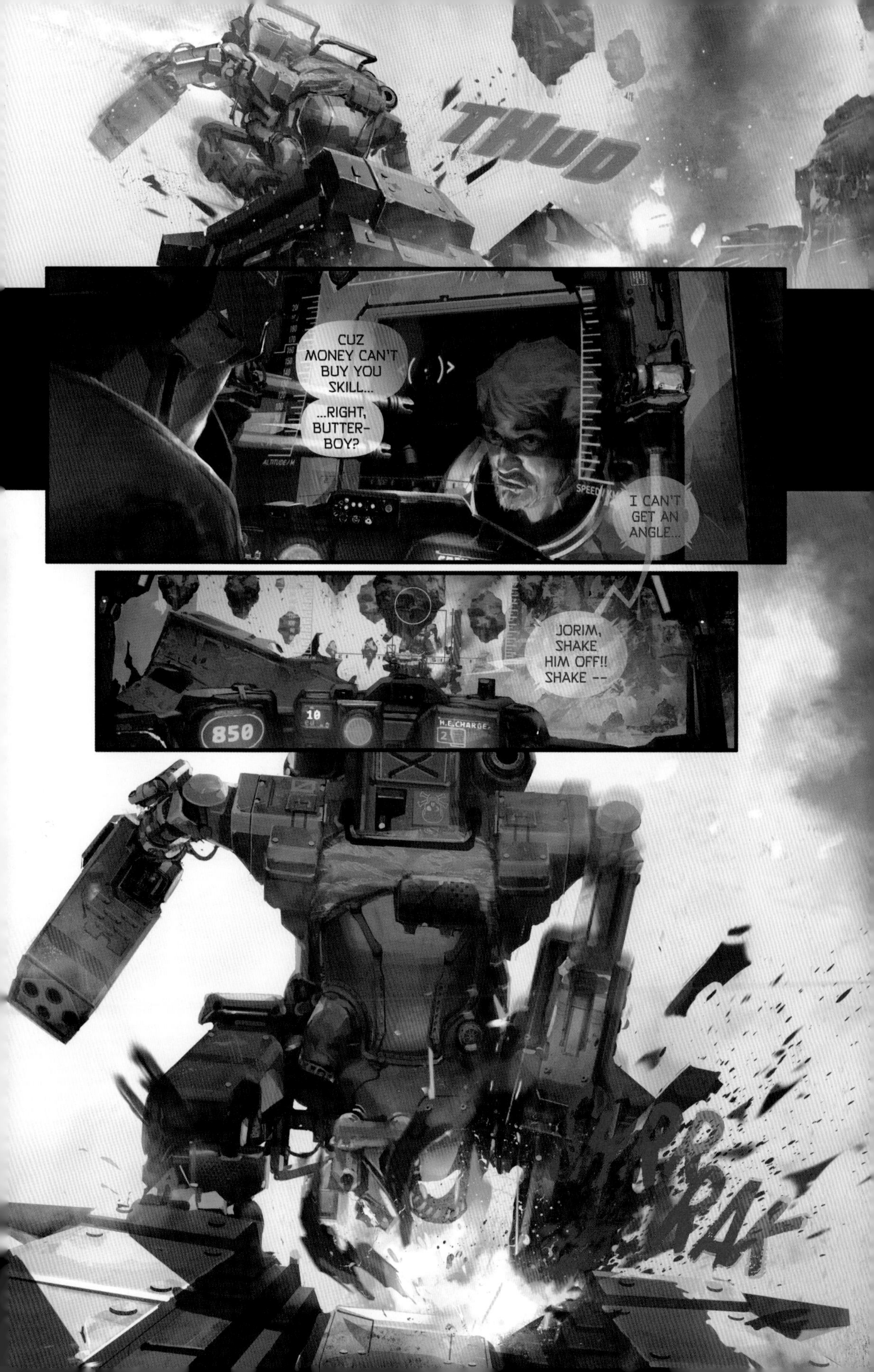
THUD
CUZ MONEY CAN'T BUY YOU SKILL...
...RIGHT, BUTTER-BOY?
I CAN'T GET AN ANGLE...
JORIM, SHAKE HIM OFF!! SHAKE --
850
10
H.E.CHARGE
2

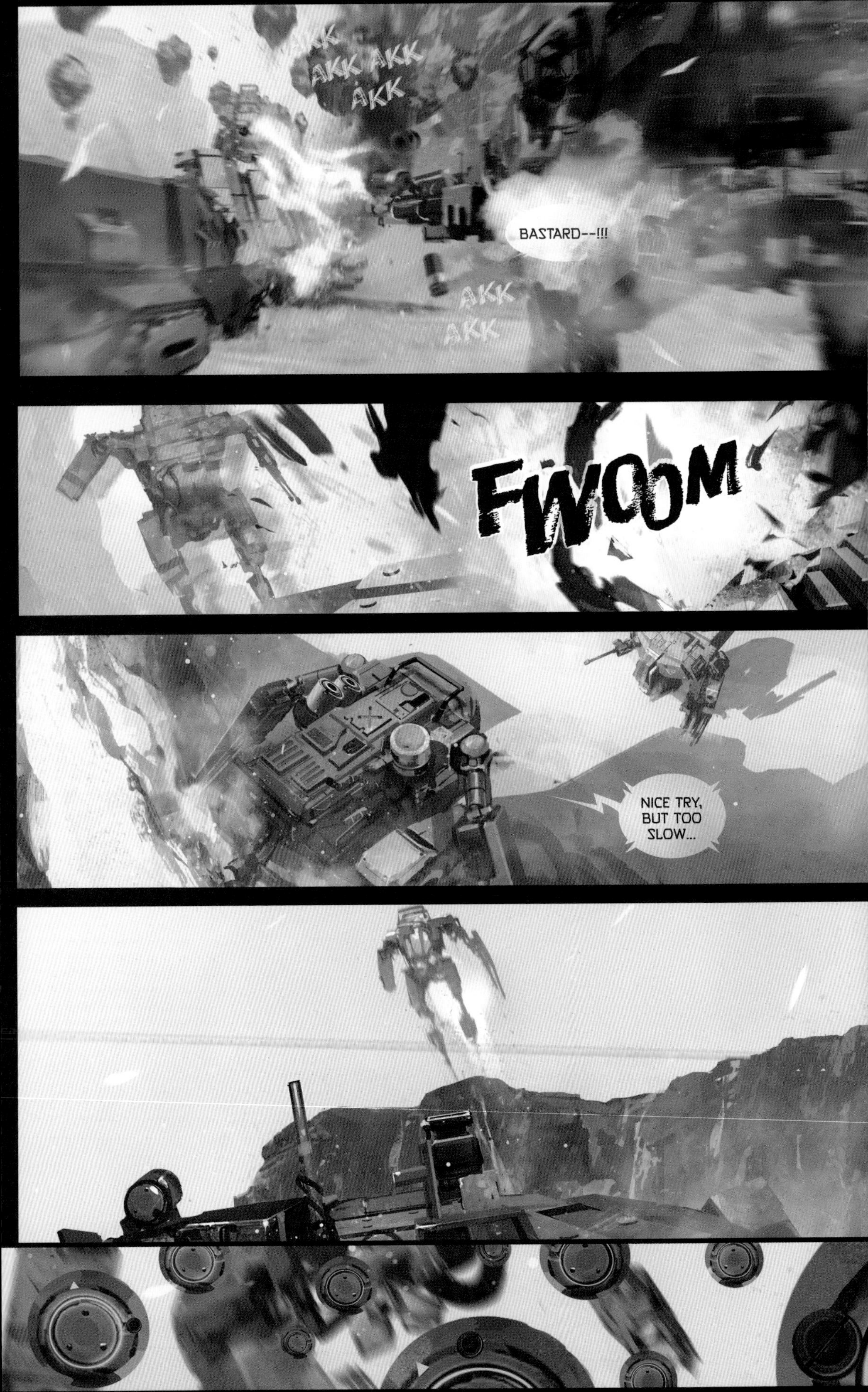
AKK
AKK AKK
AKK
BASTARD--!!!
AKK
AKK
FWOOM
NICE TRY, BUT TOO SLOW...

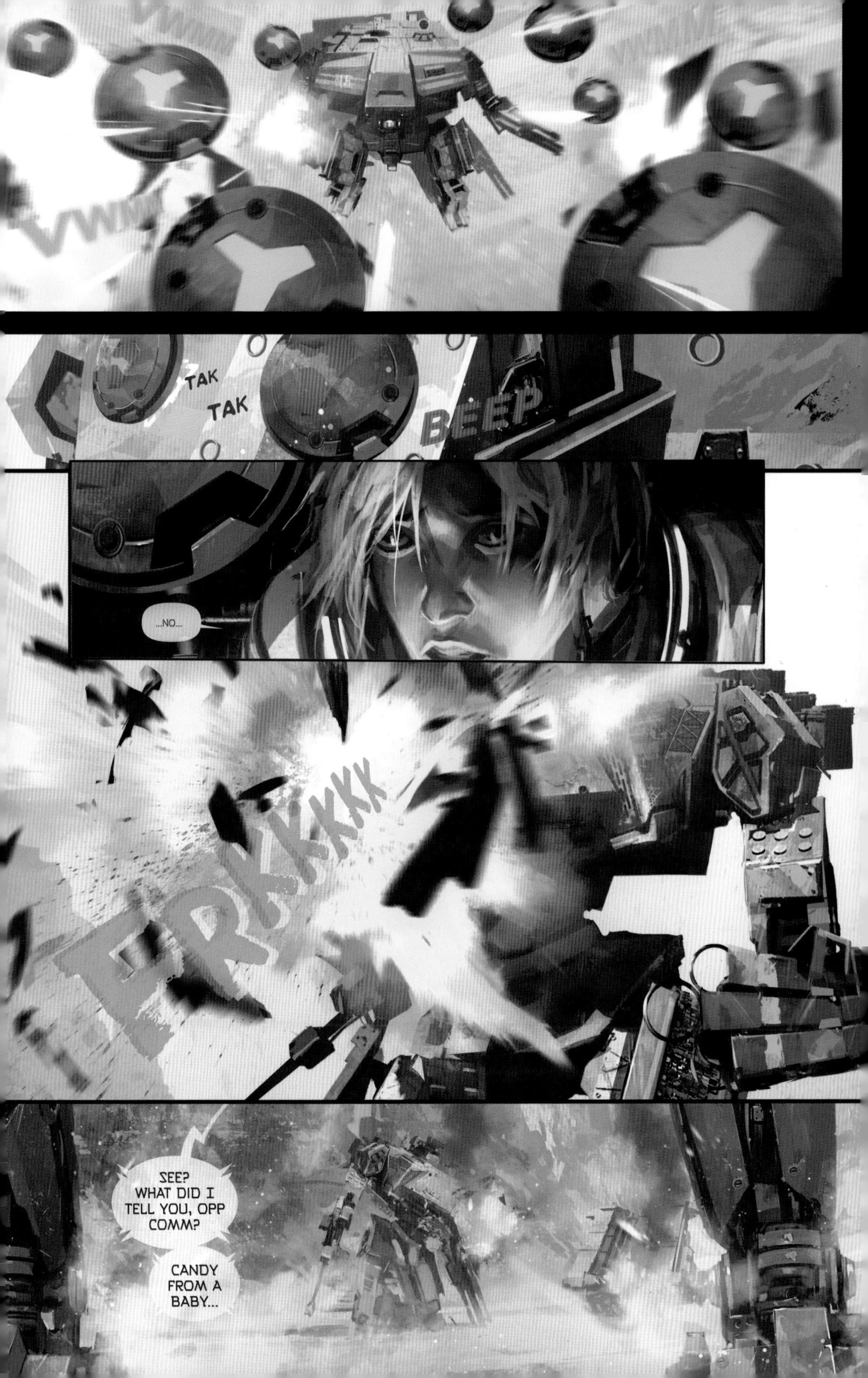
VWM
VWM
VWM
TAK
TAK
BEEP
...NO...
ERKKKKK
SEE? WHAT DID I TELL YOU, OPP COMM?
CANDY FROM A BABY...

PROSK EXFILTRATION ZONE, HOURS LATER.

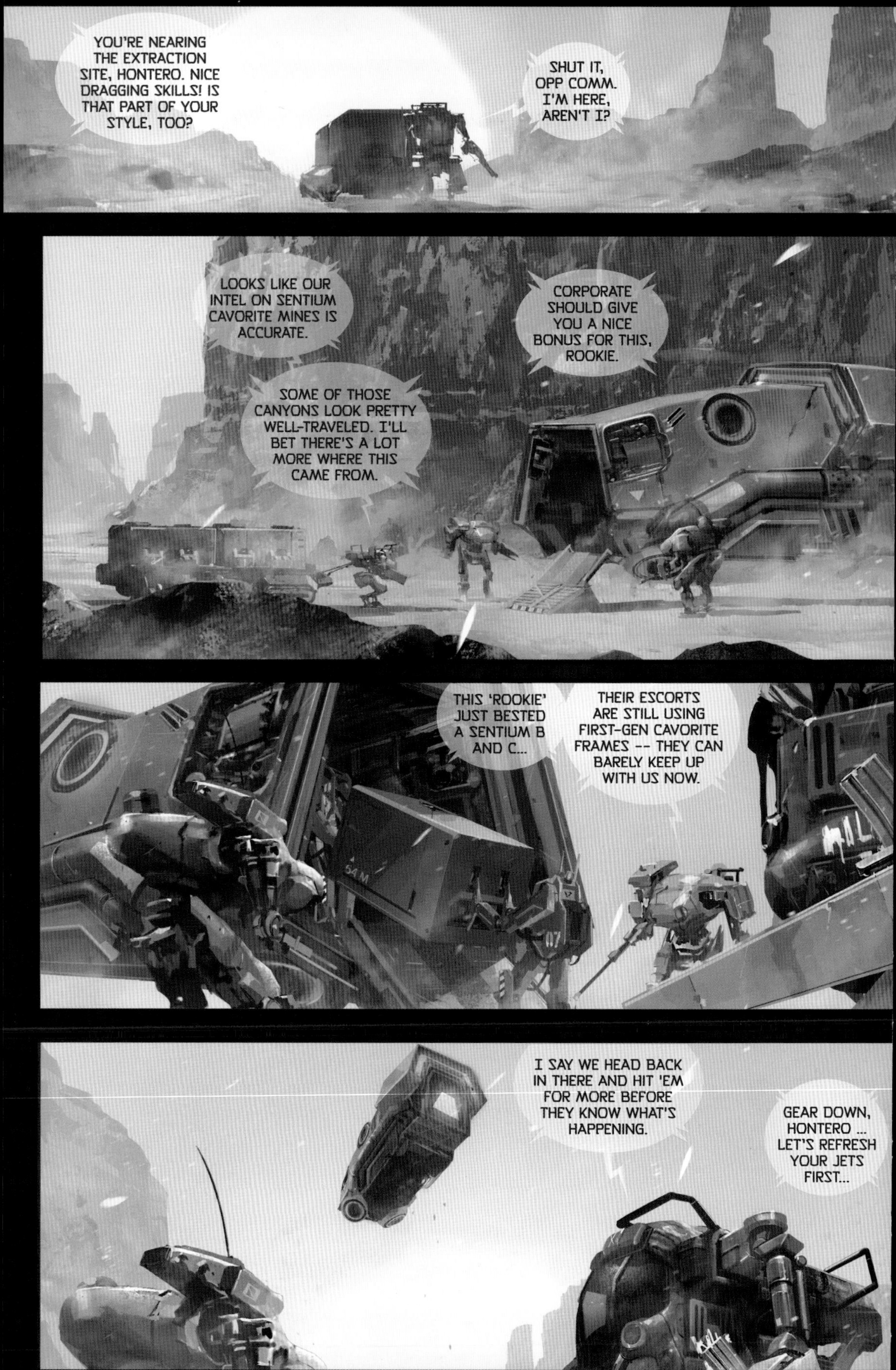
YOU'RE NEARING THE EXTRACTION SITE, HONTERO. NICE DRAGGING SKILLS! IS THAT PART OF YOUR STYLE, TOO?
SHUT IT, OPP COMM. I'M HERE, AREN'T I?
LOOKS LIKE OUR INTEL ON SENTIUM CAVORITE MINES IS ACCURATE.
CORPORATE SHOULD GIVE YOU A NICE BONUS FOR THIS, ROOKIE.
SOME OF THOSE CANYONS LOOK PRETTY WELL-TRAVELED. I'LL BET THERE'S A LOT MORE WHERE THIS CAME FROM.
THIS 'ROOKIE' JUST BESTED A SENTIUM B AND C...
THEIR ESCORTS ARE STILL USING FIRST-GEN CAVORITE FRAMES -- THEY CAN BARELY KEEP UP WITH US NOW.
I SAY WE HEAD BACK IN THERE AND HIT 'EM FOR MORE BEFORE THEY KNOW WHAT'S HAPPENING.
GEAR DOWN, HONTERO ... LET'S REFRESH YOUR JETS FIRST...

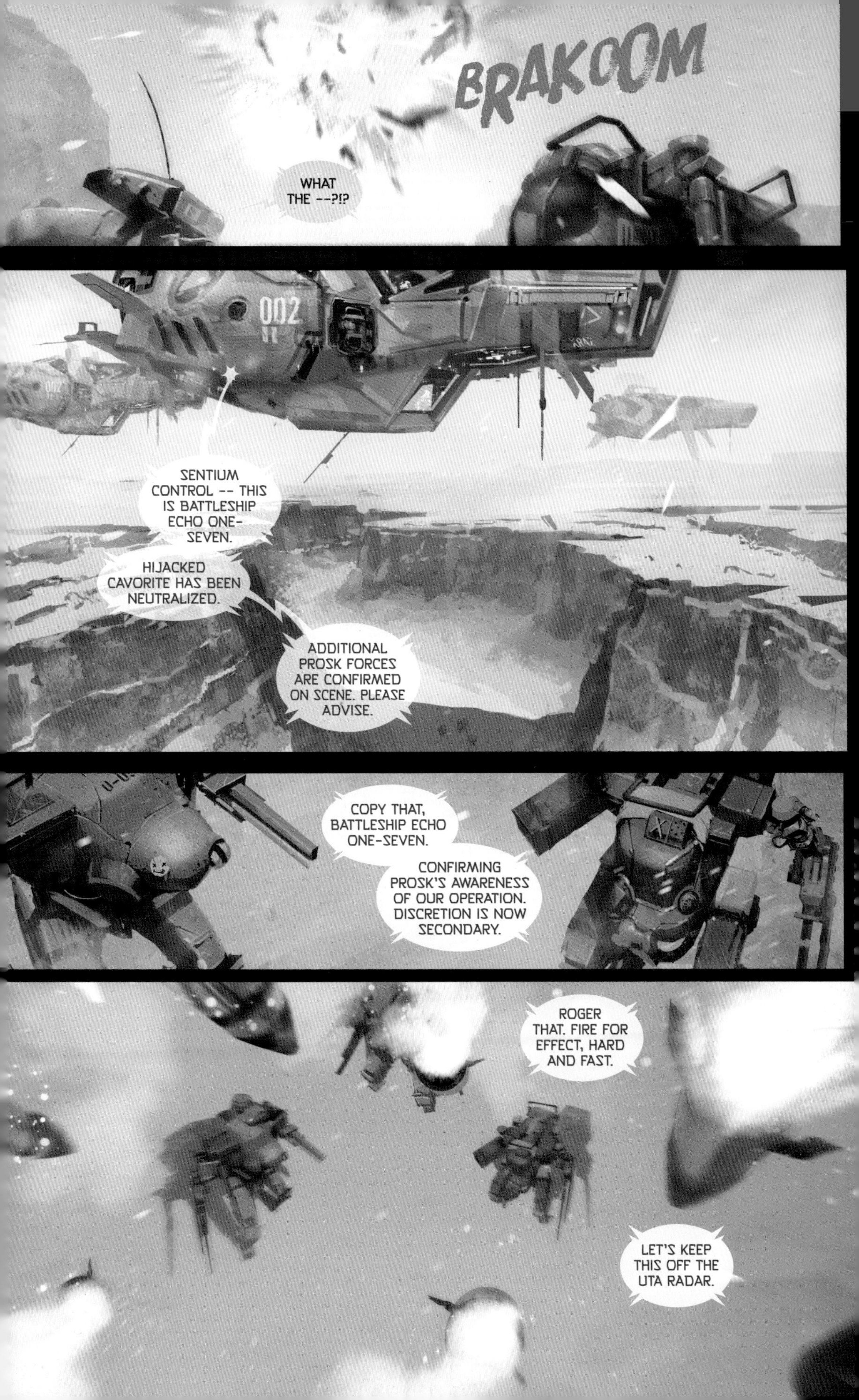
BRAKOOM
WHAT THE --?!?
SENTIUM CONTROL -- THIS IS BATTLESHIP ECHO ONE-SEVEN.
HIJACKED CAVORITE HAS BEEN NEUTRALIZED.
ADDITIONAL PROSK FORCES ARE CONFIRMED ON SCENE. PLEASE ADVISE.
COPY THAT, BATTLESHIP ECHO ONE-SEVEN.
CONFIRMING PROSK'S AWARENESS OF OUR OPERATION. DISCRETION IS NOW SECONDARY.
ROGER THAT. FIRE FOR EFFECT, HARD AND FAST.
LET'S KEEP THIS OFF THE UTA RADAR.

PROSK PORTAL
EXTRANET BROWSER

IWN - Rion Lazlo

Search - UTA Signal De...

PR

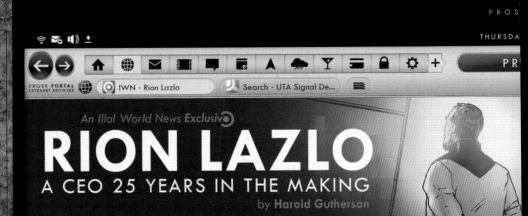

An Illal World News Exclusive

RION LAZLO
A CEO 25 YEARS IN THE MAKING
by **Harold Gutherson**

NEWS UTA **PROSK** SENTIUM CRION MPCS PQR SCRIP OFF-WORLD ENTERTAINMENT

The office is surprisingly bare. No art. No interior decor. The only life in the room a single vase of fresh flowers on his des For the office of the new colonial CEO, responsible for the multi-planetary corporation's most profitable quarter in century, one might expect more from 53-year-old Rion Lazlo. Yet there's none of his trademark swagger here. If anythir his office evokes an almost Sentium simplicity. *Sleek. Minimal. Effective.* This is the new Prosk formula, ushering in a ne era for the stalwart MPC and its latest director, with whom I recently sat down. Our chat began auspiciously wher inquired into the contents of the tumbler he was nursing. "Success," he purred with a smile. Off my expression, he adde "With a dash of humility." I laughed. "Just a dash?" Again with that smirk, "Any more and what's the point?"

Lazlo's confidence is justified. With PQRs in the billions and an export pipeline of award-winning product dominating th star chart, it's hard to believe that just a few decades ago Prosk's brand was perceived as a low cost, low quality alternativ to industry standard-bearer, Sentium Corp. No one *wanted* to buy Prosk back then. You simply made do.

ORIGINAL PROSK PROTOTYPE
INFILTRATOR™ MECH
1.01.2164.13A

The original combat capable mech developed with Nanocavorite technology; this prototype developed by Dr. James Hawken for Prosk marked the furthest leap forward in applied robotics and military defense. A rigid HV loader chassis was modified using Nanocavorite technology to allow for a weight class light enough to support a VTOL propulsion system, allowing quick deployment and movement throughout engagements.

- Nanocavorite Design
- Modified HV Loader Chassis
- VTOL Propulsion System
- Basic Weapons Suite
- Basic Counter-Measure Suite
- Light Class A-Mech

DEFENSE DIVISION

CURRENT PROSK PROTOTYPE
RAZORBACK™ MECH
1.01.2587.12C

Prosk's current mech prototype utilizes advanced Nanocavorite applications to create an even denser micro-weave, allowing for stronger armor plating and a larger cache of performance components without sacrificing mobility or functionality.

- Cross Weave Kinetic Armor
- Advanced Counter-Measure Suite
- Heavy Class C-Mech

Illal changed everything. How did this distant industri colony become a household name? After the UTA's approv of the controversial Illal Development Initiative, the Terra Hyper-Republic at large expressed only concern for wh in essence amounted to the galaxy's first privatized plane Then the public watched in awe as lesser-known MP(became fledgling nations with thriving populations eager cash in on the Illalian dream. And then came Cavorite. So th story goes, Sentium joined the terraforming conglomera already aware of the rare ore's presence on Illal. But it too Lazlo, then a young agent in Prosk's Corporate Securi Division, and a brilliant-yet-overlooked engineer name James Hawken, to alert Prosk to its existence and th potential of the now infamous gravity-defying metal.

"He was destined to change the world," recalls Lazlo, wh personally facilitated Hawken's relocation from Sentiur to Prosk. "I just gave James the resources he needed ar the spotlight he deserved." Hawken exposed Sentium use of Cavorite and led Prosk's R&D division to incorporat the element into their own product line (Lazlo is quick t downplay the reports of violent conflict preceding th

DION

10 2359

9:36PM

RTAL POWERED BY PHOENIX

File Edit View Favorites Tools Help

NEW ANDROMEDA OFF-WORLD TRANSPORTATION HUB OPENS
READ MORE

PROSK MARAUDER DEBUTS AT OVEK
READ MORE

EXCLUSIVE NEW SUPERNOVA TRAILER
WATCH IT

BLIZZARD HAULTS HV LOADER PRODUCTION
READ MORE

IWN Illal World News

SEARCH |

ABOUT OUR ADS | ADVERTISE | FEEDBACK

SHARE 2,652 SUBSCRIBE 10,714

TRAVEL SCIENCE TECHNOLOGY OBITUARIES CLASSIFIEDS VID LISTINGS HELP CONTACT

UTA's official allocation of Cavorite excavation territory). Within six months Hawken had created his own, more efficient refinement of Cavorite, Prosk's patented Nanocavorite™. The revolutionary alloy is now found in virtually every Prosk product in high demand.

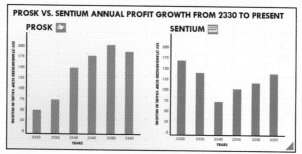

PROSK VS. SENTIUM ANNUAL PROFIT GROWTH FROM 2330 TO PRESENT
PROSK
SENTIUM
SSV (STANDARDIZED SCRIP VALUE) IN MILLIONS
0 25 50 75 100 125 150 175 200
2330 2335 2340 2345 2350 2355
YEARS

Statics provided by Illal Deparment of Financial Record Keeping VRD 1.01.625DR73.0195

Since then, Prosk has mined Hawken's ideas as much as its Cavorite quarries. Lazlo's simultaneous rise up the Prosk corporate ladder is no coincidence. His uncanny knack for predicting market trends has inspired Hawken's research from day one. In *The King of Cavorite*, Lazlo's unauthorized biography released last fall, author Marion Carthright cited internal Prosk memos as proof that Lazlo was the pivotal champion of Hawken's initial Cavorite theories. One insider even claimed that it was Lazlo, not Hawken, who commissioned the first weaponized mech. Lazlo waves off the folktale. "If only becoming CEO was so easy. The credit belongs to James." And what is Dr. Hawken up to these days? "You'll have to ask his wife. I've barely seen him since the wedding," jokes Lazlo, referring to Hawken's recent marriage to longtime Prosk research associate, Oliphia Aubrey.

Steering the conversation back toward Lazlo, we reminisce on his impressive run these past two decades as the youngest board member in Prosk history. Lazlo chuckles how stocks fell 16 points when the news first hit. Luckily, that loss preceded the record 1,455 point gain on February 7, 2336 – the unveiling of the Infiltrator™ class prototype, the first weaponized HV loader capable of VTOL (Vertical Take Off and Landing). So began the galaxy-wide arms race in mechanized warfare with Prosk as its frontrunner. "It's not like the others didn't try to compete," he adds. "They were just too late to the game." It's true. Up to that point no one had ever looked at an HV loader and thought "cavalry." Illal's new primary export has changed that perspective irreversibly, and the modern battlefield with it.

Lazlo wonders how Sentium managed to catch up so quickly. In trials Sentium's latest entry into the Class-B Mech category, the Sharpshooter™, outperformed Prosk's comparable Class-B entry, the Bruiser™, for little extra cost. Sources claim that Sentium may have developed their own equivalent of Nano-Cavorite. Lazlo isn't worried. "Even if they do develop competitive technology, our product philosophy is fundamentally different." But is there enough Cavorite to sustain the current level of demand? Or is the well running dry? "There's still enough Cavorite to go around," he assures. "We'll make it work. We may be competitors, but we're still allies in Illal's success. I'm fine being #2 for a quarter if Sentium is #1." After a sip of brandy, he adds with that smirk, "Only for one quarter, though." ■

Source Document://00.14524.74637.36tsv
Internal IP Address://834-007-2598-918-882

001

1.01

STATUS REPORT

//SentiumCSD
//[redacted]//StatusUpdate//42
//ID//[redacted]
//Attachment: **SCV.frml**

1. Had dinner with Hawken evening of 19 May. He confirmed Prosk reserve of cavorite ore is critically low. This is contrary to current public quarterly reports but dovetails with recent reports from Sentium CSD agent [redacted]. Hawken confirmed the voracity of statement citing two separate instances when he was forced to reduce amount of raw ore used during nano-cavoritic smelting. This alteration produced less dense alloy of diminished quality. Statement confirms analysis by [redacted] of Sentium's Reverse Engineering Division. Hawken expects continued decline in durability until stocks replenish, which by our reports seems unlikely.

2. Hawken's lab has been granted unlimited resources. Work on synthetic cavorite (SCV) alloy nears completion. However density and durability of this NANO-CAVORITE substitute remain low. To counteract, SCV is fortified with Hawken's latest generation of adaptive self-replicating nano-bots which pinpoint and reinforce structural weaknesses as needed. If successful, Prosk will flood market with infinite supply of SCV as confirmed by [redacted] in his 10 May report on Prosk board meeting. Analyst [redacted] believes such increased productivity and quality, along with fiscal reductions in mining, smelting, and defense threaten to return Prosk to market dominance. I have obtained and attached Hawken's latest SCV digiprints at great personal risk. My preliminary analysis generates reservations. Unless pristine, nano-cavorite is volatile and unstable. Ultimately it may be of marginal use without Hawken.

3. Lazlo operations have continued to deliver intelligence of great interest. While initially reticent, Lazlo has repeatedly intensified the nature and frequency of our meetings. Under the guise of off-site analysis, he has directed my supervisors to release me from 7-11 June and has organized a clandestine tryst. Lazlo's planned absence from Andromeda can be verified through [redacted]'s report on infiltration of Prosk computer system. It is now evident that the intensified nature of this contact increases my risk and places me in a dangerous position. Finnick grows suspicious. If he identifies the true nature of my relationship with Lazlo my mission will be compromised. There's too much at stake. I need to go communications silent until further notice. This will be my last report for the foreseeable future.

vmw xlviex

4. Proceed with caution. Lazlo's growing hubris threatirw lmw mrxiv-tivwsrep vipexmsrwlmt amxl Leaoir. Almpi Leaoir mw tvmqevmpc gsrgivrih amxl lmw asvo, li mw xss mrxippmkirx xs viqemr yreaevi jsv psrk. Gsrwmhivmrk xli zspexmpi rexyvi sj xli WGZ jsvqype, erc qmwwxit sv hipmfivexi tivzivwmsr sj xli ehetxmzi rers-fsx EM gsyph pieh xs er yrgsrxvsppefpi fviegl sj xli gsrxemrqirx jmiph. M eq gsrjmhirx sj Leaoir'w efmpmxc xs gsrxvsp xli rers-xigl, fyx li mw mrgviewmrkpc eppsamrk iqsxmsrw, sj almgl M eq gsqtpmgmx, xs mrjpyirgi lmw asvo.

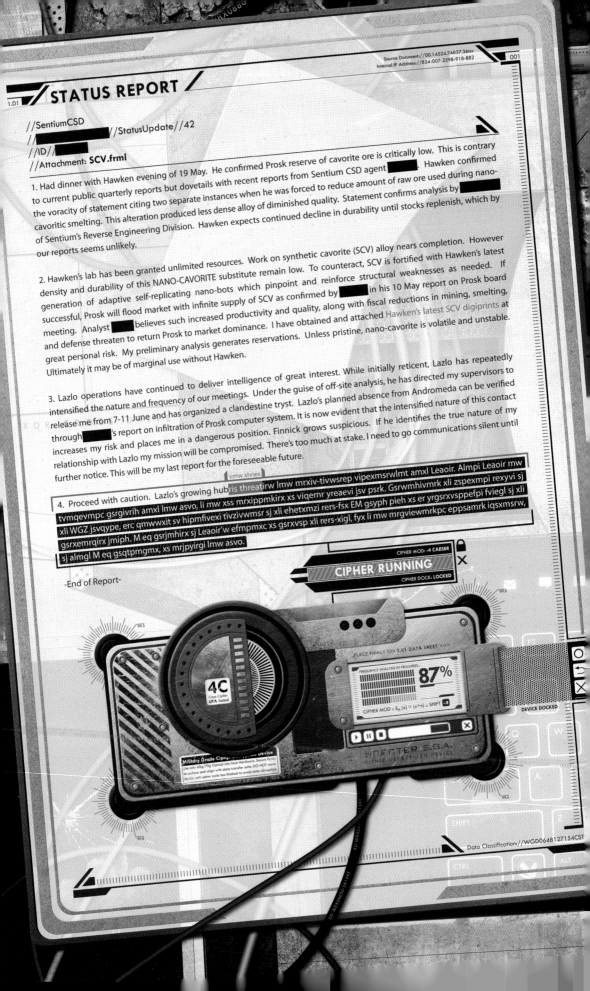

CIPHER MOD: -4 CAESER
CIPHER RUNNING
CIPHER DOCK: LOCKED

-End of Report-

4C
Class Cipher
UTA Rated
PLACE FIRMLY ON 3.01 DATA SHEET >>>
FREQUENCY ANALYSIS IN PROGRESS...
87%
CIPHER MOD :: $E_n(x) = (x+n)$ :: SHIFT -4
DEVICE DOCKED

Data Classification://WGD0648127154CST

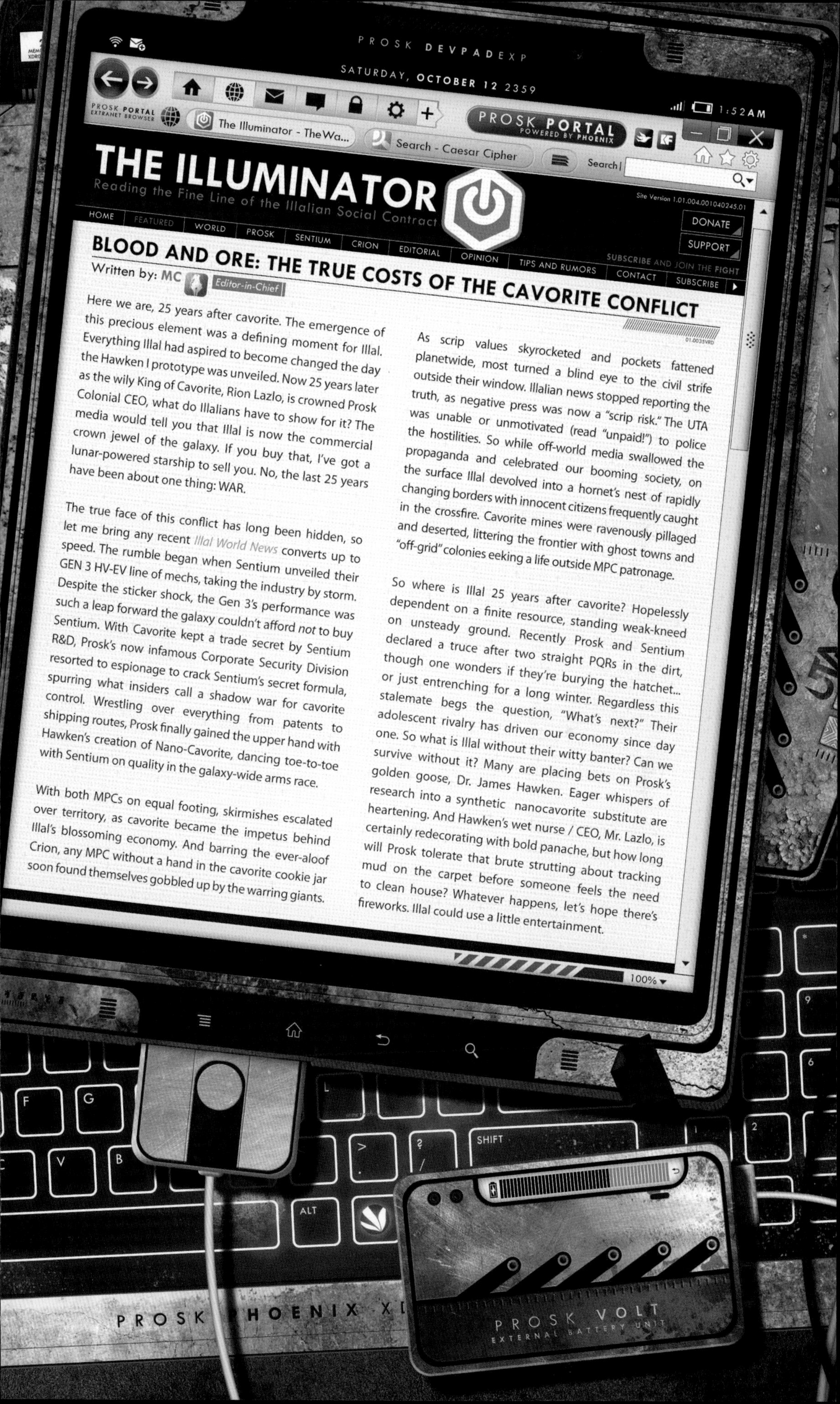

PROSK DEVPADEXP
SATURDAY, OCTOBER 12 2359
PROSK PORTAL EXTRANET BROWSER
The Illuminator - The Wa...
PROSK PORTAL POWERED BY PHOENIX
Search - Caesar Cipher
Search |
1:52AM
Site Version 1.01.004.001040245.01
HOME
FEATURED
WORLD
PROSK
SENTIUM
CRION
EDITORIAL
OPINION
TIPS AND RUMORS
CONTACT
SUBSCRIBE
DONATE
SUPPORT
SUBSCRIBE AND JOIN THE FIGHT
100%
PROSK PHOENIX XD
PROSK VOLT EXTERNAL BATTERY UNIT

THE ILLUMINATOR

Reading the Fine Line of the Illalian Social Contract

BLOOD AND ORE: THE TRUE COSTS OF THE CAVORITE CONFLICT

Written by: MC Editor-in-Chief

Here we are, 25 years after cavorite. The emergence of this precious element was a defining moment for Illal. Everything Illal had aspired to become changed the day the Hawken I prototype was unveiled. Now 25 years later as the wily King of Cavorite, Rion Lazlo, is crowned Prosk Colonial CEO, what do Illalians have to show for it? The media would tell you that Illal is now the commercial crown jewel of the galaxy. If you buy that, I've got a lunar-powered starship to sell you. No, the last 25 years have been about one thing: WAR.

The true face of this conflict has long been hidden, so let me bring any recent *Illal World News* converts up to speed. The rumble began when Sentium unveiled their GEN 3 HV-EV line of mechs, taking the industry by storm. Despite the sticker shock, the Gen 3's performance was such a leap forward the galaxy couldn't afford *not* to buy Sentium. With Cavorite kept a trade secret by Sentium R&D, Prosk's now infamous Corporate Security Division resorted to espionage to crack Sentium's secret formula, spurring what insiders call a shadow war for cavorite control. Wrestling over everything from patents to shipping routes, Prosk finally gained the upper hand with Hawken's creation of Nano-Cavorite, dancing toe-to-toe with Sentium on quality in the galaxy-wide arms race.

With both MPCs on equal footing, skirmishes escalated over territory, as cavorite became the impetus behind Illal's blossoming economy. And barring the ever-aloof Crion, any MPC without a hand in the cavorite cookie jar soon found themselves gobbled up by the warring giants.

As scrip values skyrocketed and pockets fattened planetwide, most turned a blind eye to the civil strife outside their window. Illalian news stopped reporting the truth, as negative press was now a "scrip risk." The UTA was unable or unmotivated (read "unpaid!") to police the hostilities. So while off-world media swallowed the propaganda and celebrated our booming society, on the surface Illal devolved into a hornet's nest of rapidly changing borders with innocent citizens frequently caught in the crossfire. Cavorite mines were ravenously pillaged and deserted, littering the frontier with ghost towns and "off-grid" colonies eeking a life outside MPC patronage.

So where is Illal 25 years after cavorite? Hopelessly dependent on a finite resource, standing weak-kneed on unsteady ground. Recently Prosk and Sentium declared a truce after two straight PQRs in the dirt, though one wonders if they're burying the hatchet... or just entrenching for a long winter. Regardless this stalemate begs the question, "What's next?" Their adolescent rivalry has driven our economy since day one. So what is Illal without their witty banter? Can we survive without it? Many are placing bets on Prosk's golden goose, Dr. James Hawken. Eager whispers of research into a synthetic nanocavorite substitute are heartening. And Hawken's wet nurse / CEO, Mr. Lazlo, is certainly redecorating with bold panache, but how long will Prosk tolerate that brute strutting about tracking mud on the carpet before someone feels the need to clean house? Whatever happens, let's hope there's fireworks. Illal could use a little entertainment.

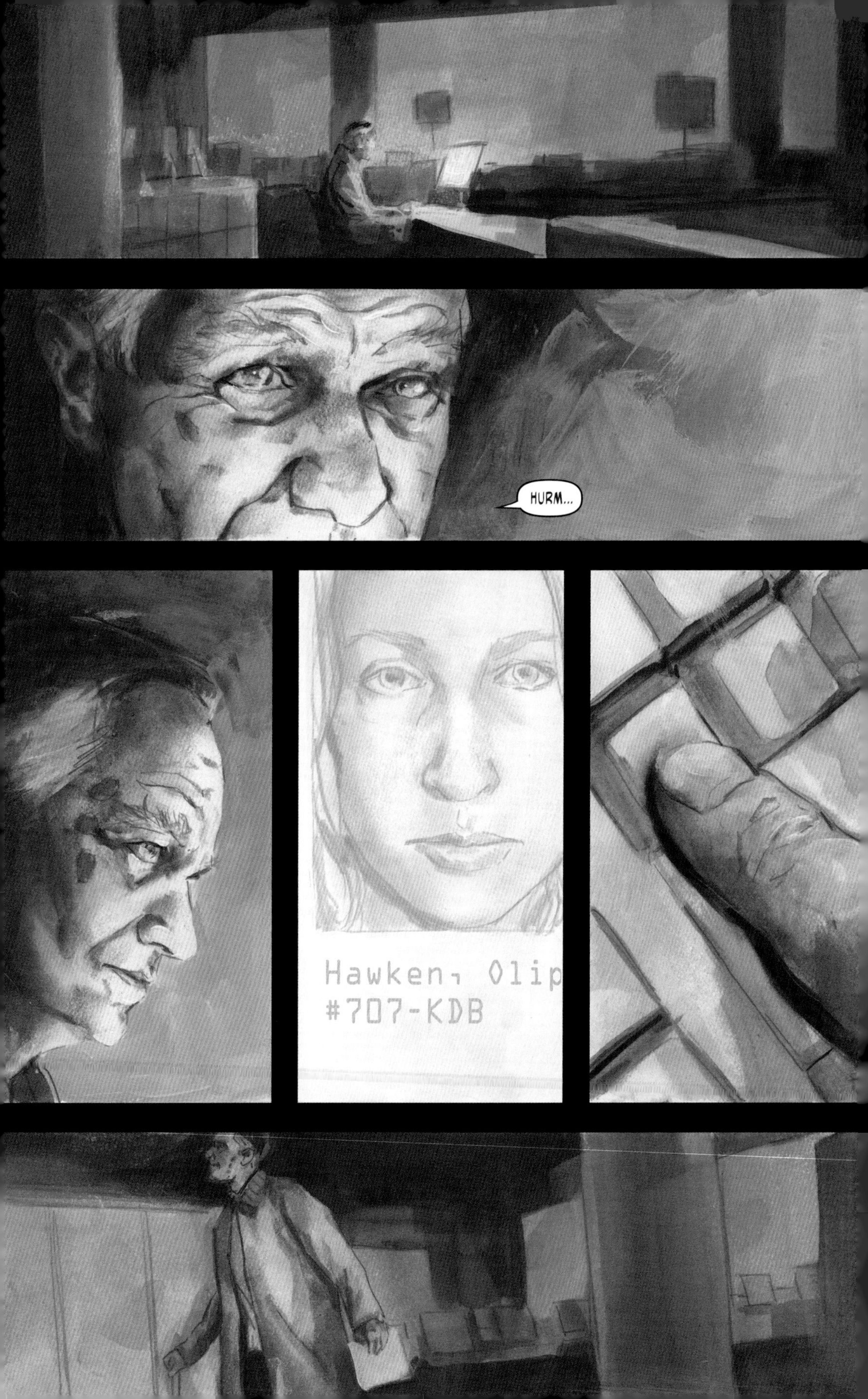
HURM...
Hawken, Olip
#707-KDB

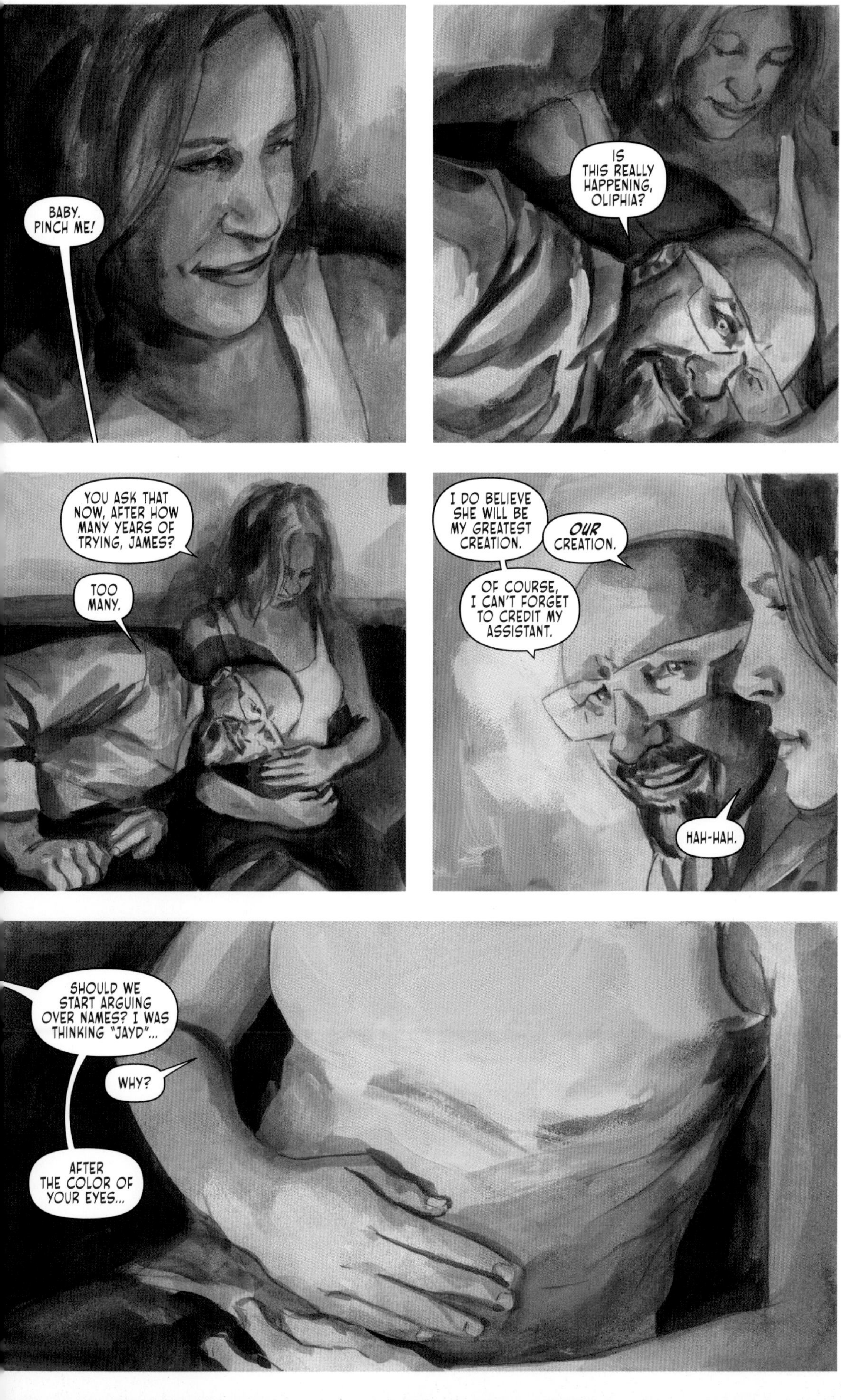
BABY. PINCH ME!
IS THIS REALLY HAPPENING, OLIPHIA?
YOU ASK THAT NOW, AFTER HOW MANY YEARS OF TRYING, JAMES?
TOO MANY.
I DO BELIEVE SHE WILL BE MY GREATEST CREATION.
OUR CREATION.
OF COURSE, I CAN'T FORGET TO CREDIT MY ASSISTANT.
HAH-HAH.
SHOULD WE START ARGUING OVER NAMES? I WAS THINKING "JAYD"...
WHY?
AFTER THE COLOR OF YOUR EYES...

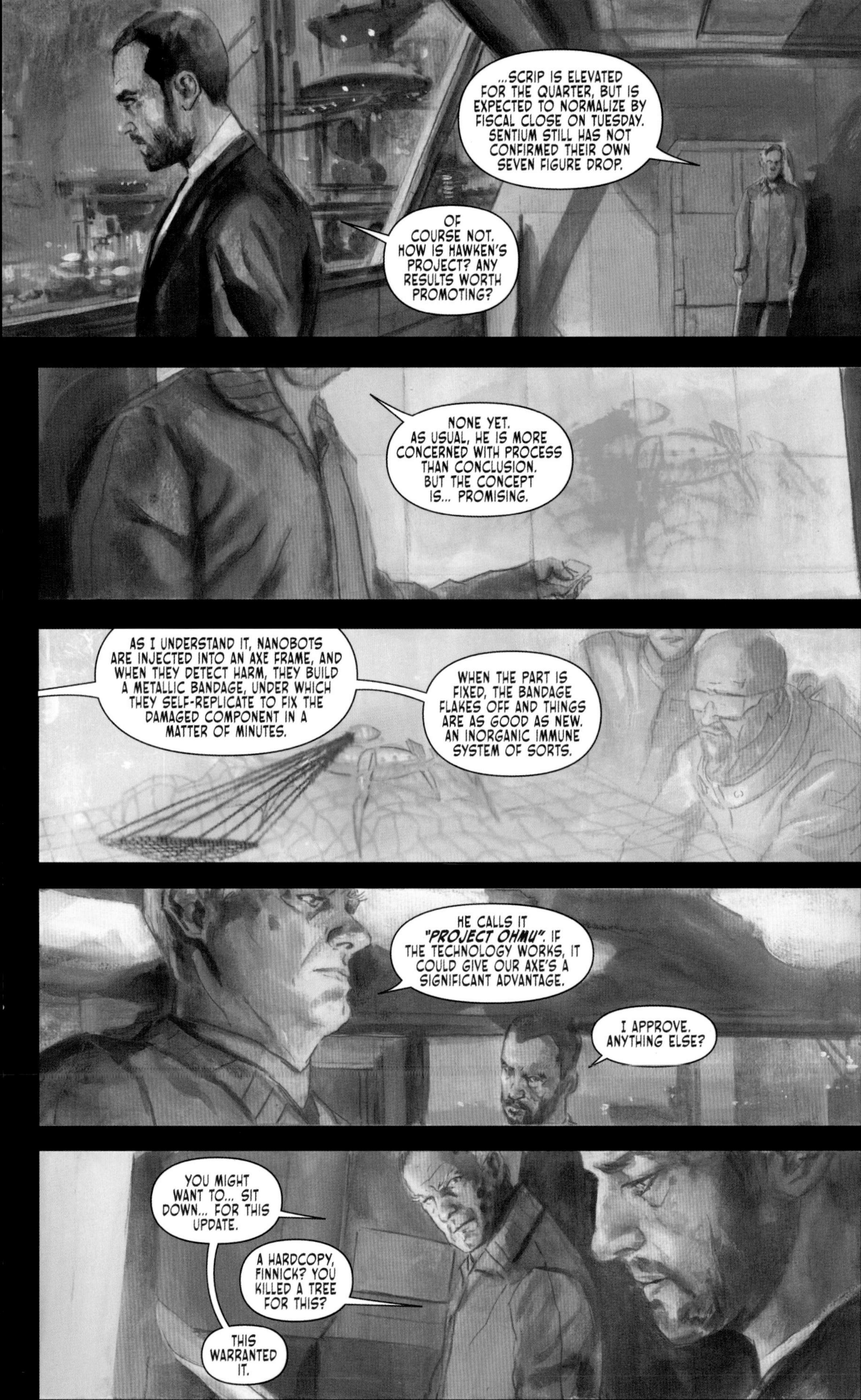
...SCRIP IS ELEVATED FOR THE QUARTER, BUT IS EXPECTED TO NORMALIZE BY FISCAL CLOSE ON TUESDAY. SENTIUM STILL HAS NOT CONFIRMED THEIR OWN SEVEN FIGURE DROP.
OF COURSE NOT. HOW IS HAWKEN'S PROJECT? ANY RESULTS WORTH PROMOTING?
NONE YET. AS USUAL, HE IS MORE CONCERNED WITH PROCESS THAN CONCLUSION. BUT THE CONCEPT IS... PROMISING.
AS I UNDERSTAND IT, NANOBOTS ARE INJECTED INTO AN AXE FRAME, AND WHEN THEY DETECT HARM, THEY BUILD A METALLIC BANDAGE, UNDER WHICH THEY SELF-REPLICATE TO FIX THE DAMAGED COMPONENT IN A MATTER OF MINUTES.
WHEN THE PART IS FIXED, THE BANDAGE FLAKES OFF AND THINGS ARE AS GOOD AS NEW. AN INORGANIC IMMUNE SYSTEM OF SORTS.
HE CALLS IT *"PROJECT OHMU"*. IF THE TECHNOLOGY WORKS, IT COULD GIVE OUR AXE'S A SIGNIFICANT ADVANTAGE.
I APPROVE. ANYTHING ELSE?
YOU MIGHT WANT TO... SIT DOWN... FOR THIS UPDATE.
A HARDCOPY, FINNICK? YOU KILLED A TREE FOR THIS?
THIS WARRANTED IT.

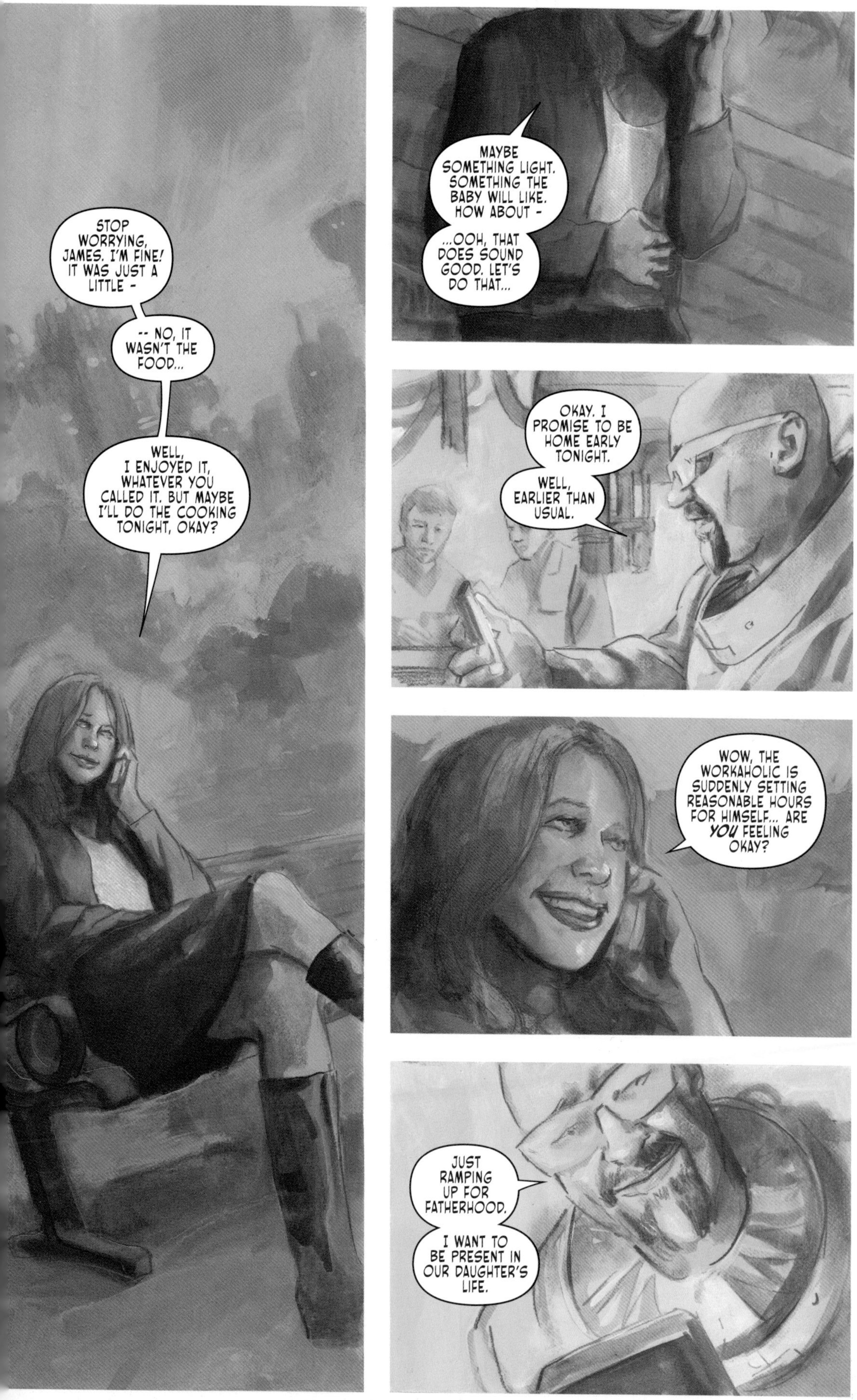
STOP WORRYING, JAMES. I'M FINE! IT WAS JUST A LITTLE -
-- NO, IT WASN'T THE FOOD...
WELL, I ENJOYED IT, WHATEVER YOU CALLED IT. BUT MAYBE I'LL DO THE COOKING TONIGHT, OKAY?
MAYBE SOMETHING LIGHT. SOMETHING THE BABY WILL LIKE. HOW ABOUT -
...OOH, THAT DOES SOUND GOOD. LET'S DO THAT...
OKAY. I PROMISE TO BE HOME EARLY TONIGHT.
WELL, EARLIER THAN USUAL.
WOW, THE WORKAHOLIC IS SUDDENLY SETTING REASONABLE HOURS FOR HIMSELF... ARE YOU FEELING OKAY?
JUST RAMPING UP FOR FATHERHOOD.
I WANT TO BE PRESENT IN OUR DAUGHTER'S LIFE.

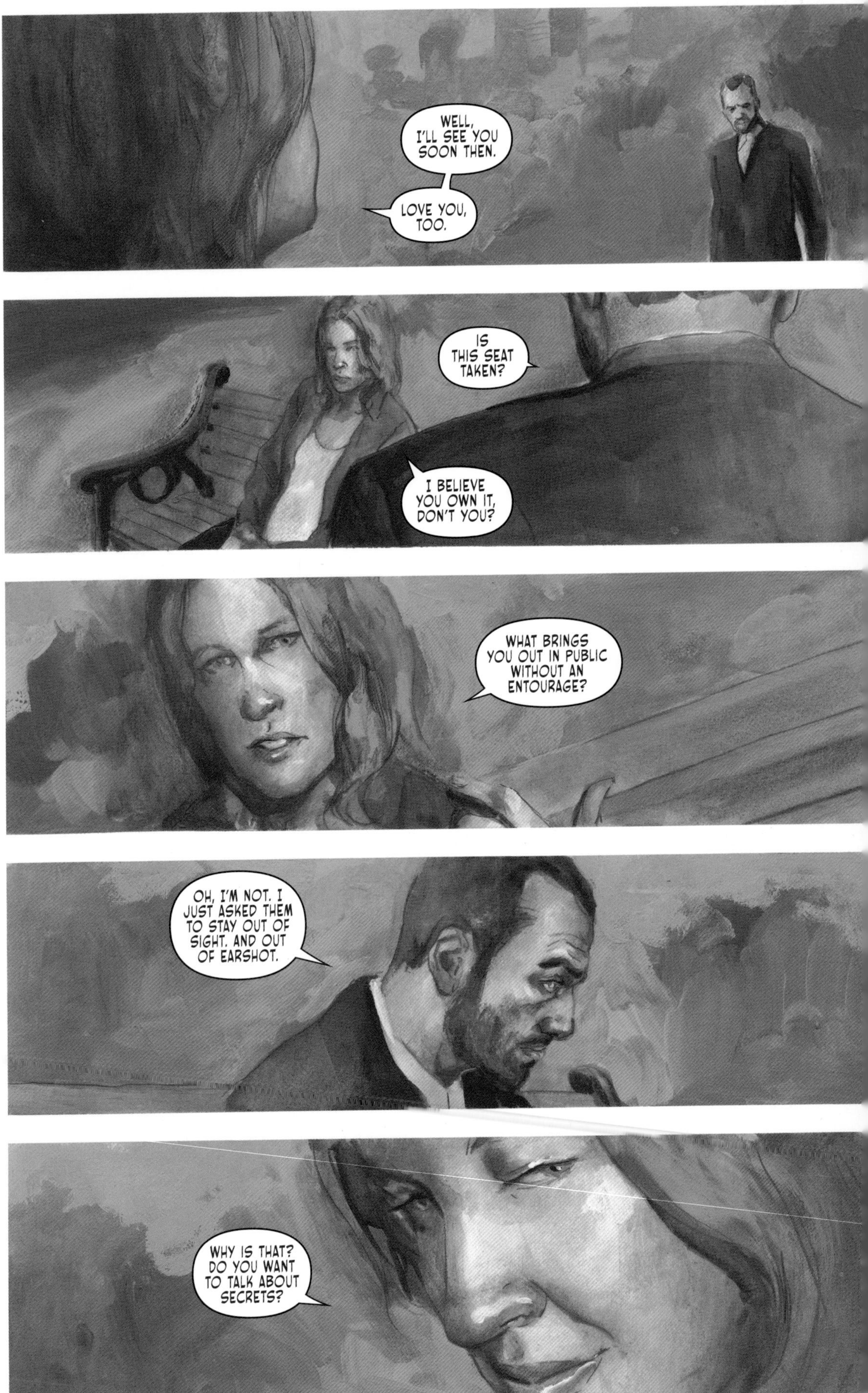

WELL, I'LL SEE YOU SOON THEN.
LOVE YOU, TOO.
IS THIS SEAT TAKEN?
I BELIEVE YOU OWN IT, DON'T YOU?
WHAT BRINGS YOU OUT IN PUBLIC WITHOUT AN ENTOURAGE?
OH, I'M NOT. I JUST ASKED THEM TO STAY OUT OF SIGHT. AND OUT OF EARSHOT.
WHY IS THAT? DO YOU WANT TO TALK ABOUT SECRETS?

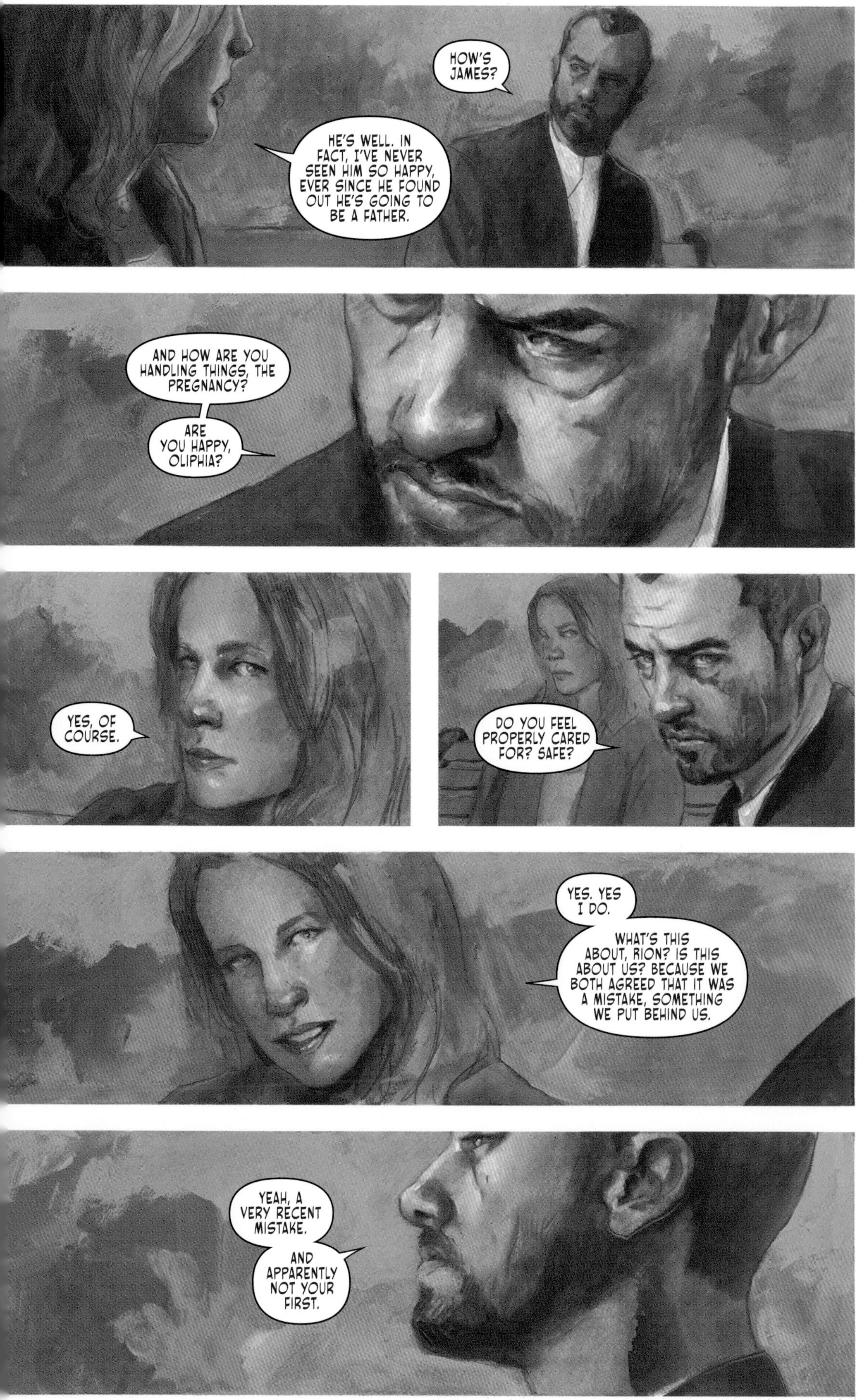
HOW'S JAMES?
HE'S WELL. IN FACT, I'VE NEVER SEEN HIM SO HAPPY, EVER SINCE HE FOUND OUT HE'S GOING TO BE A FATHER.
AND HOW ARE YOU HANDLING THINGS, THE PREGNANCY?
ARE YOU HAPPY, OLIPHIA?
YES, OF COURSE.
DO YOU FEEL PROPERLY CARED FOR? SAFE?
YES. YES I DO.
WHAT'S THIS ABOUT, RION? IS THIS ABOUT US? BECAUSE WE BOTH AGREED THAT IT WAS A MISTAKE, SOMETHING WE PUT BEHIND US.
YEAH, A VERY RECENT MISTAKE.
AND APPARENTLY NOT YOUR FIRST.

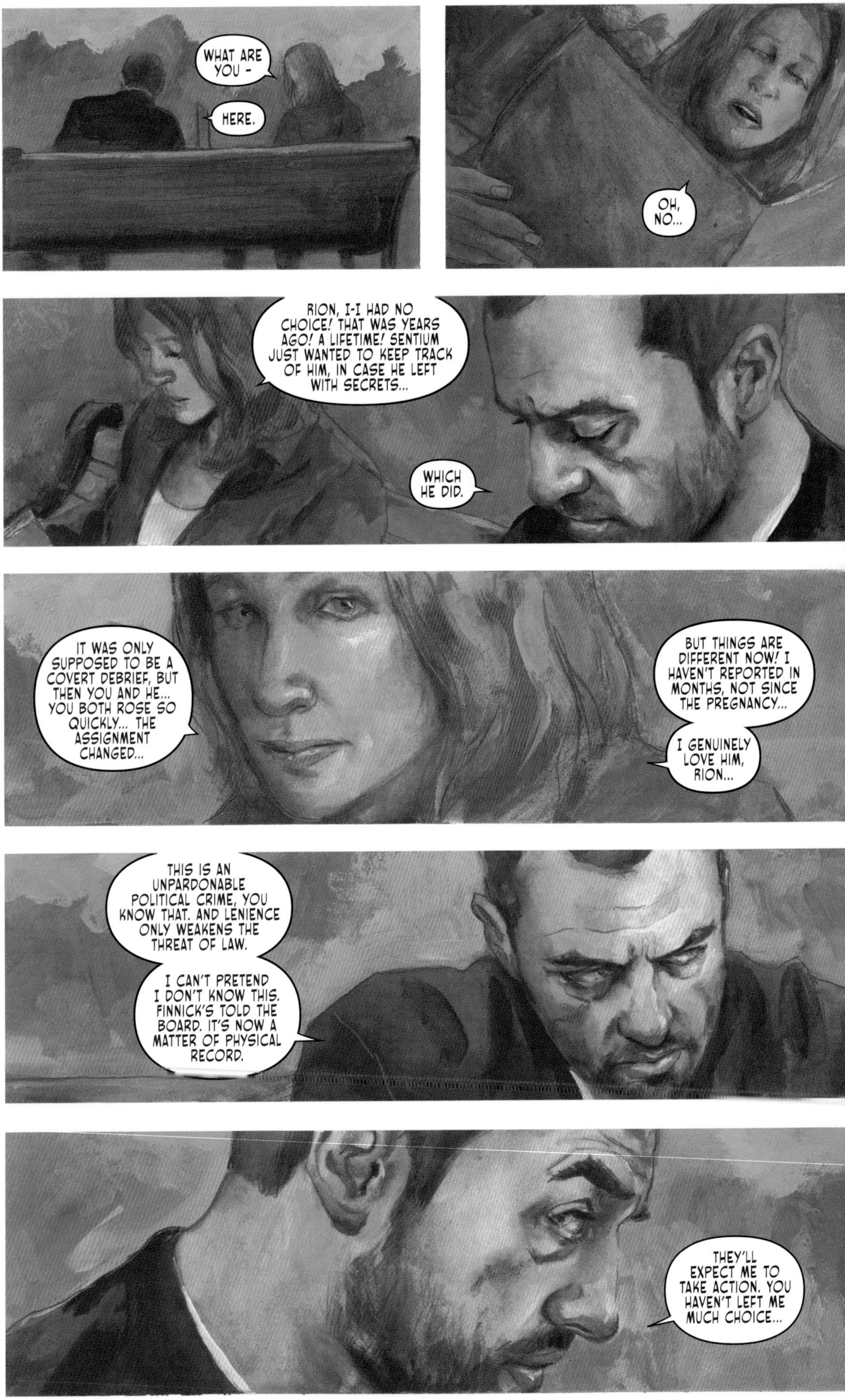
WHAT ARE YOU -
HERE.
OH, NO...
RION, I-I HAD NO CHOICE! THAT WAS YEARS AGO! A LIFETIME! SENTIUM JUST WANTED TO KEEP TRACK OF HIM, IN CASE HE LEFT WITH SECRETS...
WHICH HE DID.
IT WAS ONLY SUPPOSED TO BE A COVERT DEBRIEF, BUT THEN YOU AND HE... YOU BOTH ROSE SO QUICKLY... THE ASSIGNMENT CHANGED...
BUT THINGS ARE DIFFERENT NOW! I HAVEN'T REPORTED IN MONTHS, NOT SINCE THE PREGNANCY...
I GENUINELY LOVE HIM, RION...
THIS IS AN UNPARDONABLE POLITICAL CRIME, YOU KNOW THAT. AND LENIENCE ONLY WEAKENS THE THREAT OF LAW.
I CAN'T PRETEND I DON'T KNOW THIS. FINNICK'S TOLD THE BOARD. IT'S NOW A MATTER OF PHYSICAL RECORD.
THEY'LL EXPECT ME TO TAKE ACTION. YOU HAVEN'T LEFT ME MUCH CHOICE...

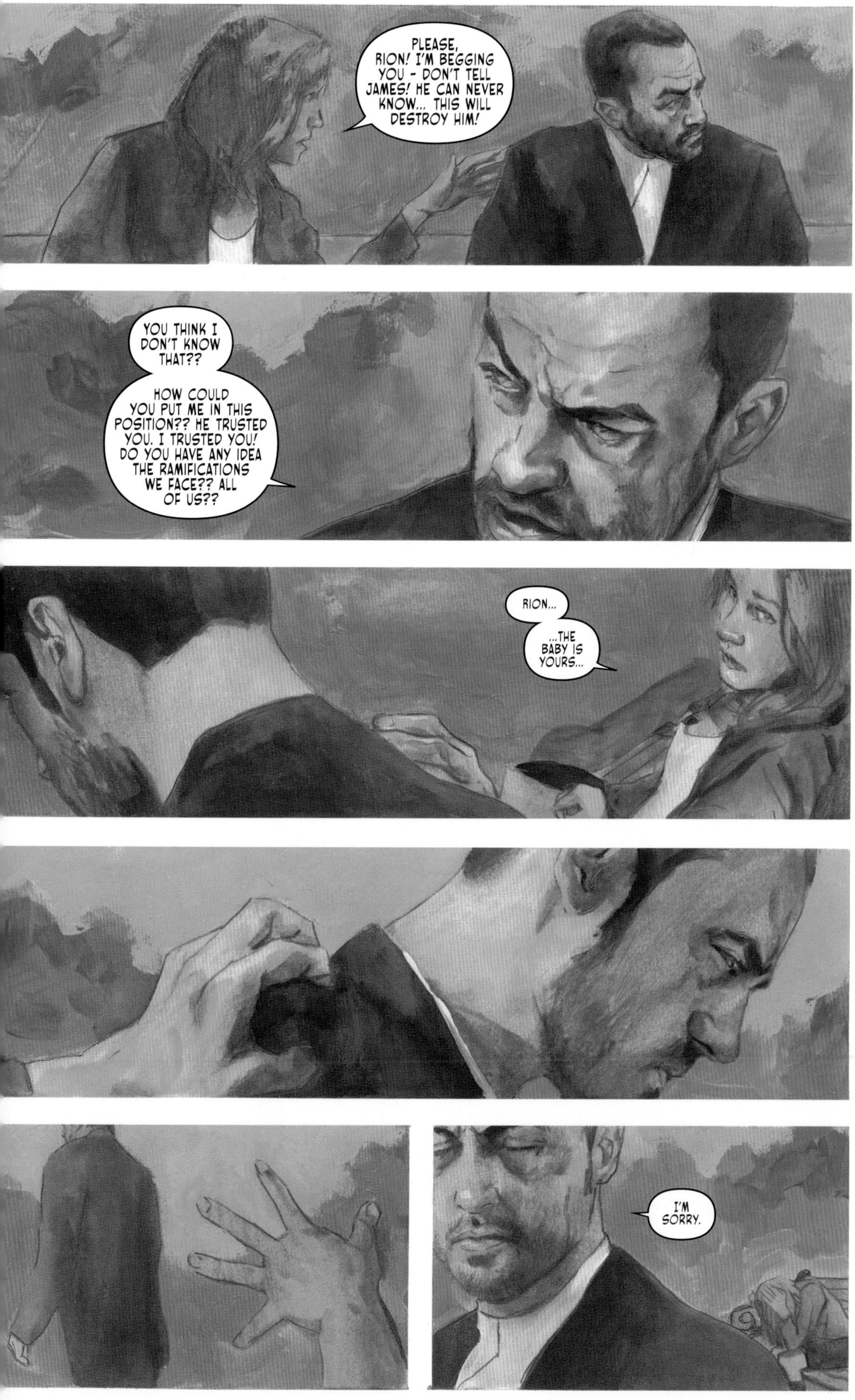
PLEASE, RION! I'M BEGGING YOU - DON'T TELL JAMES! HE CAN NEVER KNOW... THIS WILL DESTROY HIM!
YOU THINK I DON'T KNOW THAT??
HOW COULD YOU PUT ME IN THIS POSITION?? HE TRUSTED YOU. I TRUSTED YOU! DO YOU HAVE ANY IDEA THE RAMIFICATIONS WE FACE?? ALL OF US??
RION...
...THE BABY IS YOURS...
I'M SORRY.

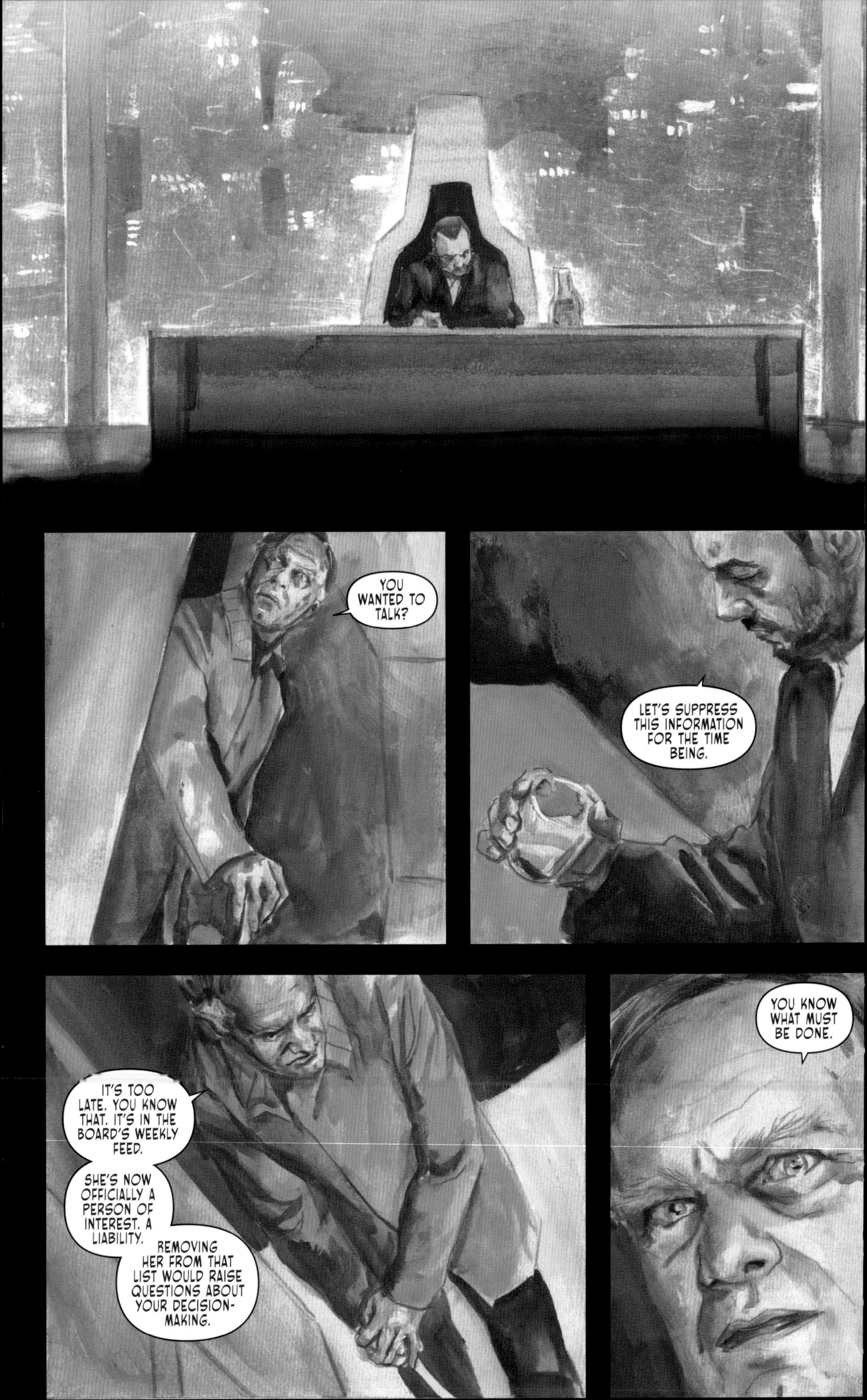
YOU WANTED TO TALK?
LET'S SUPPRESS THIS INFORMATION FOR THE TIME BEING.
IT'S TOO LATE. YOU KNOW THAT. IT'S IN THE BOARD'S WEEKLY FEED.
SHE'S NOW OFFICIALLY A PERSON OF INTEREST. A LIABILITY.
REMOVING HER FROM THAT LIST WOULD RAISE QUESTIONS ABOUT YOUR DECISION-MAKING.
YOU KNOW WHAT MUST BE DONE.

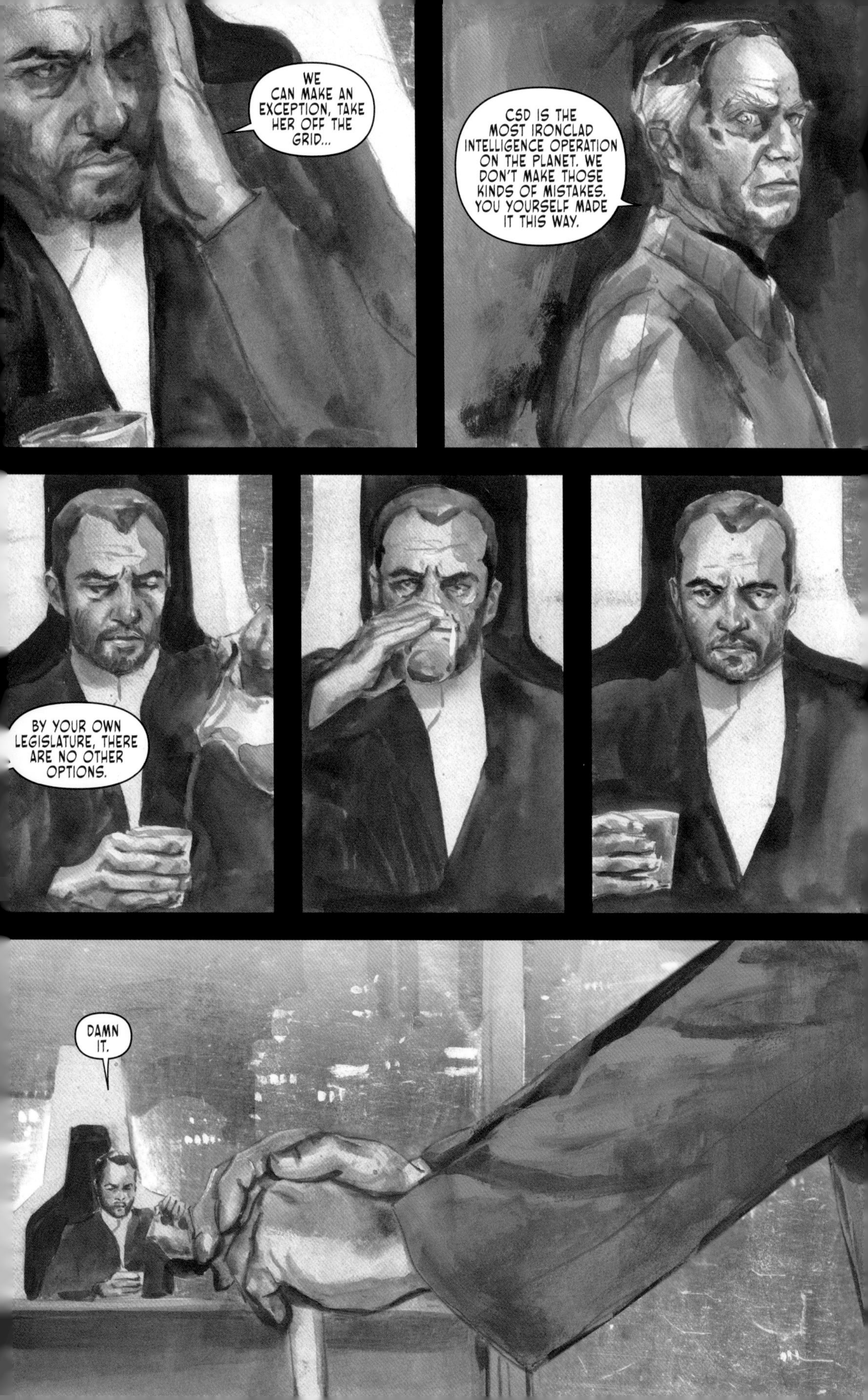
WE CAN MAKE AN EXCEPTION, TAKE HER OFF THE GRID...
CSD IS THE MOST IRONCLAD INTELLIGENCE OPERATION ON THE PLANET. WE DON'T MAKE THOSE KINDS OF MISTAKES. YOU YOURSELF MADE IT THIS WAY.
BY YOUR OWN LEGISLATURE, THERE ARE NO OTHER OPTIONS.
DAMN IT.

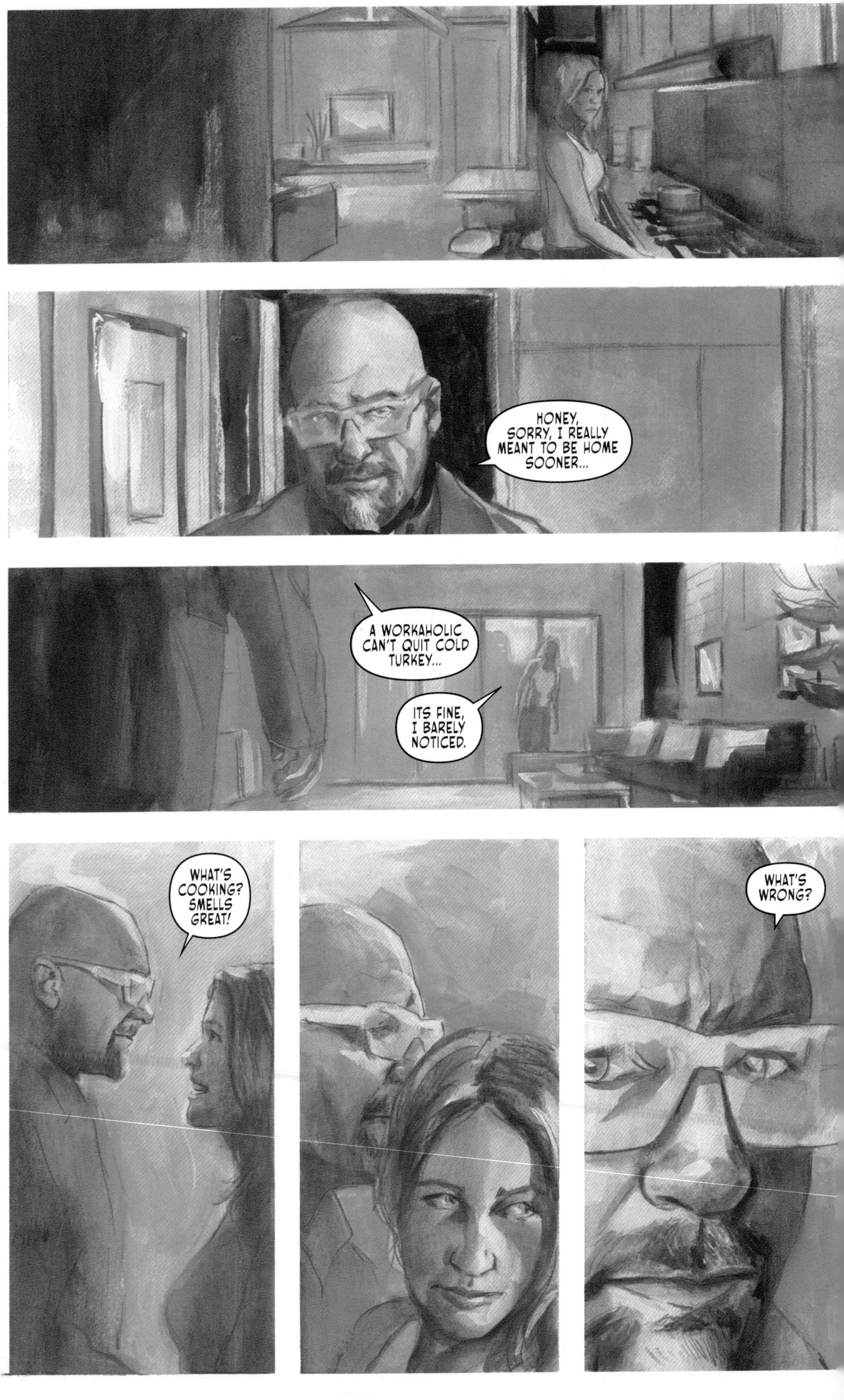
HONEY, SORRY, I REALLY MEANT TO BE HOME SOONER...
A WORKAHOLIC CAN'T QUIT COLD TURKEY...
ITS FINE, I BARELY NOTICED.
WHAT'S COOKING? SMELLS GREAT!
WHAT'S WRONG?

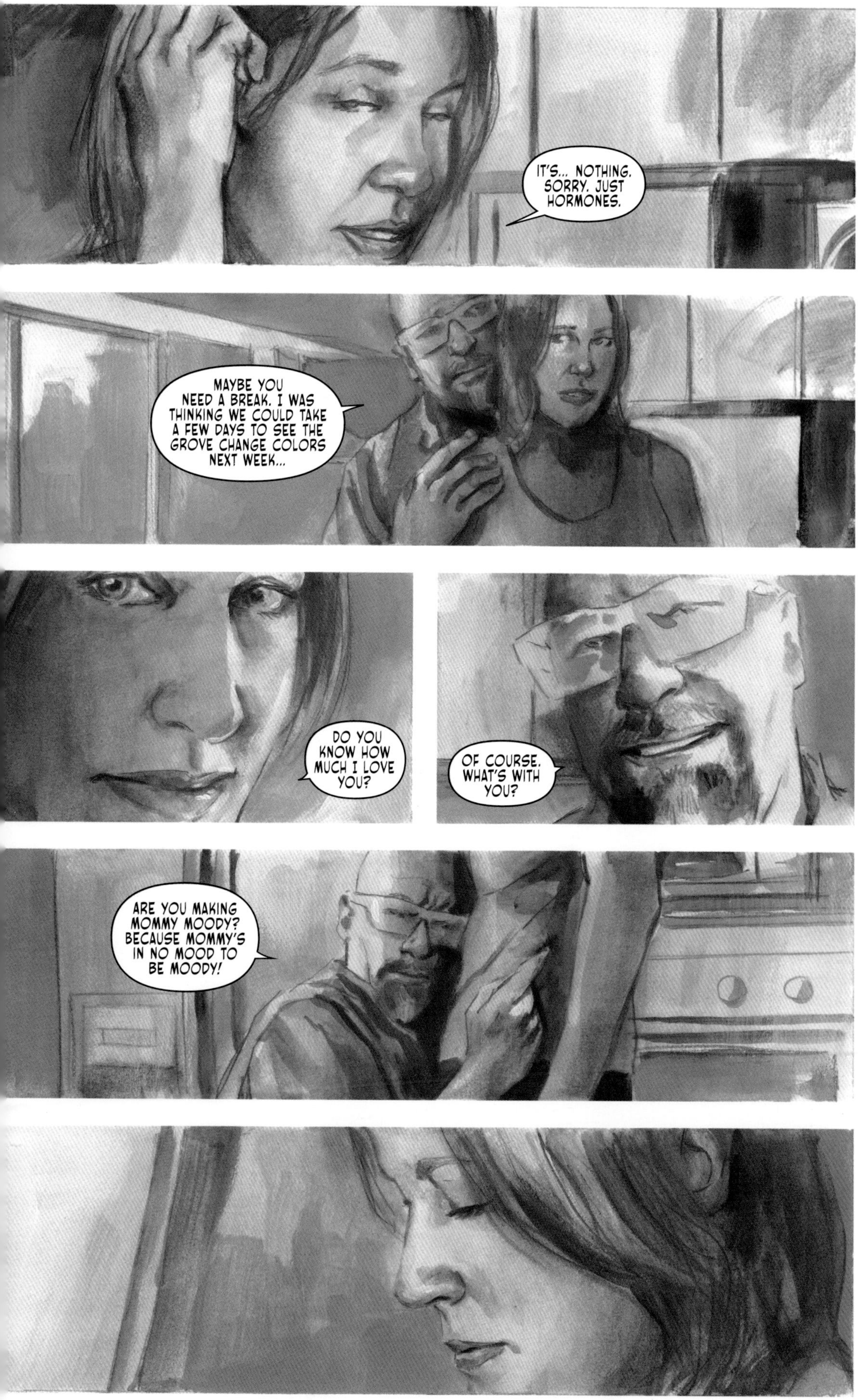
IT'S... NOTHING. SORRY. JUST HORMONES.
MAYBE YOU NEED A BREAK. I WAS THINKING WE COULD TAKE A FEW DAYS TO SEE THE GROVE CHANGE COLORS NEXT WEEK...
DO YOU KNOW HOW MUCH I LOVE YOU?
OF COURSE. WHAT'S WITH YOU?
ARE YOU MAKING MOMMY MOODY? BECAUSE MOMMY'S IN NO MOOD TO BE MOODY!

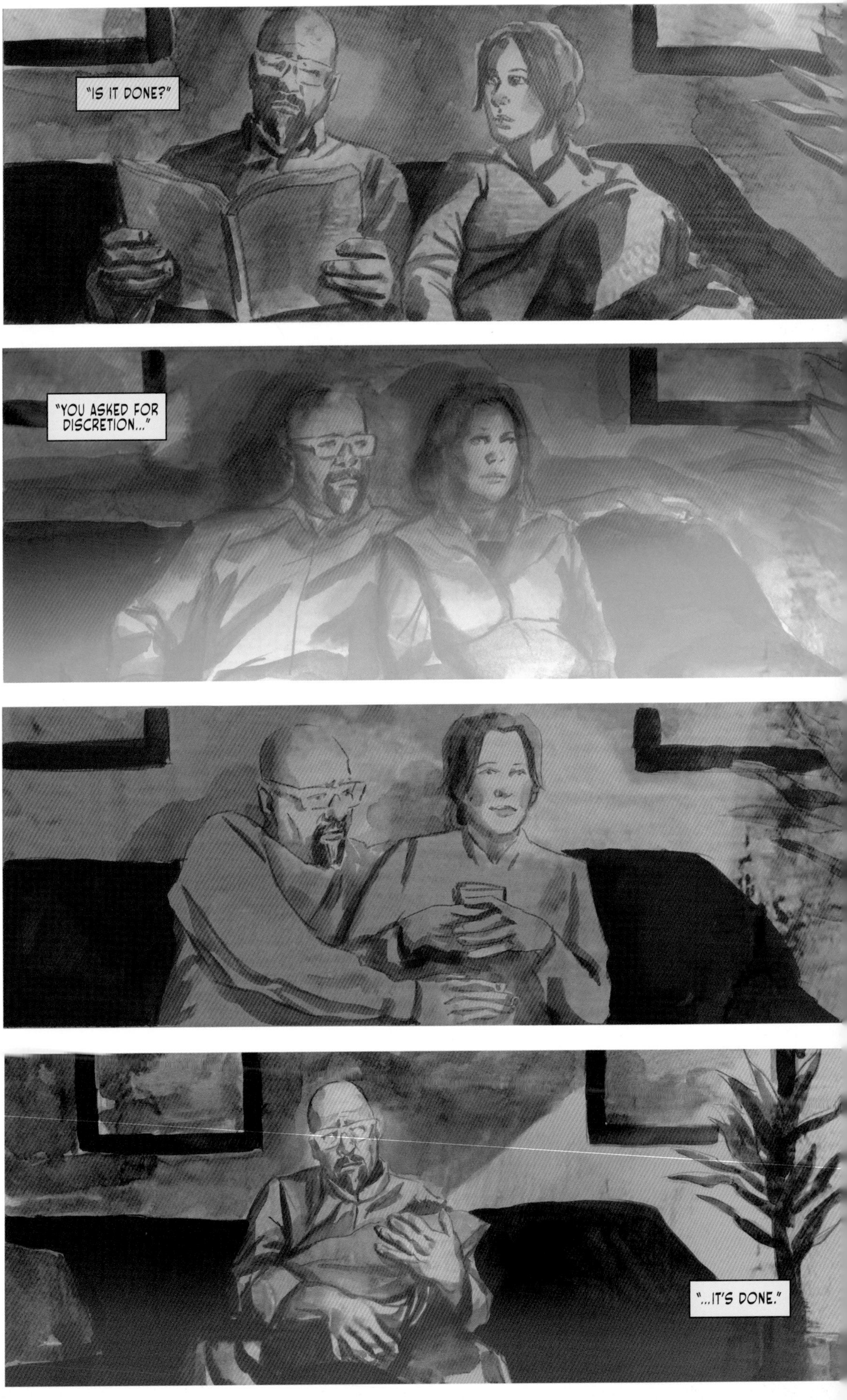
"IS IT DONE?"
"YOU ASKED FOR DISCRETION..."
"...IT'S DONE."

Source File: Illal World News :: IWN.Obituary :: 23.06.2360

IWN: OFFICIAL OBITUARIES

JUNE 23, 2360

OLIPHIA AUBREY HAWKEN

Oliphia Aubrey Hawken, a pioneer in a wide range of technological research fields, died on Wednesday in Andromeda. She was 44.

Attending physician, Dr. Richard Harris, confirmed her passing due to heart failure from unexpected complications encountered shortly after childbirth.

Working as a research assistant for Prosk since 2332, she became a key member of the preeminent Dr. James Hawken's acclaimed exploratory research team. There she contributed to numerous industry-changing scientific breakthroughs including the creation of Nano-Cavorite, along with other radical advances in nanogenetics, cryogenetics, and artificial intelligence.

PHOTO PROVIDED BY PROSK HUMAN RESOURCES.

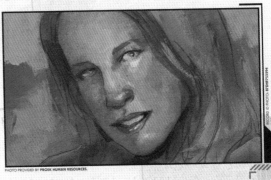

It was in that laboratory where her romance with the luminary engineer blossomed. They were married in 2348.

Known for her kindness and strong work ethic, many attest her grounding influence on Hawken was central to his inspired productivity and impact across innumerable scientific fields, culminating in his appointment as Head of Prosk's famed Experimental Sciences Division.

Mrs. Hawken was admitted to Prosk General's Maternity Clinic Wednesday morning and gave birth just hours before her death. Harris reports that the delivery itself was uneventful, with the 6 lb 5 ounces infant born in perfect health. Medical staff began to notice decreased signs of vitality in the hours following childbirth, but were unable to revive her despite their best efforts. Dr. Hawken was attending to his newborn daughter in the paternal receiving wing when he was notified of his wife's passing.

"She was the muse behind the greatest mind of our generation and a beacon of light to us all," said recently-minted Prosk CEO Rion Lazlo in a speech announcing plans for the Oliphia Aubrey Hawken Science Center, an educational science discovery center for Prosk youth, to be erected in her honor.

She is survived by daughter, Jayd, and husband, James.

Data Classification://NGC0174935B14QRN

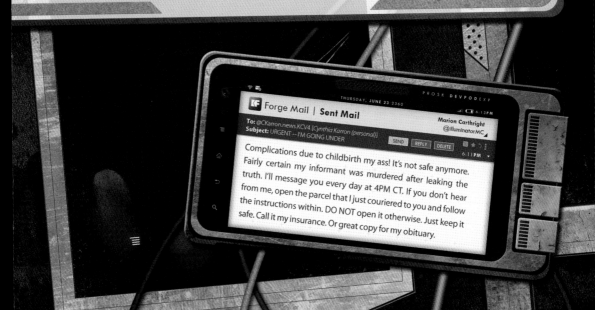

PROSK DEVPODEXP
THURSDAY, JUNE 23 2360
Forge Mail | Sent Mail
Marion Carthright
@illuminatorMC
To: @CKarron.news.KCV4 [Cynthia Karron (personal)]
Subject: URGENT -- I'M GOING UNDER
SEND
REPLY
DELETE
6:11PM
Complications due to childbirth my ass! It's not safe anymore. Fairly certain my informant was murdered after leaking the truth. I'll message you every day at 4PM CT. If you don't hear from me, open the parcel that I just couriered to you and follow the instructions within. DO NOT open it otherwise. Just keep it safe. Call it my insurance. Or great copy for my obituary.

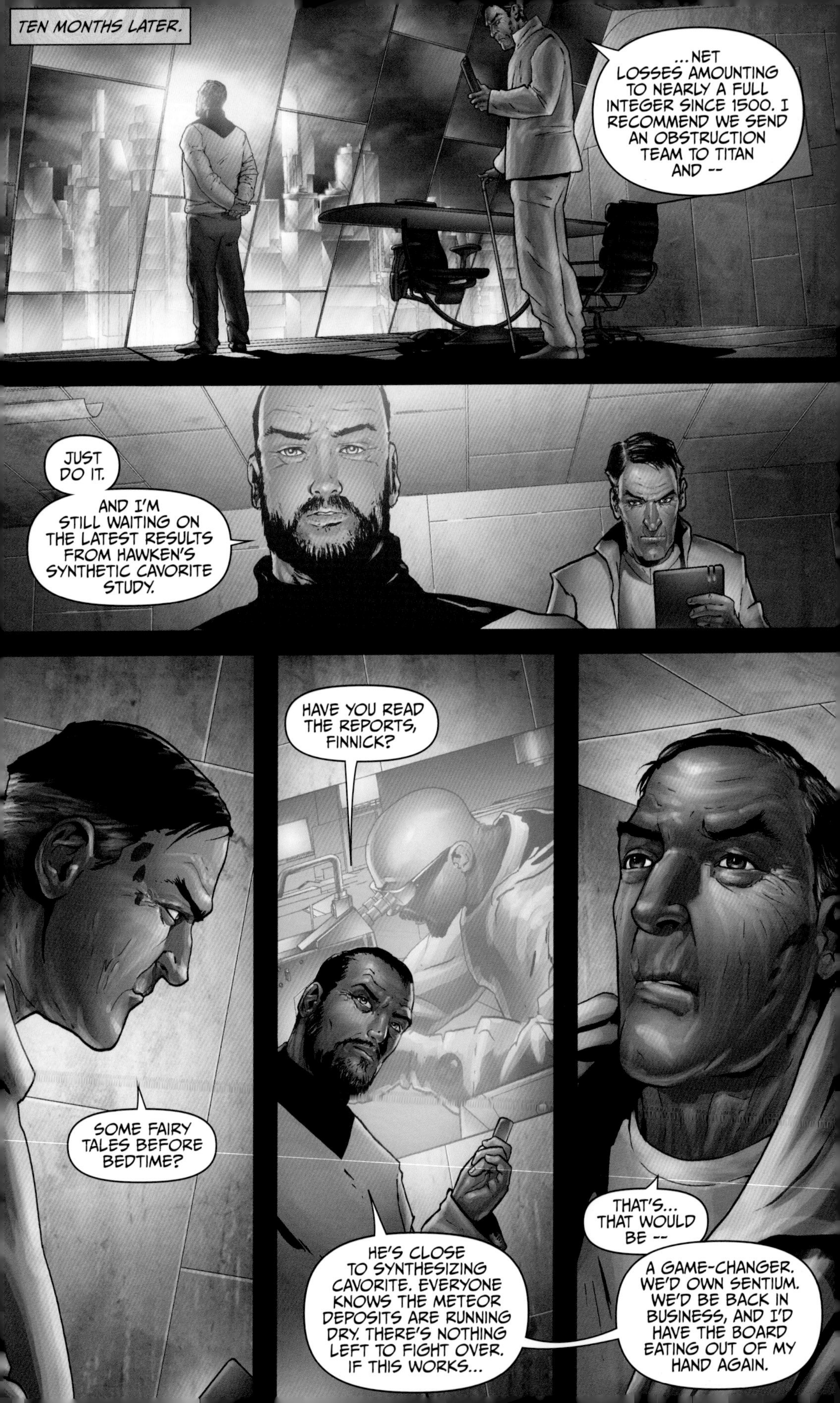
TEN MONTHS LATER.
...NET LOSSES AMOUNTING TO NEARLY A FULL INTEGER SINCE 1500. I RECOMMEND WE SEND AN OBSTRUCTION TEAM TO TITAN AND --
JUST DO IT.
AND I'M STILL WAITING ON THE LATEST RESULTS FROM HAWKEN'S SYNTHETIC CAVORITE STUDY.
SOME FAIRY TALES BEFORE BEDTIME?
HAVE YOU READ THE REPORTS, FINNICK?
HE'S CLOSE TO SYNTHESIZING CAVORITE. EVERYONE KNOWS THE METEOR DEPOSITS ARE RUNNING DRY. THERE'S NOTHING LEFT TO FIGHT OVER. IF THIS WORKS...
THAT'S... THAT WOULD BE --
A GAME-CHANGER. WE'D OWN SENTIUM. WE'D BE BACK IN BUSINESS, AND I'D HAVE THE BOARD EATING OUT OF MY HAND AGAIN.

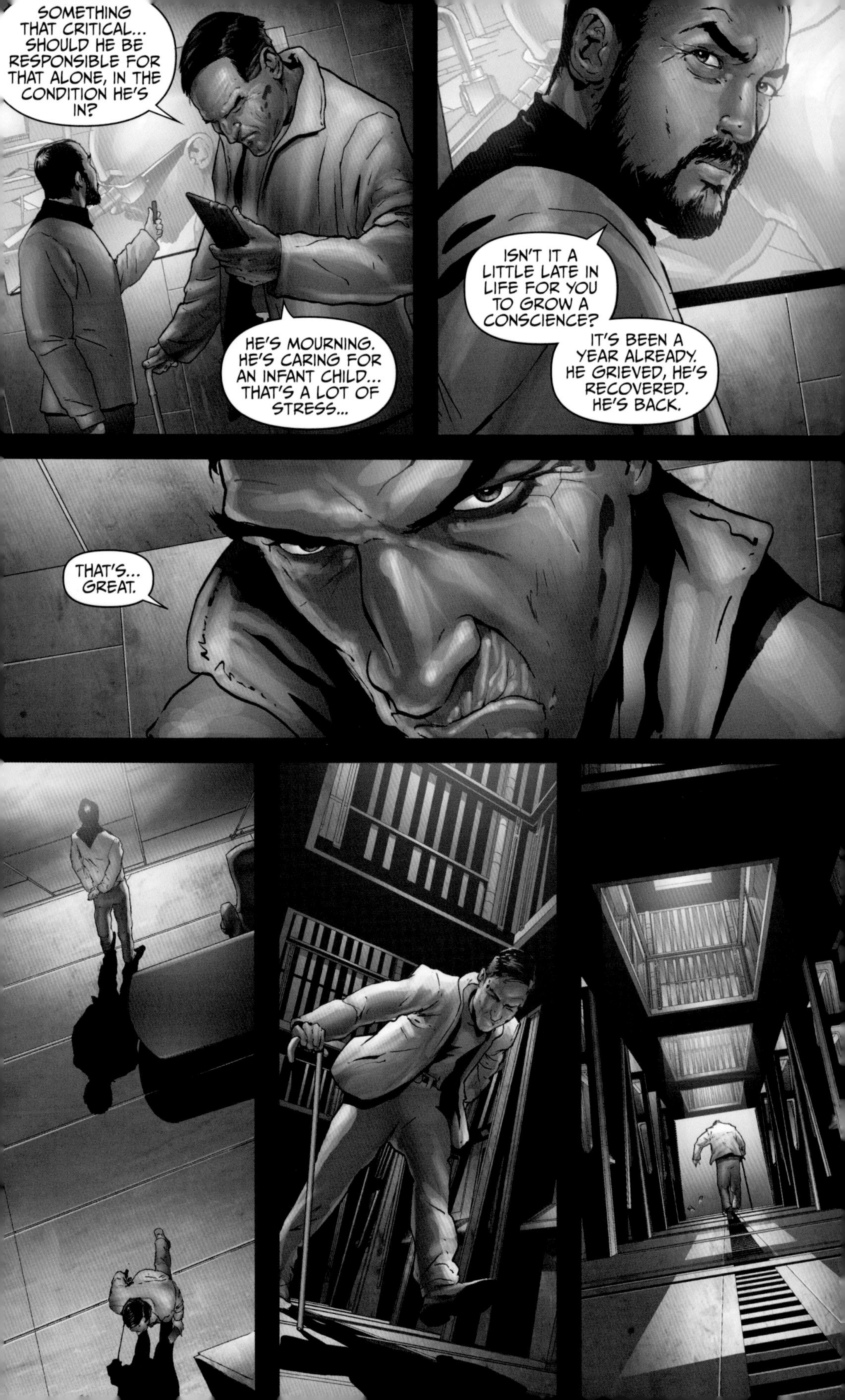
SOMETHING THAT CRITICAL... SHOULD HE BE RESPONSIBLE FOR THAT ALONE, IN THE CONDITION HE'S IN?
HE'S MOURNING. HE'S CARING FOR AN INFANT CHILD... THAT'S A LOT OF STRESS...
ISN'T IT A LITTLE LATE IN LIFE FOR YOU TO GROW A CONSCIENCE?
IT'S BEEN A YEAR ALREADY. HE GRIEVED, HE'S RECOVERED. HE'S BACK.
THAT'S... GREAT.

RE-EVALUATED TERMS. ASSET CAN B...
AVAILABLE FOR AN ADDITIONAL 10%.
>> 4% IS AS HIGH AS WE CAN GO, WITH GUARANTE...
   DISCRETION.
>> AND LIVE ACCESS TO PROGRESS REPORTS?
>> WE AREN'T PROSK. FINNICK. CRION IS COMMON...
   SOURCE. WE FREELY SHARE ALL STUDY RESULT...
   WITH THE COMMUNITY.
>> WILL RETURN 2% FOR A 60 DAY EXCLUSIVE ON ALL
   PROGRESS.
>> RETURN ALL 4% AND WE'RE IN AGREEMENT.

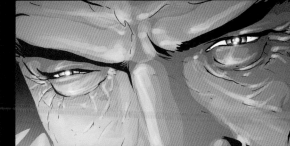

>> RETURN ALL 4% AN...
>> DONE.
>> HOW WILL YOU GET
   HAWKEN TO AGREE
   TO THE TRADE?

HAWKEN T...
TO THE TRADE?
NOT YOUR PROBLEM

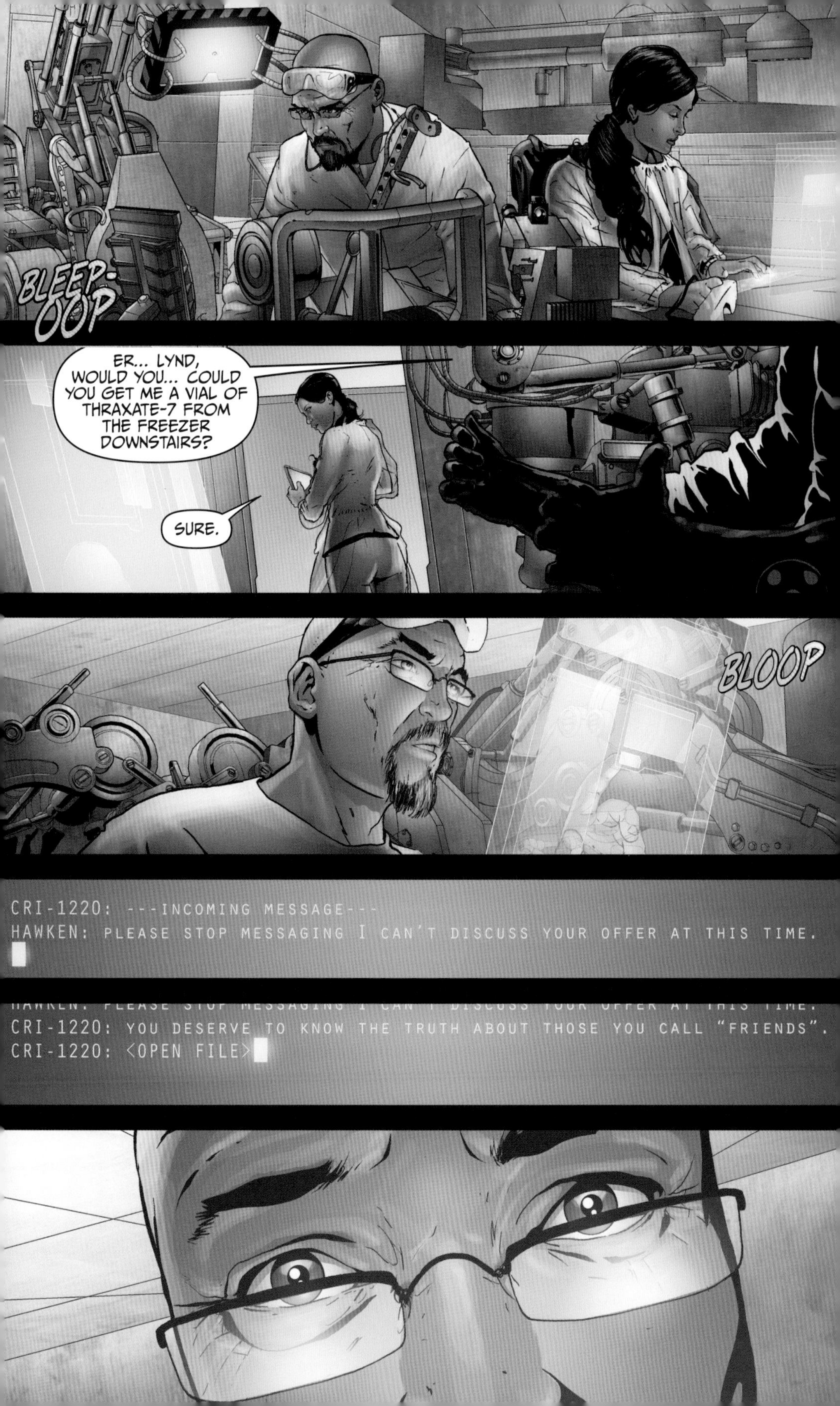
BLEEP-OOP
ER... LYND, WOULD YOU... COULD YOU GET ME A VIAL OF THRAXATE-7 FROM THE FREEZER DOWNSTAIRS?
SURE.
BLOOP
CRI-1220: ---INCOMING MESSAGE---
HAWKEN: PLEASE STOP MESSAGING I CAN'T DISCUSS YOUR OFFER AT THIS TIME.
CRI-1220: YOU DESERVE TO KNOW THE TRUTH ABOUT THOSE YOU CALL "FRIENDS".
CRI-1220: <OPEN FILE>

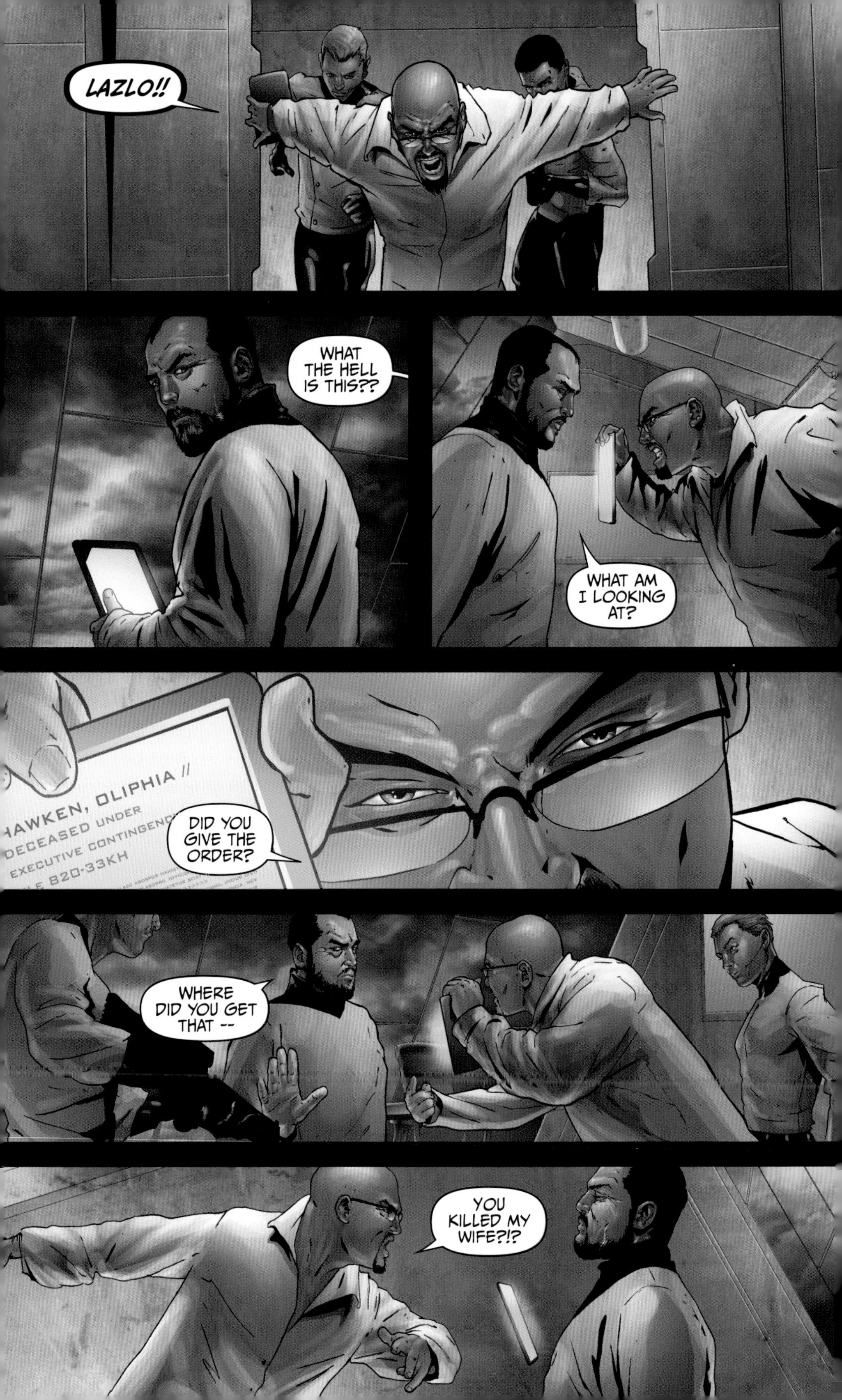
LAZLO!!
WHAT THE HELL IS THIS??
WHAT AM I LOOKING AT?
DECEASED UNDER
DID YOU GIVE THE ORDER?
WHERE DID YOU GET THAT --
YOU KILLED MY WIFE?!?

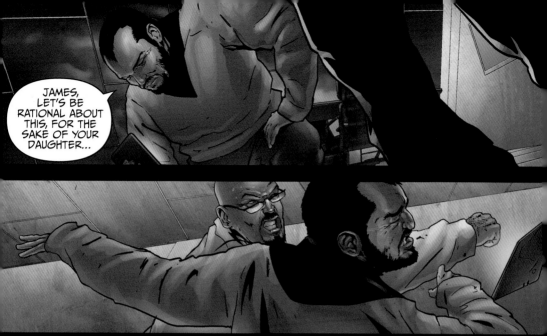

JAMES, LET'S BE RATIONAL ABOUT THIS, FOR THE SAKE OF YOUR DAUGHTER...

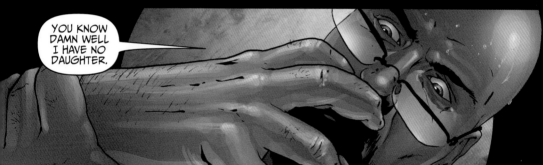

YOU KNOW DAMN WELL I HAVE NO DAUGHTER.

NO! LET HIM GO...

GET ME FINNICK. NOW!

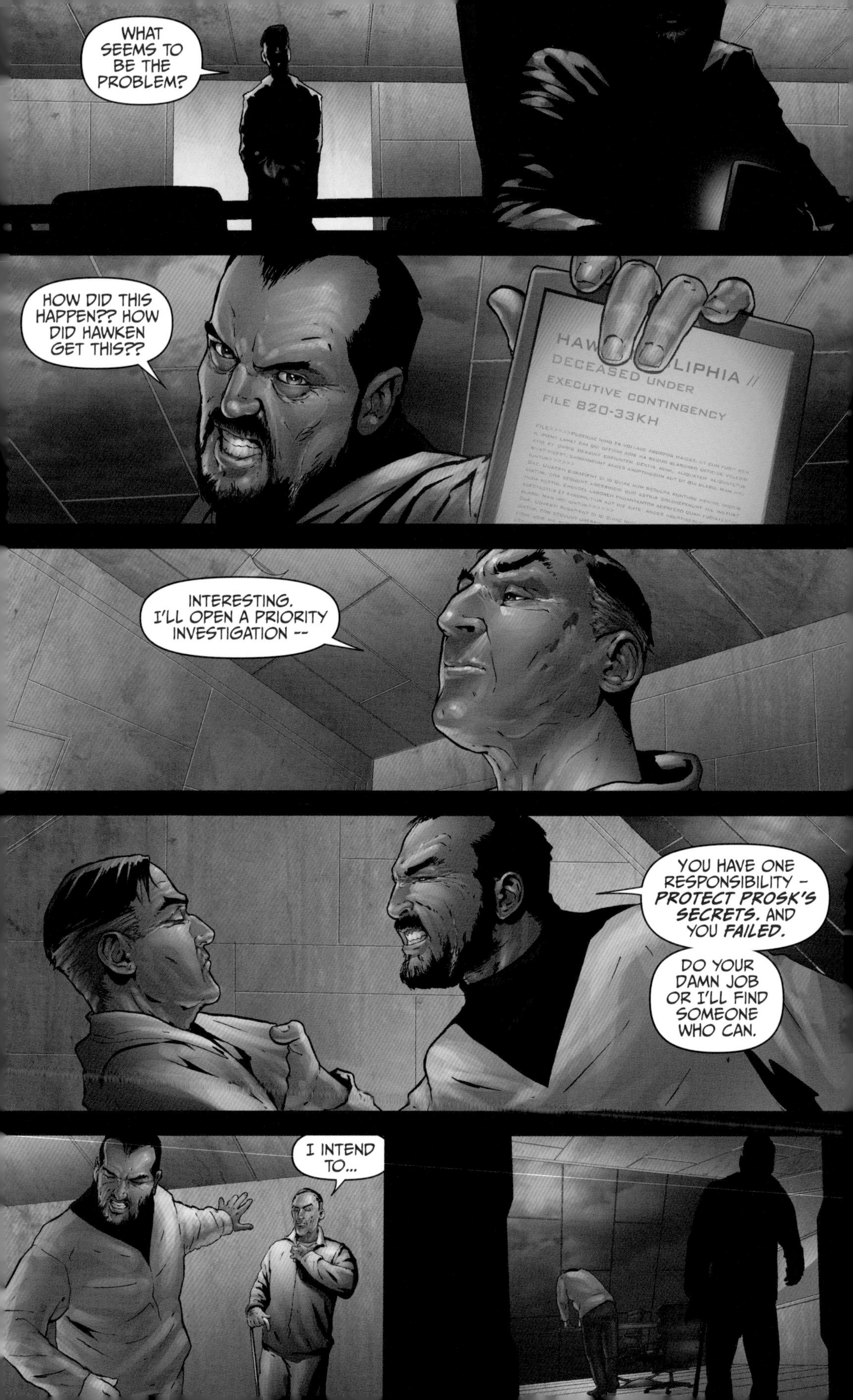
WHAT SEEMS TO BE THE PROBLEM?
HOW DID THIS HAPPEN?? HOW DID HAWKEN GET THIS??
DECEASED UNDER
EXECUTIVE CONTINGENCY
FILE 820-33KH
INTERESTING. I'LL OPEN A PRIORITY INVESTIGATION --
YOU HAVE ONE RESPONSIBILITY - *PROTECT PROSK'S SECRETS.* AND YOU *FAILED.*
DO YOUR DAMN JOB OR I'LL FIND SOMEONE WHO CAN.
I INTEND TO...

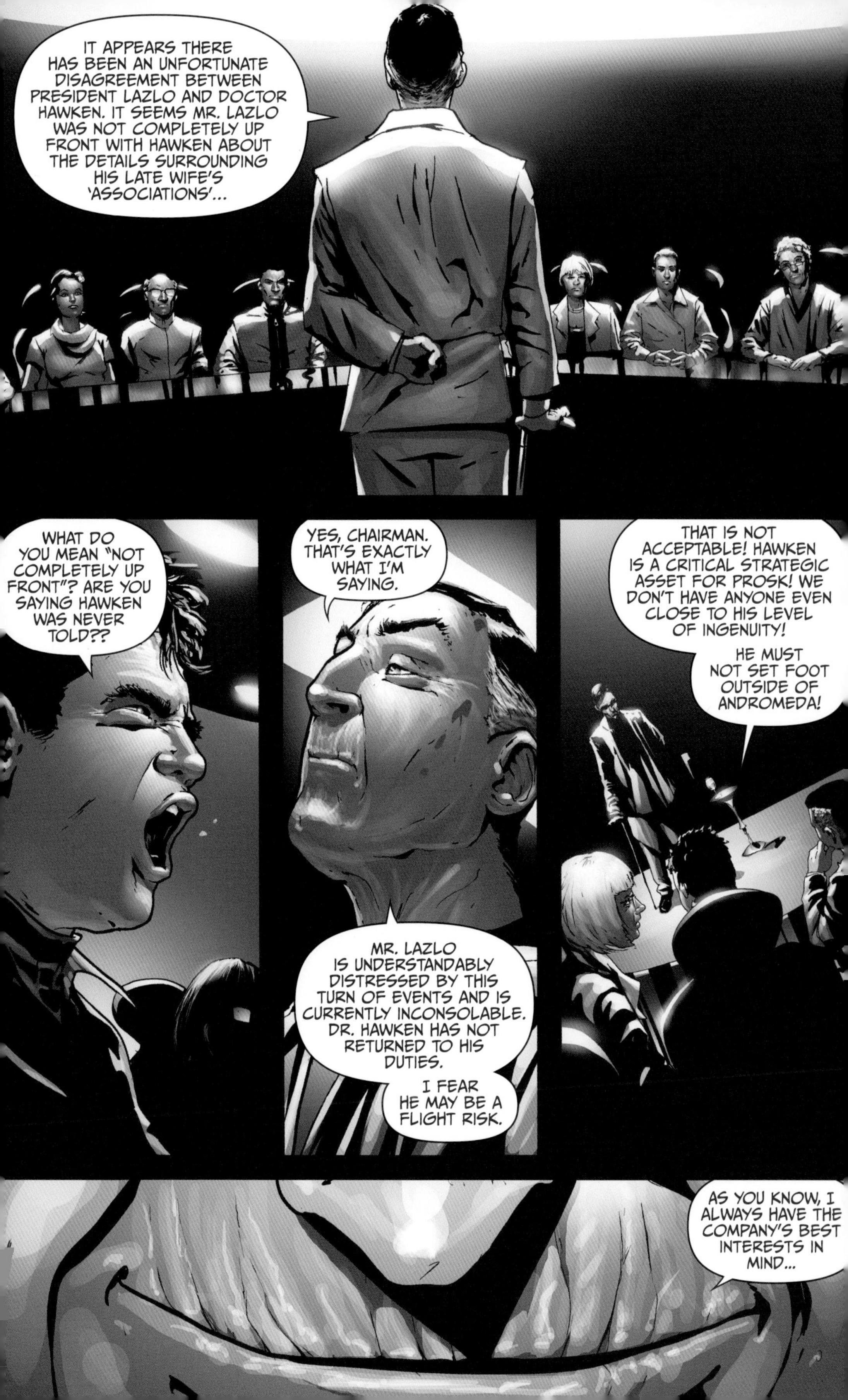
IT APPEARS THERE HAS BEEN AN UNFORTUNATE DISAGREEMENT BETWEEN PRESIDENT LAZLO AND DOCTOR HAWKEN. IT SEEMS MR. LAZLO WAS NOT COMPLETELY UP FRONT WITH HAWKEN ABOUT THE DETAILS SURROUNDING HIS LATE WIFE'S 'ASSOCIATIONS'...
WHAT DO YOU MEAN "NOT COMPLETELY UP FRONT"? ARE YOU SAYING HAWKEN WAS NEVER TOLD??
YES, CHAIRMAN. THAT'S EXACTLY WHAT I'M SAYING.
MR. LAZLO IS UNDERSTANDABLY DISTRESSED BY THIS TURN OF EVENTS AND IS CURRENTLY INCONSOLABLE. DR. HAWKEN HAS NOT RETURNED TO HIS DUTIES.
I FEAR HE MAY BE A FLIGHT RISK.
THAT IS NOT ACCEPTABLE! HAWKEN IS A CRITICAL STRATEGIC ASSET FOR PROSK! WE DON'T HAVE ANYONE EVEN CLOSE TO HIS LEVEL OF INGENUITY!
HE MUST NOT SET FOOT OUTSIDE OF ANDROMEDA!
AS YOU KNOW, I ALWAYS HAVE THE COMPANY'S BEST INTERESTS IN MIND...

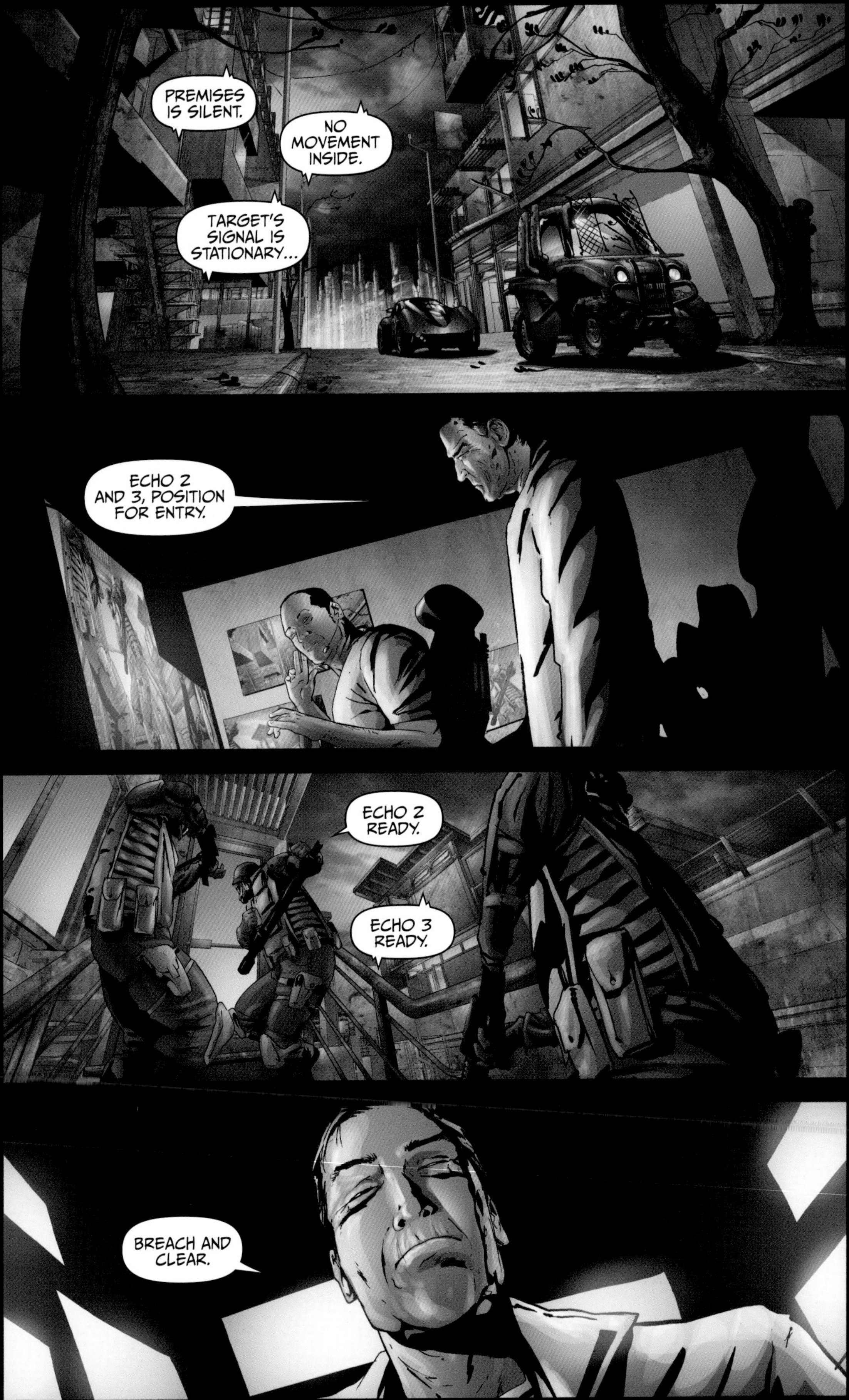
PREMISES IS SILENT.
NO MOVEMENT INSIDE.
TARGET'S SIGNAL IS STATIONARY...
ECHO 2 AND 3, POSITION FOR ENTRY.
ECHO 2 READY.
ECHO 3 READY.
BREACH AND CLEAR.

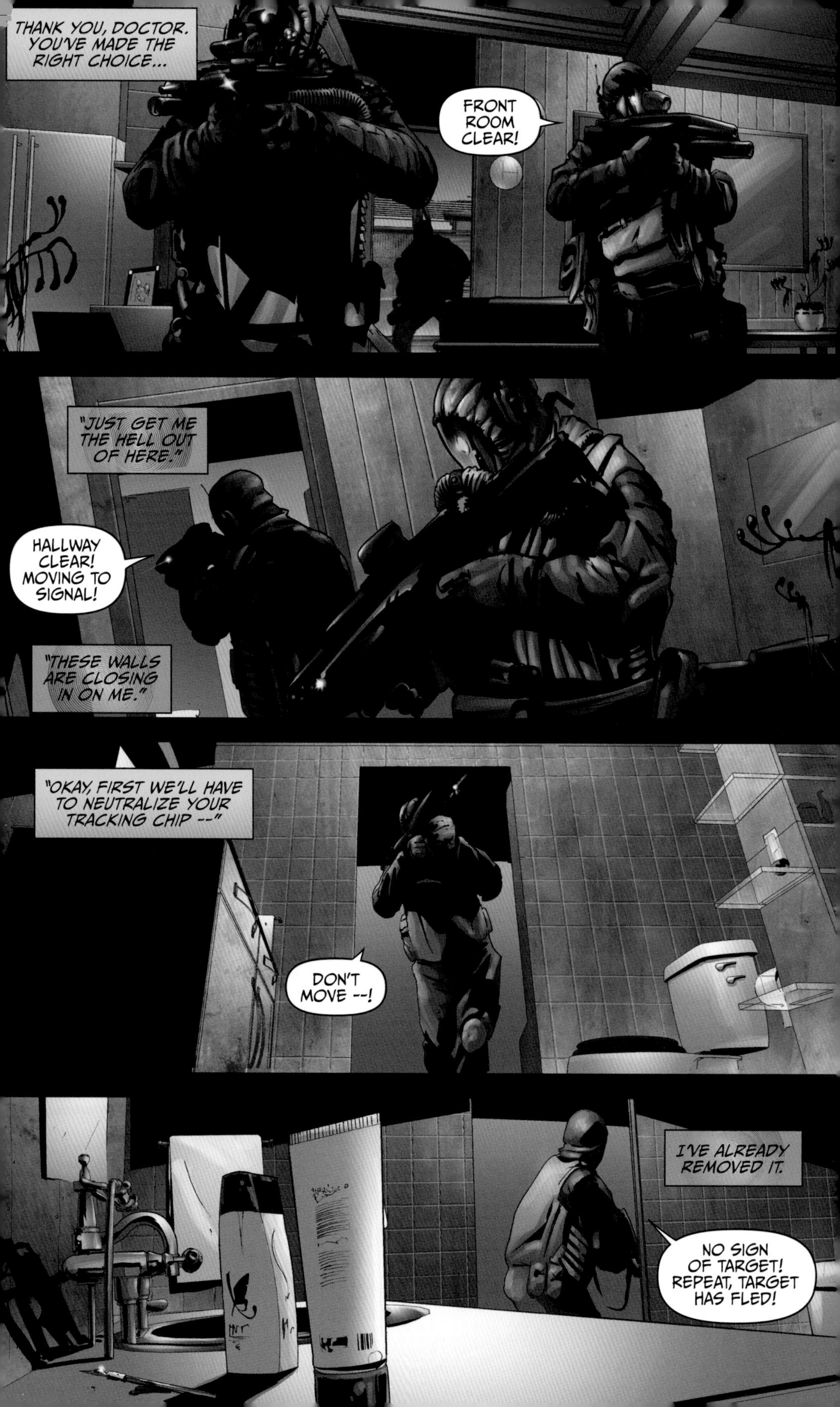
THANK YOU, DOCTOR. YOU'VE MADE THE RIGHT CHOICE...
FRONT ROOM CLEAR!
"JUST GET ME THE HELL OUT OF HERE."
HALLWAY CLEAR! MOVING TO SIGNAL!
"THESE WALLS ARE CLOSING IN ON ME."
"OKAY, FIRST WE'LL HAVE TO NEUTRALIZE YOUR TRACKING CHIP --"
DON'T MOVE --!
I'VE ALREADY REMOVED IT.
NO SIGN OF TARGET! REPEAT, TARGET HAS FLED!

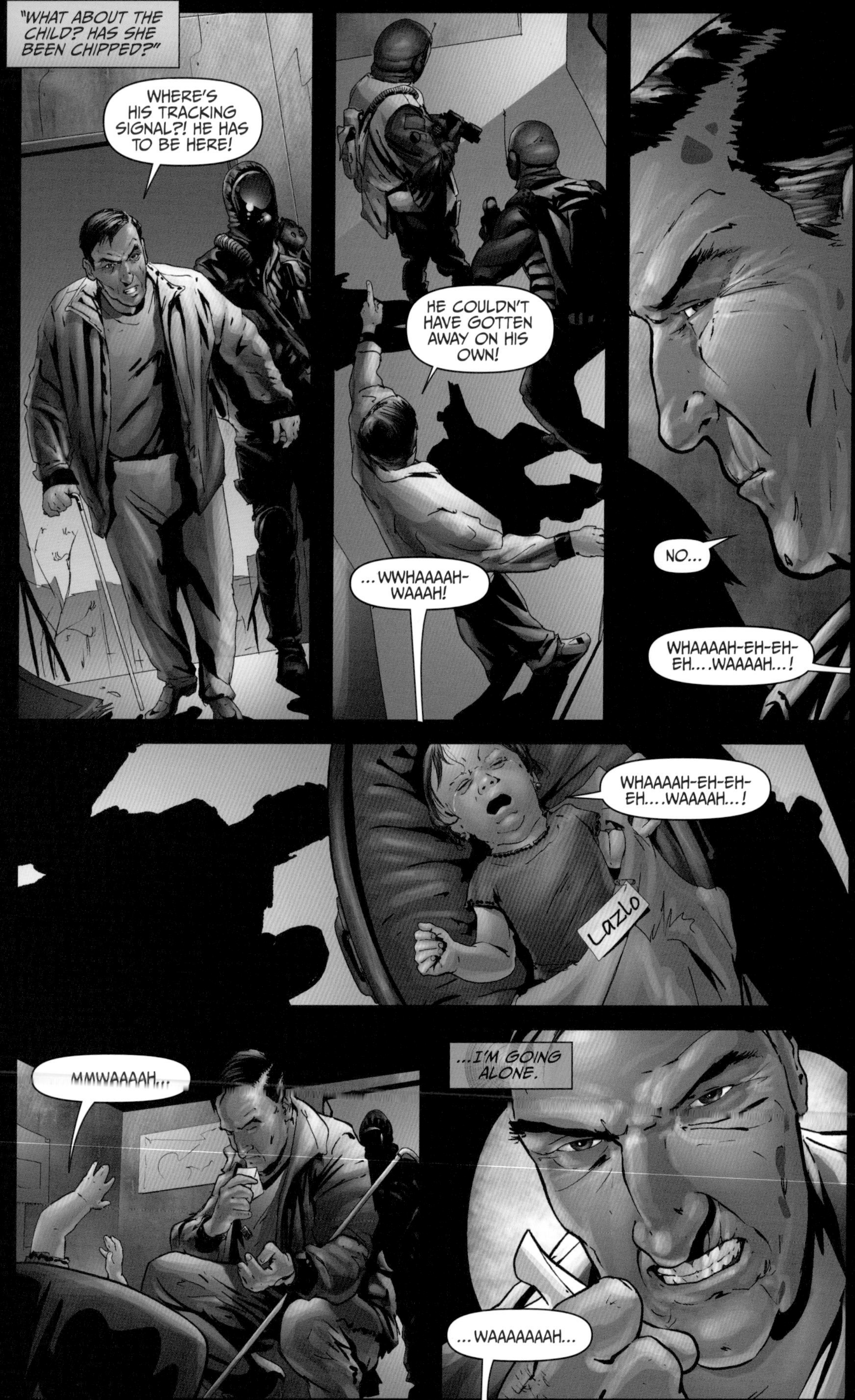
"WHAT ABOUT THE CHILD? HAS SHE BEEN CHIPPED?"
WHERE'S HIS TRACKING SIGNAL?! HE HAS TO BE HERE!
HE COULDN'T HAVE GOTTEN AWAY ON HIS OWN!
...WWHAAAAH-WAAAH!
NO...
WHAAAAH-EH-EH-EH....WAAAAH...!
WHAAAAH-EH-EH-EH....WAAAAH...!
Lazlo
MMWAAAAH...
...I'M GOING ALONE.
...WAAAAAAAH...

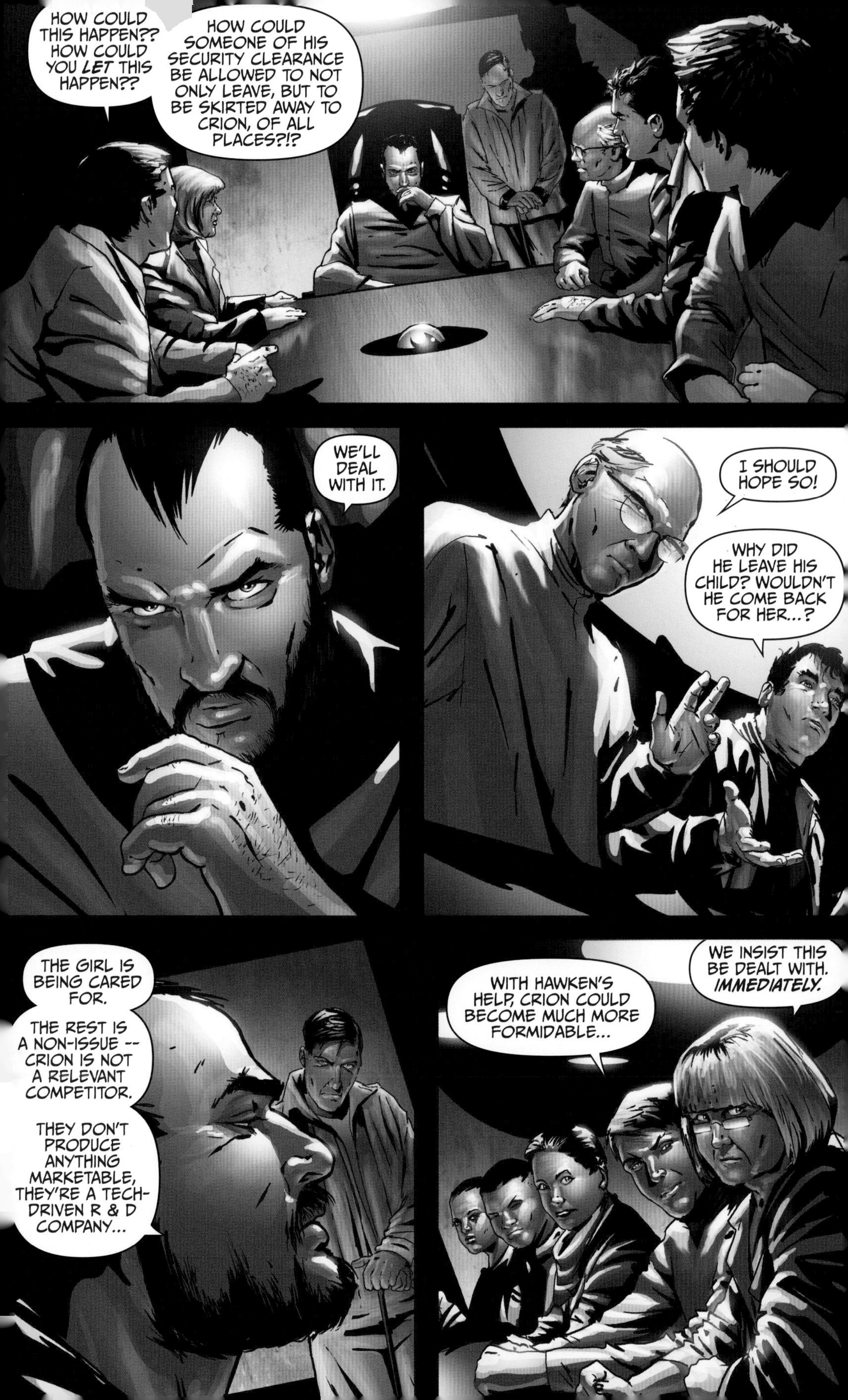
HOW COULD THIS HAPPEN?? HOW COULD YOU *LET* THIS HAPPEN??
HOW COULD SOMEONE OF HIS SECURITY CLEARANCE BE ALLOWED TO NOT ONLY LEAVE, BUT TO BE SKIRTED AWAY TO CRION, OF ALL PLACES?!?
WE'LL DEAL WITH IT.
I SHOULD HOPE SO!
WHY DID HE LEAVE HIS CHILD? WOULDN'T HE COME BACK FOR HER...?
THE GIRL IS BEING CARED FOR.
THE REST IS A NON-ISSUE -- CRION IS NOT A RELEVANT COMPETITOR.
THEY DON'T PRODUCE ANYTHING MARKETABLE, THEY'RE A TECH-DRIVEN R & D COMPANY...
WITH HAWKEN'S HELP, CRION COULD BECOME MUCH MORE FORMIDABLE...
WE INSIST THIS BE DEALT WITH. ***IMMEDIATELY.***

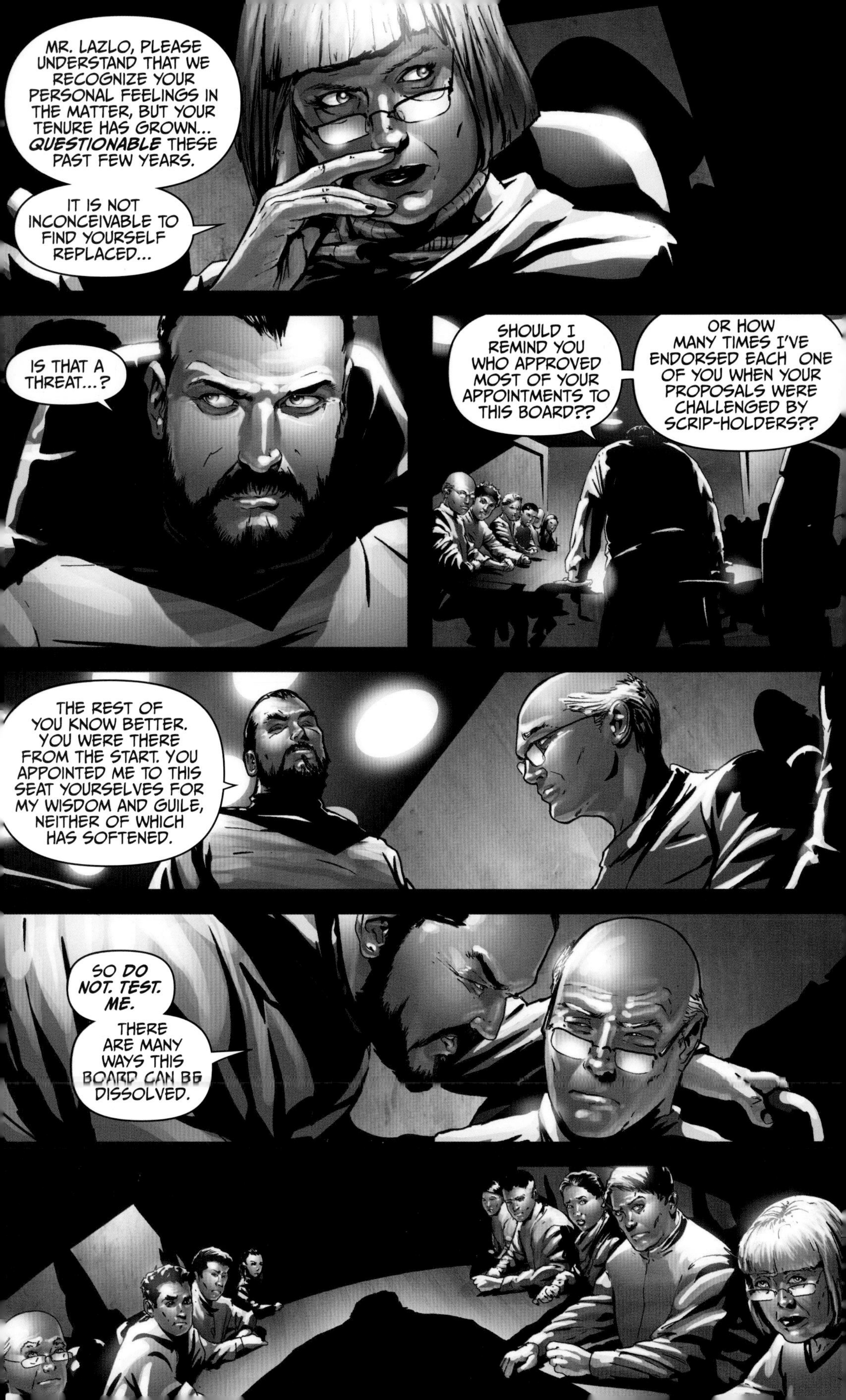
MR. LAZLO, PLEASE UNDERSTAND THAT WE RECOGNIZE YOUR PERSONAL FEELINGS IN THE MATTER, BUT YOUR TENURE HAS GROWN... *QUESTIONABLE* THESE PAST FEW YEARS.
IT IS NOT INCONCEIVABLE TO FIND YOURSELF REPLACED...
IS THAT A THREAT...?
SHOULD I REMIND YOU WHO APPROVED MOST OF YOUR APPOINTMENTS TO THIS BOARD??
OR HOW MANY TIMES I'VE ENDORSED EACH ONE OF YOU WHEN YOUR PROPOSALS WERE CHALLENGED BY SCRIP-HOLDERS??
THE REST OF YOU KNOW BETTER. YOU WERE THERE FROM THE START. YOU APPOINTED ME TO THIS SEAT YOURSELVES FOR MY WISDOM AND GUILE, NEITHER OF WHICH HAS SOFTENED.
SO *DO NOT. TEST. ME.*
THERE ARE MANY WAYS THIS BOARD CAN BE DISSOLVED.

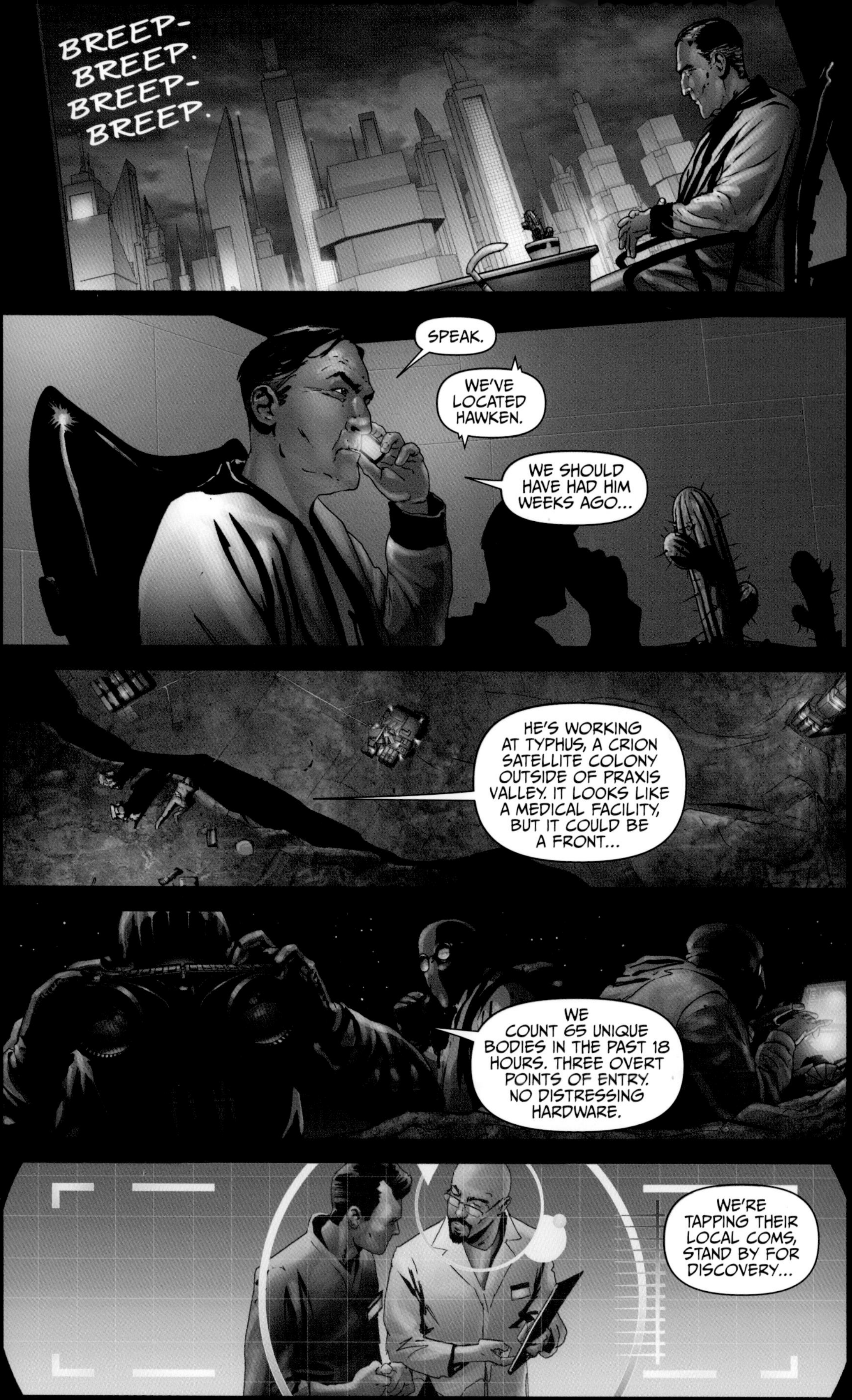
BREEP-
BREEP.
BREEP-
BREEP.
SPEAK.
WE'VE LOCATED HAWKEN.
WE SHOULD HAVE HAD HIM WEEKS AGO...
HE'S WORKING AT TYPHUS, A CRION SATELLITE COLONY OUTSIDE OF PRAXIS VALLEY. IT LOOKS LIKE A MEDICAL FACILITY, BUT IT COULD BE A FRONT...
WE COUNT 65 UNIQUE BODIES IN THE PAST 18 HOURS. THREE OVERT POINTS OF ENTRY. NO DISTRESSING HARDWARE.
WE'RE TAPPING THEIR LOCAL COMS, STAND BY FOR DISCOVERY...

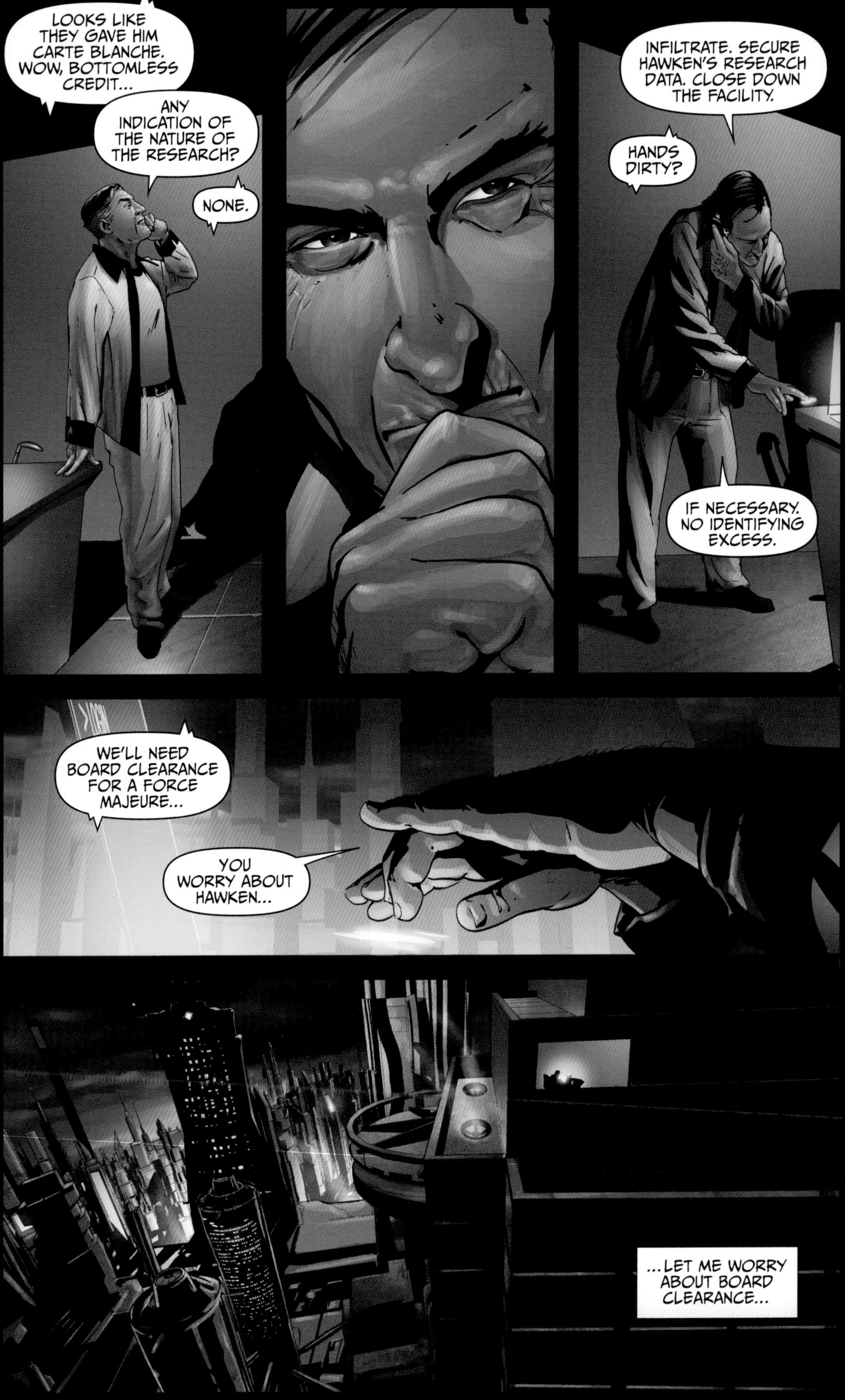
LOOKS LIKE THEY GAVE HIM CARTE BLANCHE. WOW, BOTTOMLESS CREDIT...
ANY INDICATION OF THE NATURE OF THE RESEARCH?
NONE.
INFILTRATE. SECURE HAWKEN'S RESEARCH DATA. CLOSE DOWN THE FACILITY.
HANDS DIRTY?
IF NECESSARY. NO IDENTIFYING EXCESS.
WE'LL NEED BOARD CLEARANCE FOR A FORCE MAJEURE...
YOU WORRY ABOUT HAWKEN...
...LET ME WORRY ABOUT BOARD CLEARANCE...

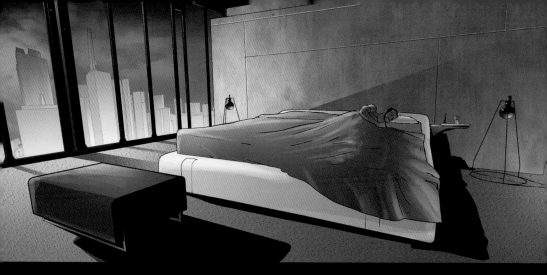

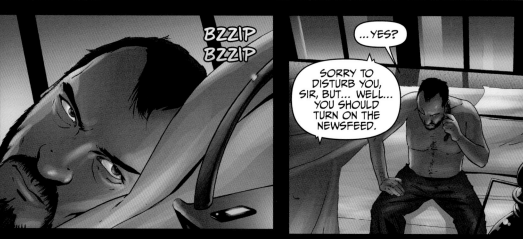

BZZIP
BZZIP

...YES?

SORRY TO DISTURB YOU, SIR, BUT... WELL... YOU SHOULD TURN ON THE NEWSFEED.

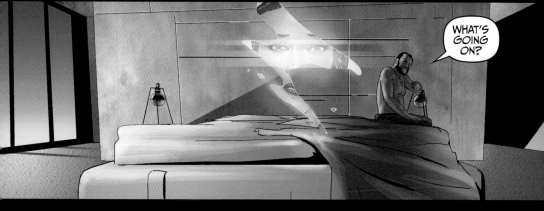

WHAT'S GOING ON?

network

-- MASSIVE EXPLOSION AT ONE OF CRION'S RESEARCH AND DEVELOPMENT LABORATORIES JUST MOMENTS AGO...

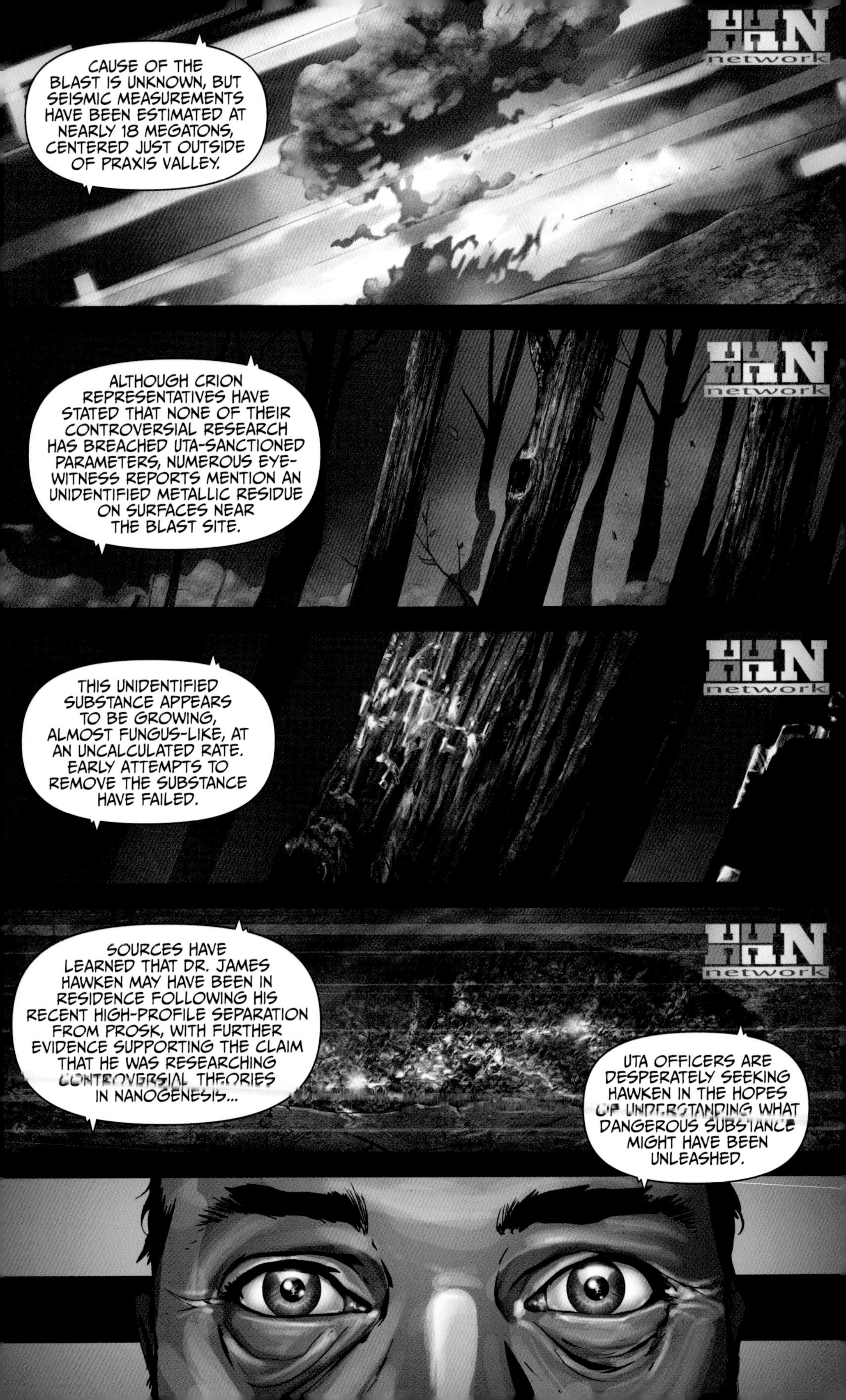
CAUSE OF THE BLAST IS UNKNOWN, BUT SEISMIC MEASUREMENTS HAVE BEEN ESTIMATED AT NEARLY 18 MEGATONS, CENTERED JUST OUTSIDE OF PRAXIS VALLEY.
ALTHOUGH CRION REPRESENTATIVES HAVE STATED THAT NONE OF THEIR CONTROVERSIAL RESEARCH HAS BREACHED UTA-SANCTIONED PARAMETERS, NUMEROUS EYE-WITNESS REPORTS MENTION AN UNIDENTIFIED METALLIC RESIDUE ON SURFACES NEAR THE BLAST SITE.
THIS UNIDENTIFIED SUBSTANCE APPEARS TO BE GROWING, ALMOST FUNGUS-LIKE, AT AN UNCALCULATED RATE. EARLY ATTEMPTS TO REMOVE THE SUBSTANCE HAVE FAILED.
SOURCES HAVE LEARNED THAT DR. JAMES HAWKEN MAY HAVE BEEN IN RESIDENCE FOLLOWING HIS RECENT HIGH-PROFILE SEPARATION FROM PROSK, WITH FURTHER EVIDENCE SUPPORTING THE CLAIM THAT HE WAS RESEARCHING CONTROVERSIAL THEORIES IN NANOGENESIS...
UTA OFFICERS ARE DESPERATELY SEEKING HAWKEN IN THE HOPES OF UNDERSTANDING WHAT DANGEROUS SUBSTANCE MIGHT HAVE BEEN UNLEASHED.

AT THIS MOMENT, HOWEVER, HE IS PRESUMED TO HAVE DIED IN THE BLAST, ALONG WITH THE CURRENTLY ESTIMATED 34,000 REPORTED CASUALTIES AS OF THE HOUR.

AUTHORITIES RECOMMEND EVERYONE LIVING WITHIN FOUR ZONES OF THE BLAST TO STAY INDOORS AND AWAY FROM ANY FOREIGN SUBSTANCE THAT MAY FALL FROM THE UPPER ATMOSPHERE.

OPERATION: PRODIGAL SON

>> E-6
TREMILL

>> E-5
BLAKE RO

>> E-5
LOY MONROE

UNTIL THE SPREAD OF CONTAMINATION CAN BE PROPERLY ASSESSED, IT IS BEST TO KEEP ALL WINDOWS, DOORS, AND VENTS SEALED SHUT.

OPERATION

>> KIA/DISAVOWED
TREMILL FRANCIS

>> KIA/DISAVOWED
BLAKE

WHILE NO ADVERSE RADIATION HAS BEEN MEASURED, THE THREAT OF FALLOUT SHOULD BE OBSERVED.

WE WILL CONTINUE TO REPORT ON THIS TRAGIC EVENT AS NEW INFORMATION IS RECEIVED.

PROSK
FRIDA
PROSK PORTAL
EXTRANET BROWSER
UTA Today - Illal Accide...   The Illuminator - Blocked
PRO

UTA TODAY
Your World. Your News.

THE CRION INCID

HOME | BREAKING | NEWS | WORLD | PLANETARY | MPCS | ENTERTAINMENT | SPORTS | HEALTH | SCIENCE | TE

THE ACCIDENT THAT SHATTERED THE ILLALIAN DREAM

Written by Senior Reporter Elizabeth O'Roarke

We call them *turning points*. Pivotal events that change the course of human history. A radical new technology. A lifesaving cure. An unforgivable act of aggression. An unforgettable catastrophe. Ask any Illalian where they were on May 3rd, 2361 when they heard the news. When this industrial mecca woke up from the "Illalian Dream" to greet a new reality. The day of "The Crion Incident" is a moment burned into our collective consciousness. Now on its fifth anniversary, we look back on the origins of the Hawken Virus, and the end of a golden age of commerce.

The Incident

The cause is still a mystery. Though Crion (and conspiracy theorists at large) blame corporate sabotage, the UTA investigation ultimately faulted Crion's lax safety regulations. Crion's stake in Illal was, after all, a thinly veiled refuge from the UTA's Scientific Ethics Commission. All we can verify is that energy fluctuations recorded at 03:17 AM CT suggest an acute meltdown at Typhus, a top-secret R&D facility five miles outside Kobalt proper. The resulting 18-megaton blast vaporized the lab and everything else within a 20-mile radius, including 70% of Praxis Valley.

To date over 54,000 deaths have been confirmed with hundreds more still missing, most notably Crion's high-profile acquisition, Dr. James Hawken. Hawken was a costly loss to Illal and the first death from the tragedy to resonate with the galactic community, making him forever synonymous with the aftermath of the blast that took his life. While many speculate, no record linking Hawken's lab at Typhus and the ensuing horror has been found.

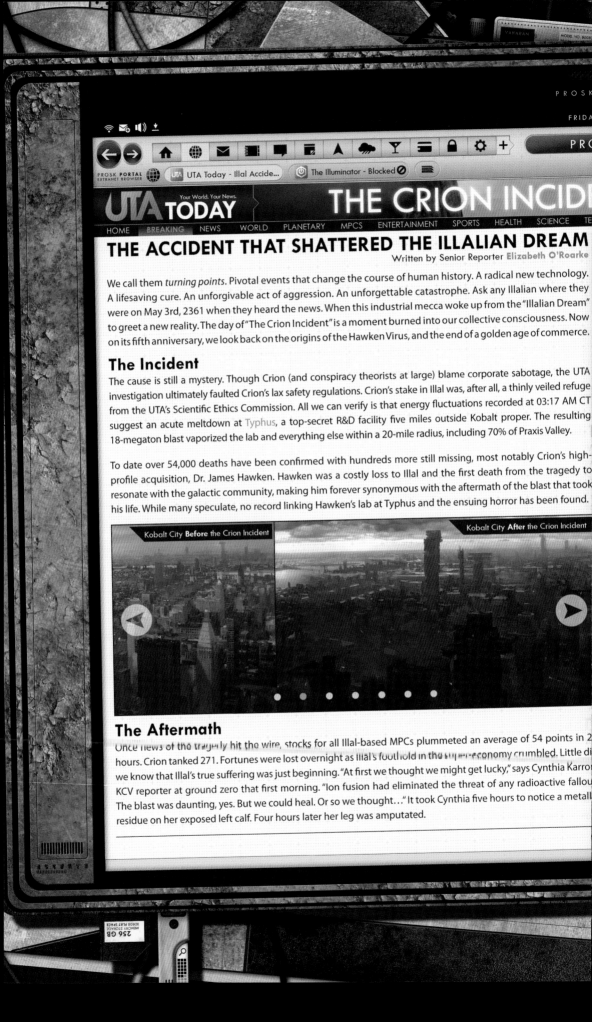

Kobalt City **Before** the Crion Incident   Kobalt City **After** the Crion Incident

The Aftermath

Once news of the tragedy hit the wire, stocks for all Illal-based MPCs plummeted an average of 54 points in 2 hours. Crion tanked 271. Fortunes were lost overnight as Illal's foothold in the super-economy crumbled. Little di we know that Illal's true suffering was just beginning. "At first we thought we might get lucky," says Cynthia Karro KCV reporter at ground zero that first morning. "Ion fusion had eliminated the threat of any radioactive fallou The blast was daunting, yes. But we could heal. Or so we thought…" It took Cynthia five hours to notice a metall residue on her exposed left calf. Four hours later her leg was amputated.

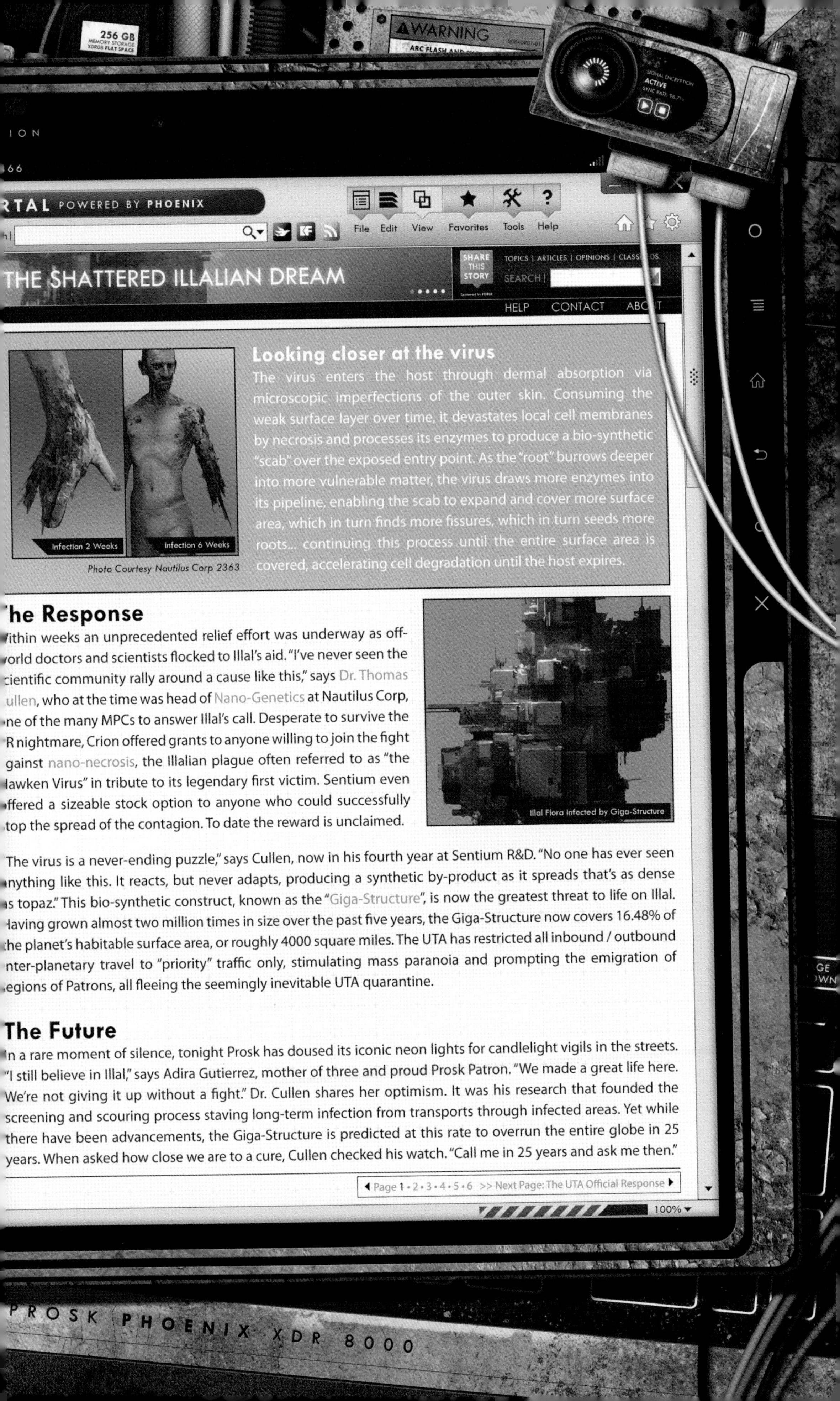
256 GB
MEMORY STORAGE
XDR08 FLAT SPACE
WARNING
ARC FLASH AND
SIGNAL ENCRYPTION
ACTIVE
ION
66
RTAL POWERED BY PHOENIX
File
Edit
View
Favorites
Tools
Help
SHARE THIS STORY
TOPICS | ARTICLES | OPINIONS | CLASS DS
SEARCH |
HELP
CONTACT
ABC T
PROSK PHOENIX XDR 8000

THE SHATTERED ILLALIAN DREAM

Looking closer at the virus

The virus enters the host through dermal absorption via microscopic imperfections of the outer skin. Consuming the weak surface layer over time, it devastates local cell membranes by necrosis and processes its enzymes to produce a bio-synthetic "scab" over the exposed entry point. As the "root" burrows deeper into more vulnerable matter, the virus draws more enzymes into its pipeline, enabling the scab to expand and cover more surface area, which in turn finds more fissures, which in turn seeds more roots... continuing this process until the entire surface area is covered, accelerating cell degradation until the host expires.

Infection 2 Weeks

Infection 6 Weeks

Photo Courtesy Nautilus Corp 2363

'he Response

/ithin weeks an unprecedented relief effort was underway as off-/orld doctors and scientists flocked to Illal's aid. "I've never seen the cientific community rally around a cause like this," says Dr. Thomas ullen, who at the time was head of Nano-Genetics at Nautilus Corp, ne of the many MPCs to answer Illal's call. Desperate to survive the R nightmare, Crion offered grants to anyone willing to join the fight gainst nano-necrosis, the Illalian plague often referred to as "the lawken Virus" in tribute to its legendary first victim. Sentium even ffered a sizeable stock option to anyone who could successfully top the spread of the contagion. To date the reward is unclaimed.

Illal Flora Infected by Giga-Structure

The virus is a never-ending puzzle," says Cullen, now in his fourth year at Sentium R&D. "No one has ever seen nything like this. It reacts, but never adapts, producing a synthetic by-product as it spreads that's as dense s topaz." This bio-synthetic construct, known as the "Giga-Structure", is now the greatest threat to life on Illal. Having grown almost two million times in size over the past five years, the Giga-Structure now covers 16.48% of the planet's habitable surface area, or roughly 4000 square miles. The UTA has restricted all inbound / outbound nter-planetary travel to "priority" traffic only, stimulating mass paranoia and prompting the emigration of egions of Patrons, all fleeing the seemingly inevitable UTA quarantine.

The Future

In a rare moment of silence, tonight Prosk has doused its iconic neon lights for candlelight vigils in the streets. "I still believe in Illal," says Adira Gutierrez, mother of three and proud Prosk Patron. "We made a great life here. We're not giving it up without a fight." Dr. Cullen shares her optimism. It was his research that founded the screening and scouring process staving long-term infection from transports through infected areas. Yet while there have been advancements, the Giga-Structure is predicted at this rate to overrun the entire globe in 25 years. When asked how close we are to a cure, Cullen checked his watch. "Call me in 25 years and ask me then."

◀ Page 1 • 2 • 3 • 4 • 5 • 6 >> Next Page: The UTA Official Response ▶

100% ▾

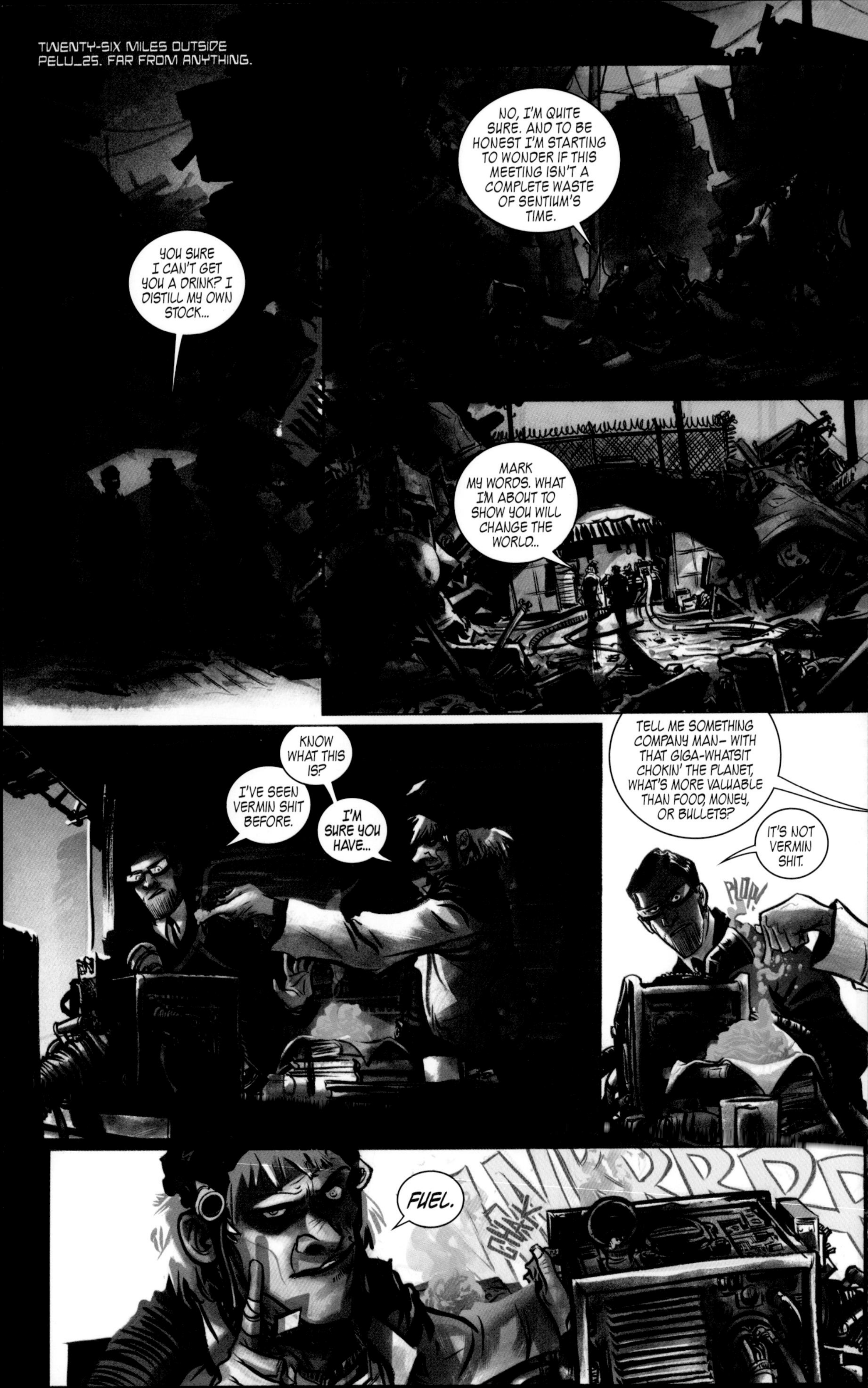

TWENTY-SIX MILES OUTSIDE PELU_25. FAR FROM ANYTHING.
YOU SURE I CAN'T GET YOU A DRINK? I DISTILL MY OWN STOCK...
NO, I'M QUITE SURE. AND TO BE HONEST I'M STARTING TO WONDER IF THIS MEETING ISN'T A COMPLETE WASTE OF SENTIUM'S TIME.
MARK MY WORDS. WHAT I'M ABOUT TO SHOW YOU WILL CHANGE THE WORLD...
KNOW WHAT THIS IS?
I'VE SEEN VERMIN SHIT BEFORE.
I'M SURE YOU HAVE...
TELL ME SOMETHING COMPANY MAN– WITH THAT GIGA-WHATSIT CHOKIN' THE PLANET, WHAT'S MORE VALUABLE THAN FOOD, MONEY, OR BULLETS?
IT'S NOT VERMIN SHIT.
PLOP!
FUEL.
CHAK

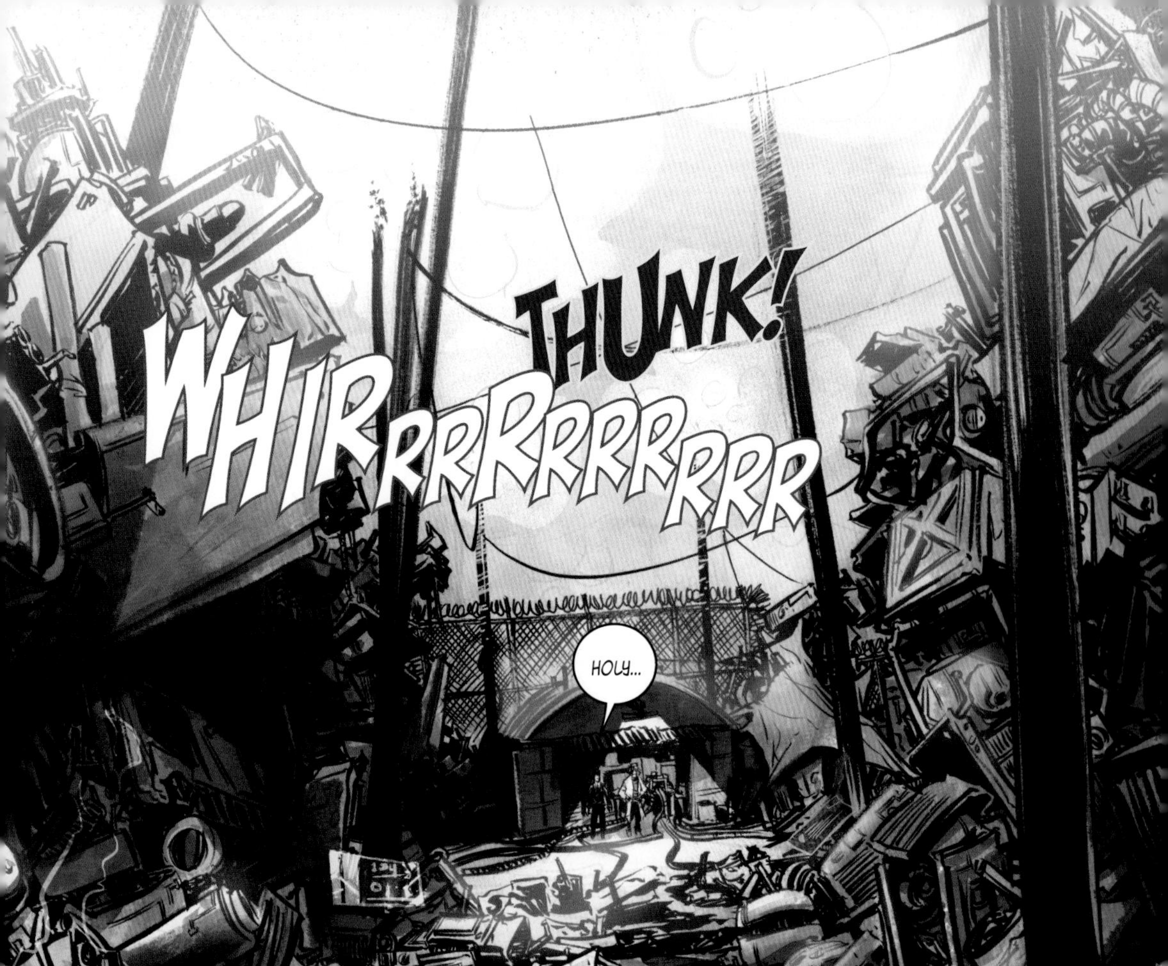
THUNK!
WHIRRRRRRRRRRR
HOLY...

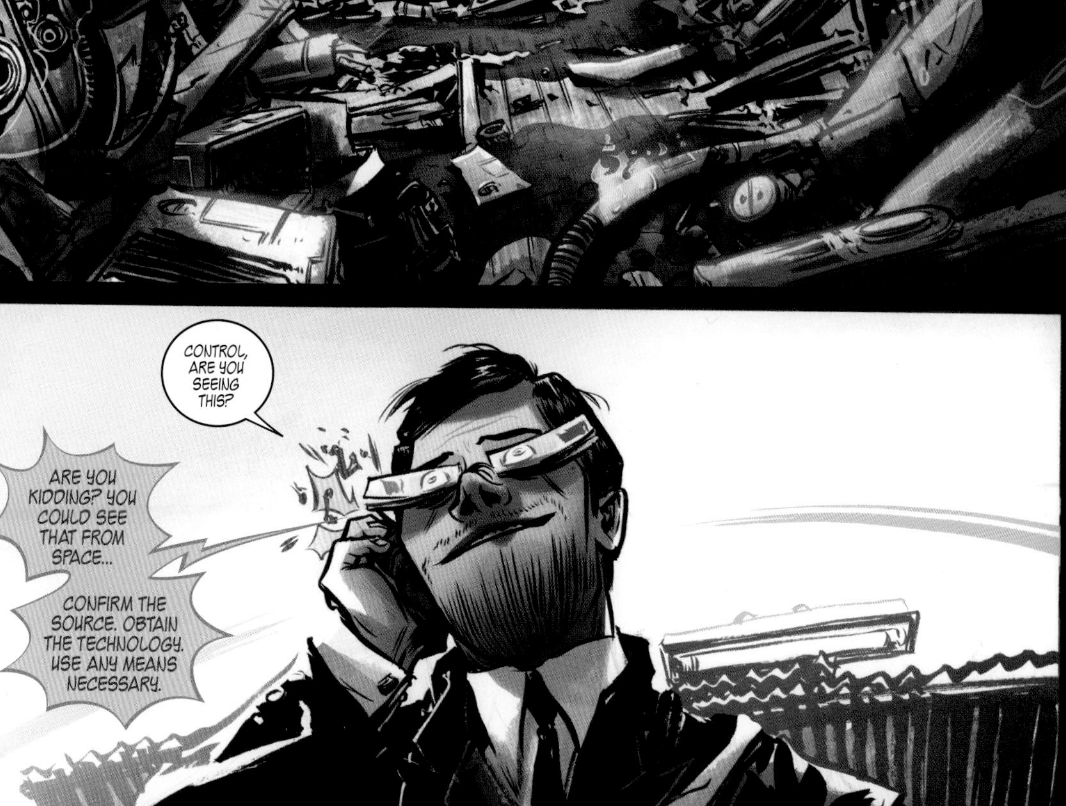
CONTROL, ARE YOU SEEING THIS?
ARE YOU KIDDING? YOU COULD SEE THAT FROM SPACE...
CONFIRM THE SOURCE. OBTAIN THE TECHNOLOGY. USE ANY MEANS NECESSARY.

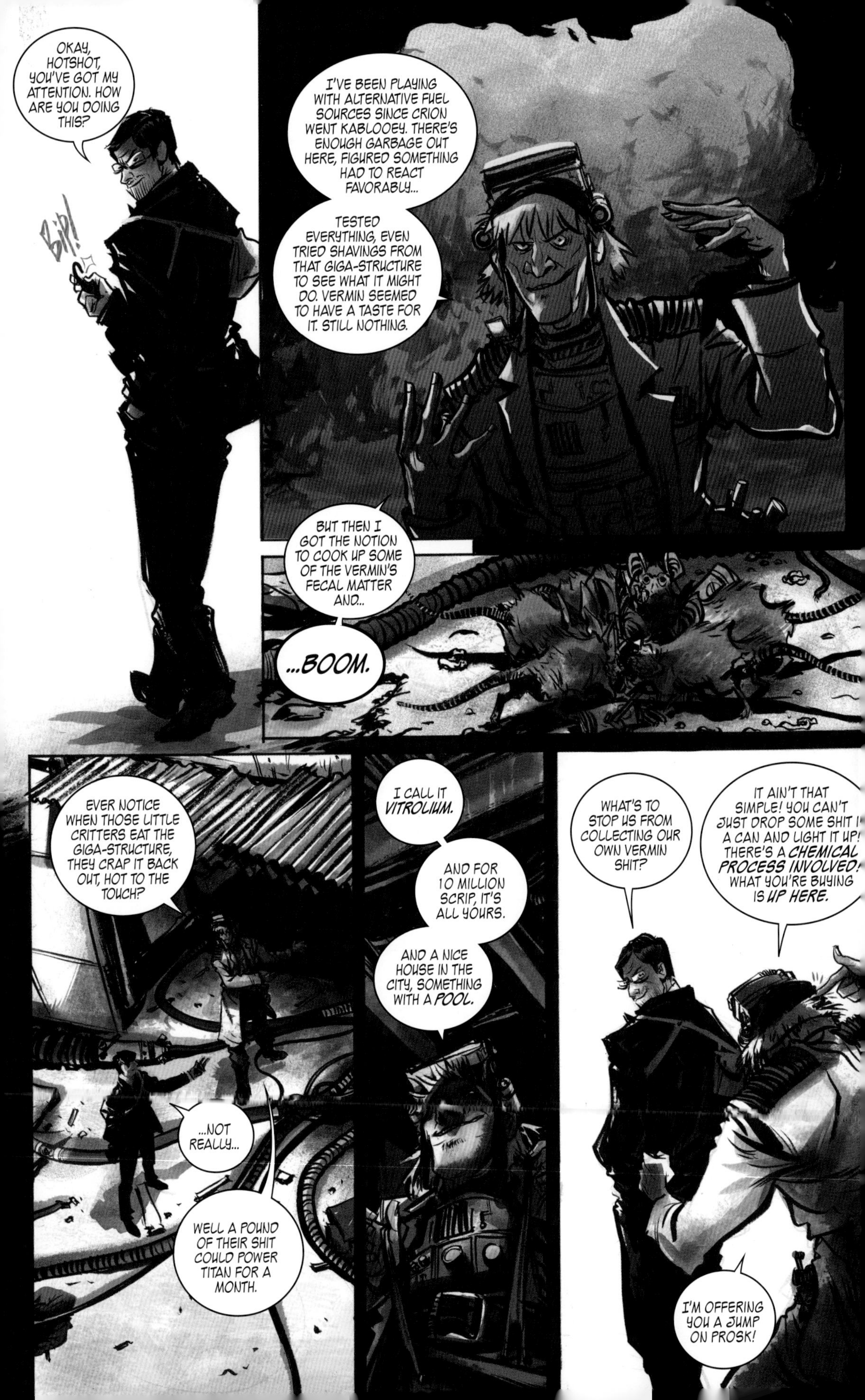
OKAY, HOTSHOT, YOU'VE GOT MY ATTENTION. HOW ARE YOU DOING THIS?
BIP!
I'VE BEEN PLAYING WITH ALTERNATIVE FUEL SOURCES SINCE CRION WENT KABLOOEY. THERE'S ENOUGH GARBAGE OUT HERE, FIGURED SOMETHING HAD TO REACT FAVORABLY...
TESTED EVERYTHING, EVEN TRIED SHAVINGS FROM THAT GIGA-STRUCTURE TO SEE WHAT IT MIGHT DO. VERMIN SEEMED TO HAVE A TASTE FOR IT. STILL NOTHING.
BUT THEN I GOT THE NOTION TO COOK UP SOME OF THE VERMIN'S FECAL MATTER AND...
...BOOM.
EVER NOTICE WHEN THOSE LITTLE CRITTERS EAT THE GIGA-STRUCTURE, THEY CRAP IT BACK OUT, HOT TO THE TOUCH?
...NOT REALLY...
WELL A POUND OF THEIR SHIT COULD POWER TITAN FOR A MONTH.
I CALL IT *VITROLIUM.*
AND FOR 10 MILLION SCRIP, IT'S ALL YOURS.
AND A NICE HOUSE IN THE CITY, SOMETHING WITH A *POOL.*
WHAT'S TO STOP US FROM COLLECTING OUR OWN VERMIN SHIT?
IT AIN'T THAT SIMPLE! YOU CAN'T JUST DROP SOME SHIT I A CAN AND LIGHT IT UP! THERE'S A *CHEMICAL PROCESS INVOLVED!* WHAT YOU'RE BUYING IS *UP HERE.*
I'M OFFERING YOU A JUMP ON PROSK!

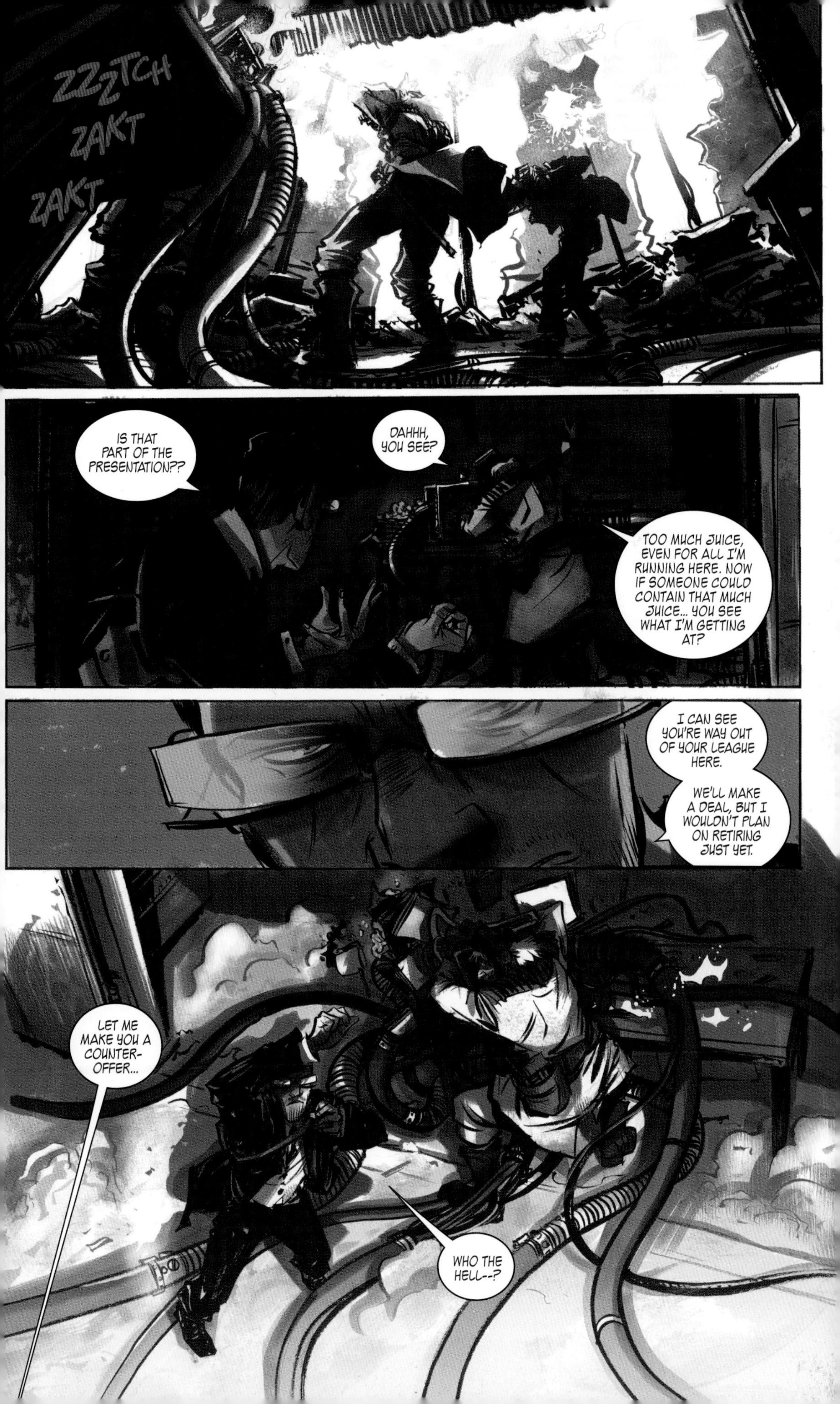

ZZZTCH
ZAKT
ZAKT
IS THAT PART OF THE PRESENTATION??
DAHHH, YOU SEE?
TOO MUCH JUICE, EVEN FOR ALL I'M RUNNING HERE. NOW IF SOMEONE COULD CONTAIN THAT MUCH JUICE... YOU SEE WHAT I'M GETTING AT?
I CAN SEE YOU'RE WAY OUT OF YOUR LEAGUE HERE.
WE'LL MAKE A DEAL, BUT I WOULDN'T PLAN ON RETIRING JUST YET.
LET ME MAKE YOU A COUNTER-OFFER...
WHO THE HELL--?

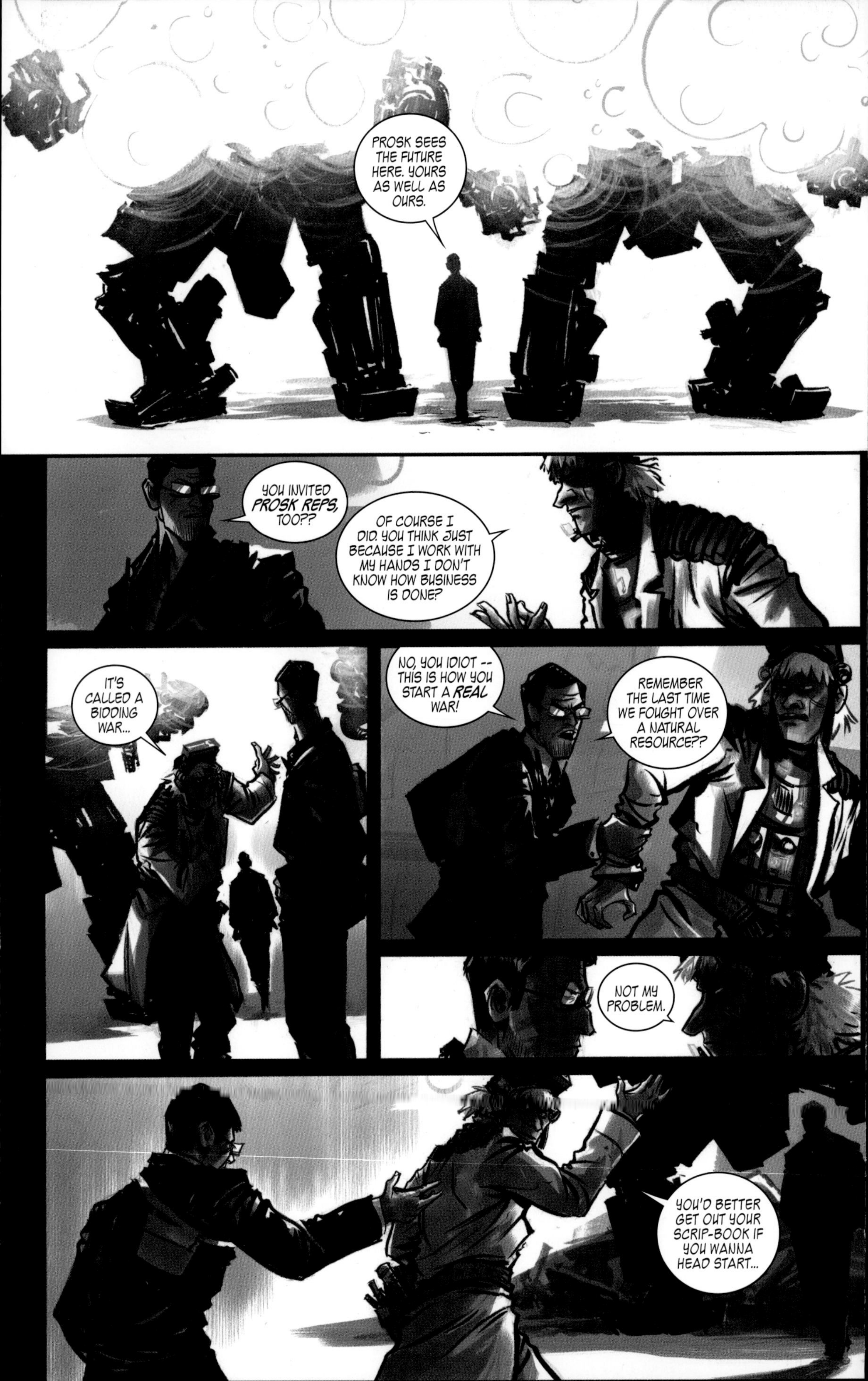
PROSK SEES THE FUTURE HERE. YOURS AS WELL AS OURS.
YOU INVITED PROSK REPS, TOO??
OF COURSE I DID. YOU THINK JUST BECAUSE I WORK WITH MY HANDS I DON'T KNOW HOW BUSINESS IS DONE?
IT'S CALLED A BIDDING WAR...
NO, YOU IDIOT -- THIS IS HOW YOU START A REAL WAR!
REMEMBER THE LAST TIME WE FOUGHT OVER A NATURAL RESOURCE??
NOT MY PROBLEM.
YOU'D BETTER GET OUT YOUR SCRIP-BOOK IF YOU WANNA HEAD START...

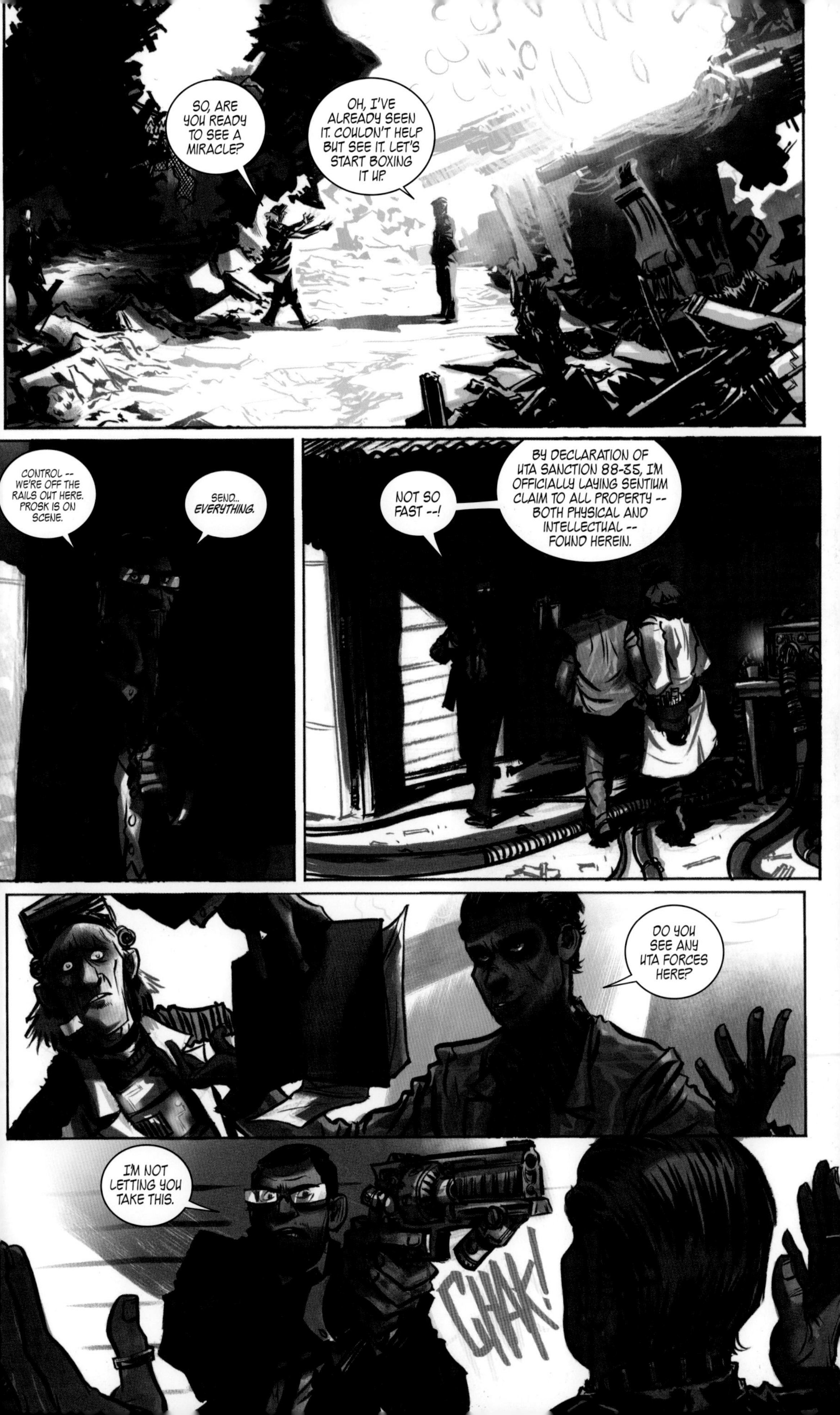
SO, ARE YOU READY TO SEE A MIRACLE?
OH, I'VE ALREADY SEEN IT. COULDN'T HELP BUT SEE IT. LET'S START BOXING IT UP.
CONTROL -- WE'RE OFF THE RAILS OUT HERE. PROSK IS ON SCENE.
SEND... EVERYTHING.
BY DECLARATION OF UTA SANCTION 88-35, I'M OFFICIALLY LAYING SENTIUM CLAIM TO ALL PROPERTY -- BOTH PHYSICAL AND INTELLECTUAL -- FOUND HEREIN.
NOT SO FAST --!
DO YOU SEE ANY UTA FORCES HERE?
I'M NOT LETTING YOU TAKE THIS.
CHAK!

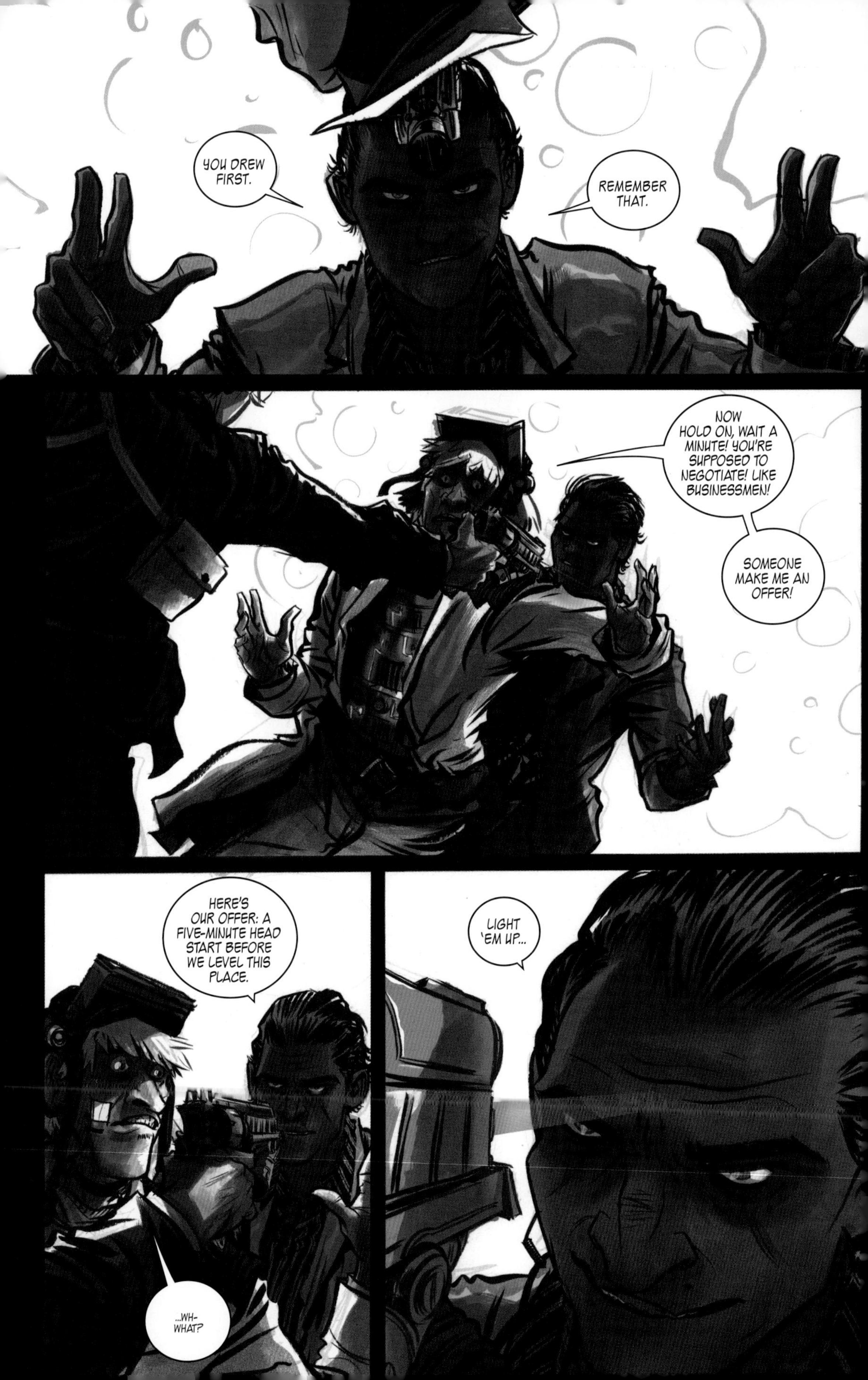
YOU DREW FIRST.
REMEMBER THAT.
NOW HOLD ON, WAIT A MINUTE! YOU'RE SUPPOSED TO NEGOTIATE! LIKE BUSINESSMEN!
SOMEONE MAKE ME AN OFFER!
HERE'S OUR OFFER: A FIVE-MINUTE HEAD START BEFORE WE LEVEL THIS PLACE.
...WH-WHAT?
LIGHT 'EM UP...

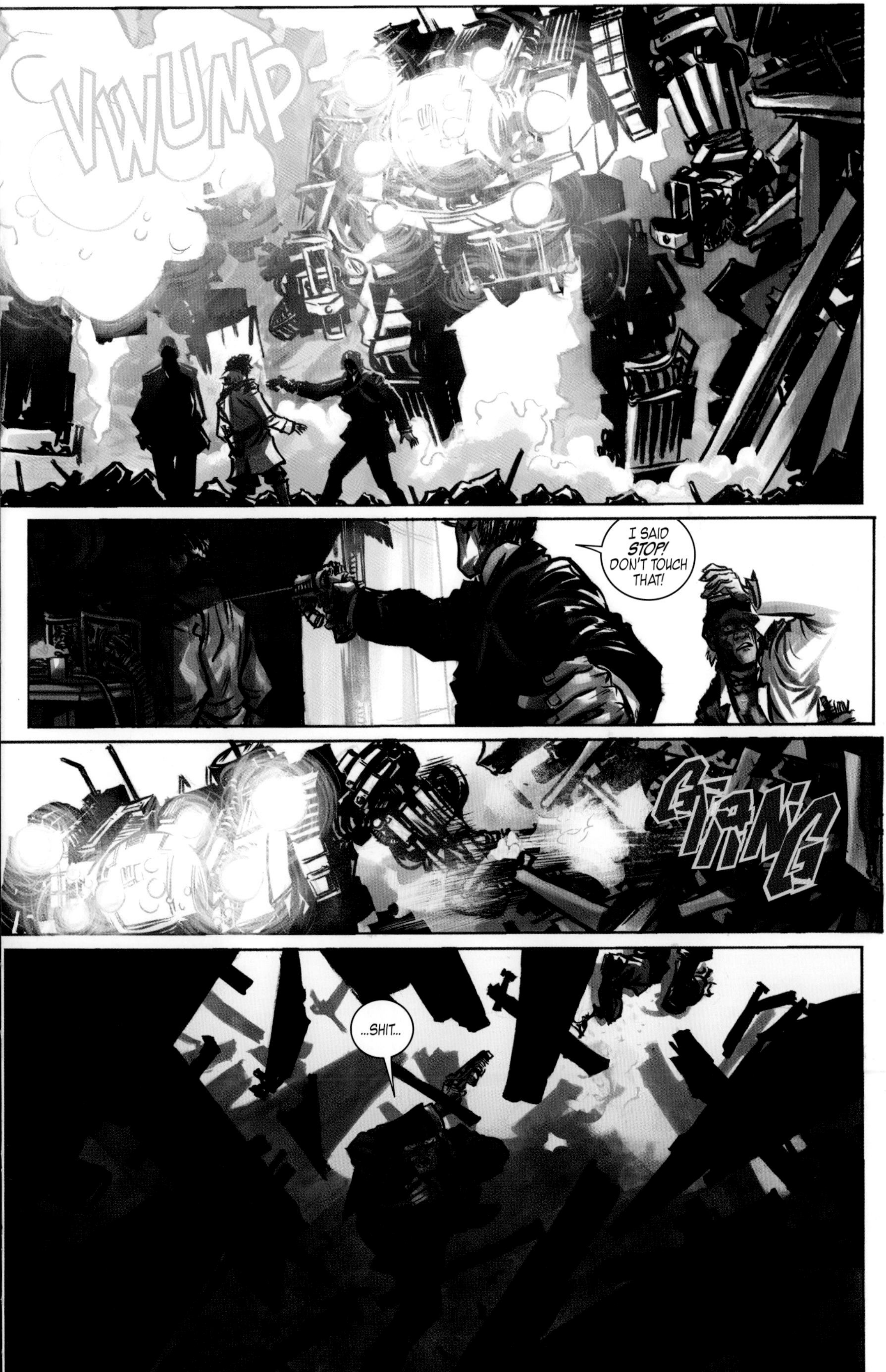
VWUMP
I SAID *STOP!* DON'T TOUCH THAT!
...SHIT...

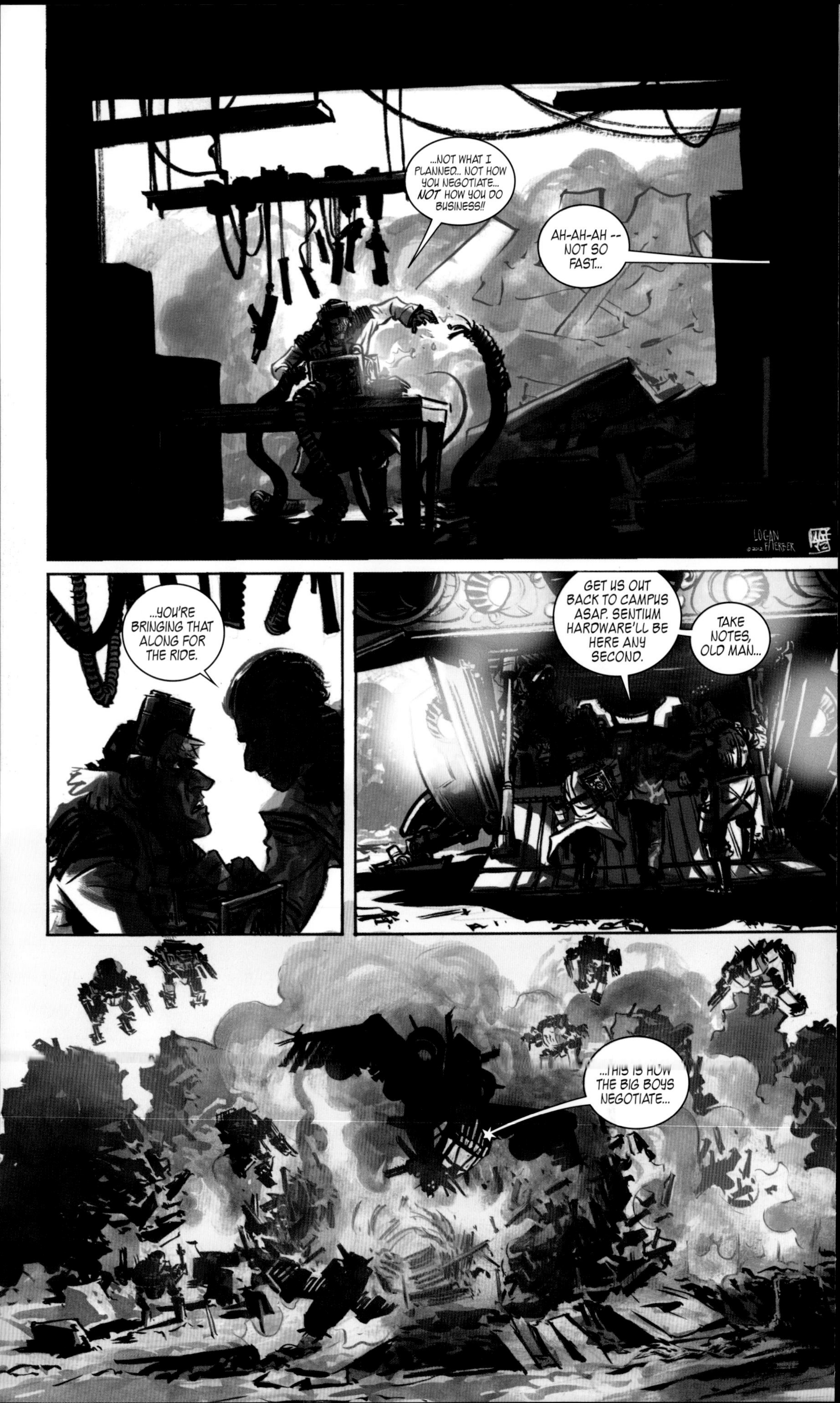
...NOT WHAT I PLANNED... NOT HOW YOU NEGOTIATE... NOT HOW YOU DO BUSINESS!!
AH-AH-AH -- NOT SO FAST...
LOGAN ©2012 F/TERBER
...YOU'RE BRINGING THAT ALONG FOR THE RIDE.
GET US OUT BACK TO CAMPUS ASAP. SENTIUM HARDWARE'LL BE HERE ANY SECOND.
TAKE NOTES, OLD MAN...
...THIS IS HOW THE BIG BOYS NEGOTIATE...

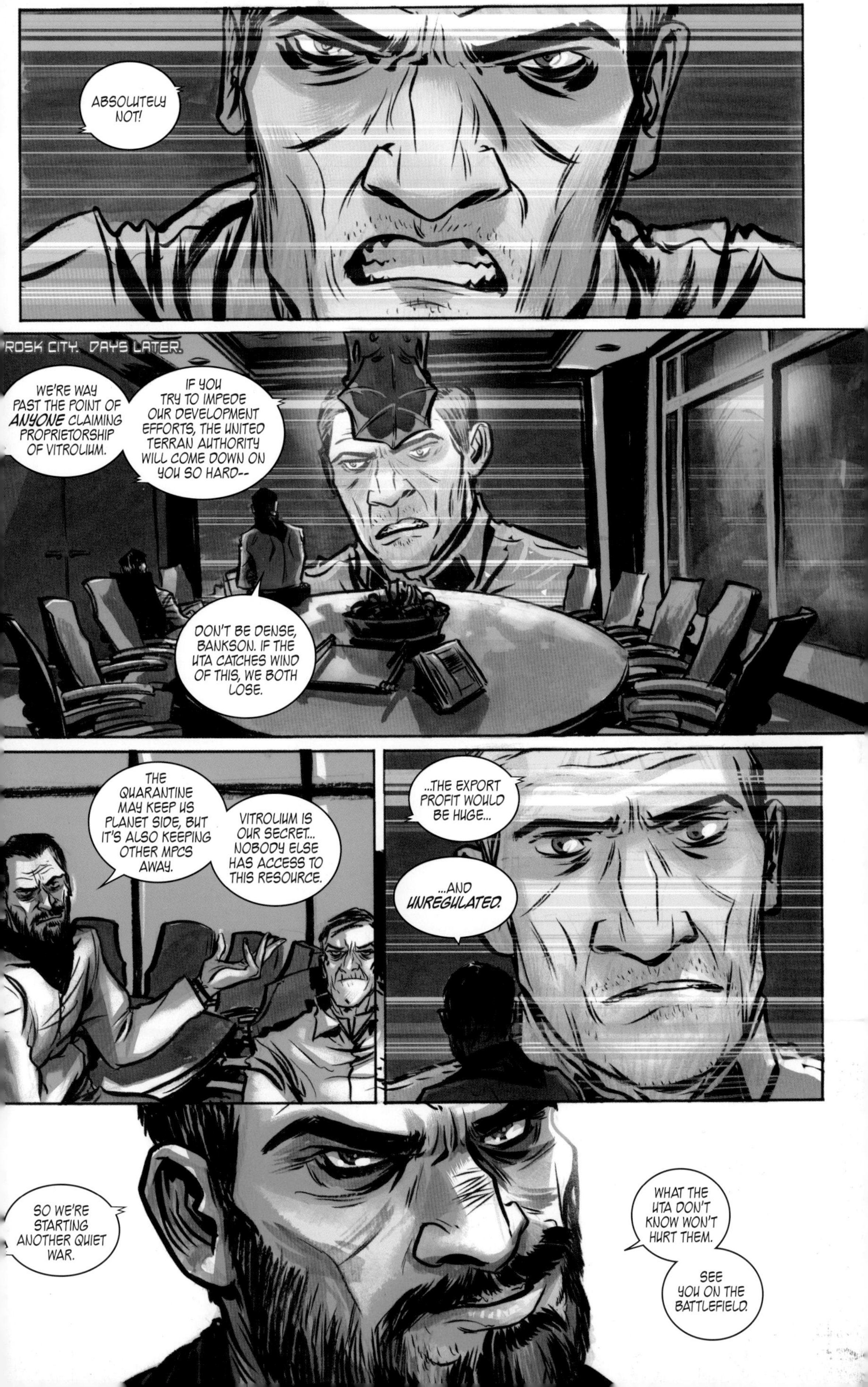
ABSOLUTELY NOT!
ROSK CITY. DAYS LATER.
WE'RE WAY PAST THE POINT OF *ANYONE* CLAIMING PROPRIETORSHIP OF VITROLIUM.
IF YOU TRY TO IMPEDE OUR DEVELOPMENT EFFORTS, THE UNITED TERRAN AUTHORITY WILL COME DOWN ON YOU SO HARD--
DON'T BE DENSE, BANKSON. IF THE UTA CATCHES WIND OF THIS, WE BOTH LOSE.
THE QUARANTINE MAY KEEP US PLANET SIDE, BUT IT'S ALSO KEEPING OTHER MPCS AWAY.
VITROLIUM IS OUR SECRET... NOBODY ELSE HAS ACCESS TO THIS RESOURCE.
...THE EXPORT PROFIT WOULD BE HUGE...
...AND *UNREGULATED.*
SO WE'RE STARTING ANOTHER QUIET WAR.
WHAT THE UTA DON'T KNOW WON'T HURT THEM.
SEE YOU ON THE BATTLEFIELD.

UTA Today - Quarantin... Search - UTA Signal Encr...

UTA TODAY Your World. Your News.

ILLAL QUARANTIN

HOME BREAKING NEWS WORLD PLANETARY MPCS ENTERTAINMENT SPORTS HEALTH SCIENCE

WORLDWIDE QUARANTINE MARKS END OF AN ERA FOR ILLAL

Written by Senior Reporter Elizabeth O'Roarke

The latest round of MPC appeals were rejected by the UTA Special Investigations Committee today, marking wh is now over three months since the UTA halted evacuation efforts on Illal. The quarantine was initially impos as part of a UTA-sanctioned emergency plan to prevent the spread of the Hawken Virus to other colonies. Ma presumed the quarantine would be lifted after conclusive information on the virus was uncovered. Yet, as t root and nature of the virus remain unknown, UTA officials are concerned that the virus could easily contamina surrounding planets if not contained or neutralized. One source not willing to speak on record added, "No-o knows what we're dealing with here. It's clearly nanotech, but it's self-replicating in a manner we've never se before. We aren't sure of its purpose, let alone its capabilities."

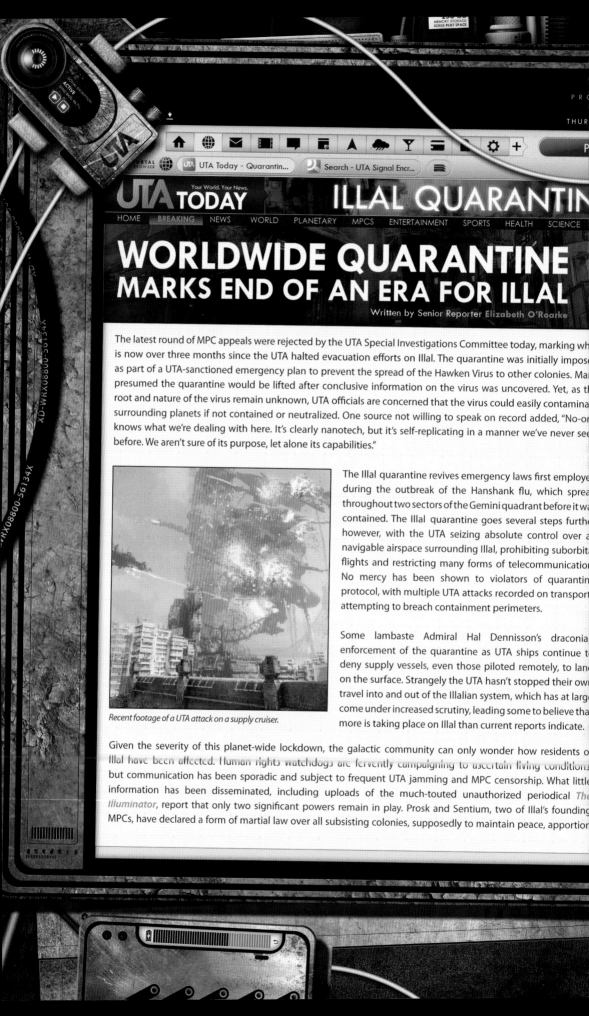

Recent footage of a UTA attack on a supply cruiser.

The Illal quarantine revives emergency laws first employe during the outbreak of the Hanshank flu, which sprea throughout two sectors of the Gemini quadrant before it wa contained. The Illal quarantine goes several steps furth however, with the UTA seizing absolute control over a navigable airspace surrounding Illal, prohibiting suborbit flights and restricting many forms of telecommunicatio No mercy has been shown to violators of quarantin protocol, with multiple UTA attacks recorded on transport attempting to breach containment perimeters.

Some lambaste Admiral Hal Dennisson's draconia enforcement of the quarantine as UTA ships continue t deny supply vessels, even those piloted remotely, to lan on the surface. Strangely the UTA hasn't stopped their ow travel into and out of the Illalian system, which has at larg come under increased scrutiny, leading some to believe tha more is taking place on Illal than current reports indicate.

Given the severity of this planet-wide lockdown, the galactic community can only wonder how residents o Illal have been affected. Human rights watchdogs are fervently campaigning to ascertain living condition but communication has been sporadic and subject to frequent UTA jamming and MPC censorship. What littl information has been disseminated, including uploads of the much-touted unauthorized periodical *The Illuminator*, report that only two significant powers remain in play. Prosk and Sentium, two of Illal's foundin MPCs, have declared a form of martial law over all subsisting colonies, supposedly to maintain peace, apportio

ORTAL POWERED BY PHOENIX

earch | Q ▼   File Edit View   Favorites Tools Help

2:53 PM

'S ORBITAL BLOCKADE CONTINUES

SHARE THIS STORY   TOPICS | ARTICLES | OPINIONS | CLASSIFIEDS   SEARCH |

HELP   CONTACT   ABOUT

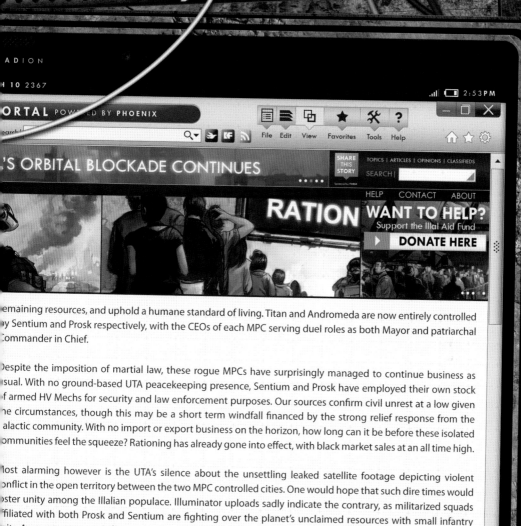

RATION WANT TO HELP?
Support the Illal Aid Fund
▶ DONATE HERE

...emaining resources, and uphold a humane standard of living. Titan and Andromeda are now entirely controlled
by Sentium and Prosk respectively, with the CEOs of each MPC serving duel roles as both Mayor and patriarchal
Commander in Chief.

Despite the imposition of martial law, these rogue MPCs have surprisingly managed to continue business as
usual. With no ground-based UTA peacekeeping presence, Sentium and Prosk have employed their own stock
of armed HV Mechs for security and law enforcement purposes. Our sources confirm civil unrest at a low given
the circumstances, though this may be a short term windfall financed by the strong relief response from the
galactic community. With no import or export business on the horizon, how long can it be before these isolated
communities feel the squeeze? Rationing has already gone into effect, with black market sales at an all time high.

Most alarming however is the UTA's silence about the unsettling leaked satellite footage depicting violent
conflict in the open territory between the two MPC controlled cities. One would hope that such dire times would
foster unity among the Illalian populace. Illuminator uploads sadly indicate the contrary, as militarized squads
affiliated with both Prosk and Sentium are fighting over the planet's unclaimed resources with small infantry
units. Accounts suggest civilian and collateral damage in frontier and mining colonies are quite common. Exactly
what Prosk and Sentium hope to gain from feigned tranquility undermined by these shadow skirmishes is yet to
be seen. Regardless of their agenda, these are uncertain times for the industrious planet of great infamy.

Courtesy of Illuminator MC © 2367

Recent ground skirmishes between Prosk and Sentium units.

100% ▼

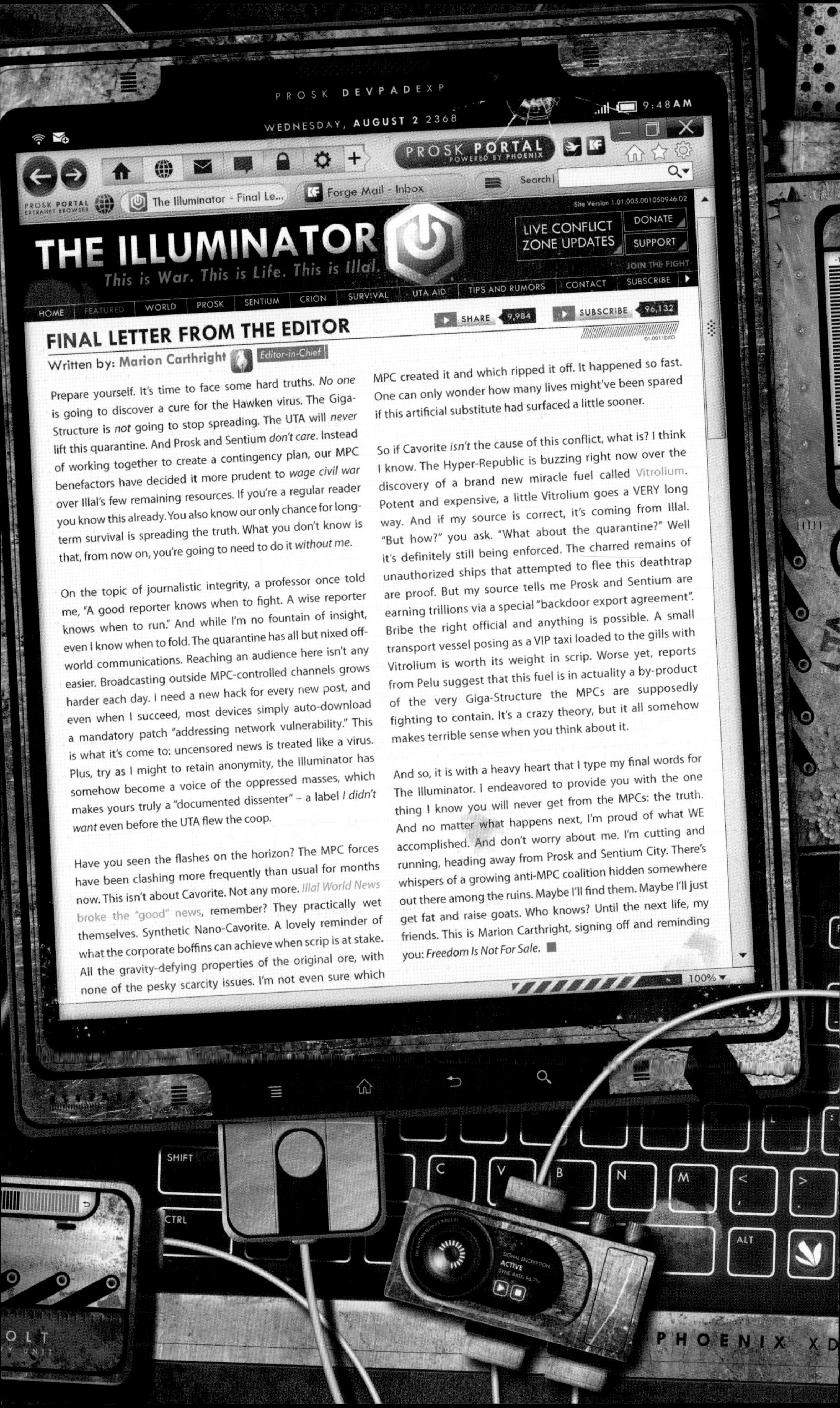
PROSK DEVPADEXP
WEDNESDAY, AUGUST 2 2368
9:48AM
PROSK PORTAL
POWERED BY PHOENIX
Search|
PROSK PORTAL EXTRANET BROWSER
The Illuminator - Final Le...
Forge Mail - Inbox
Site Version 1.01.005.001050946.02
THE ILLUMINATOR
This is War. This is Life. This is Illal.
LIVE CONFLICT ZONE UPDATES
DONATE
SUPPORT
JOIN THE FIGHT
HOME
FEATURED
WORLD
PROSK
SENTIUM
CRION
SURVIVAL
UTA AID
TIPS AND RUMORS
CONTACT
SUBSCRIBE
SHARE 9,984
SUBSCRIBE 96,132
100%
SHIFT
CTRL
ALT
SIGNAL ENCRYPTION ACTIVE
PHOENIX XD

FINAL LETTER FROM THE EDITOR

Written by: **Marion Carthright** Editor-in-Chief

Prepare yourself. It's time to face some hard truths. *No one* is going to discover a cure for the Hawken virus. The Giga-Structure is *not* going to stop spreading. The UTA will *never* lift this quarantine. And Prosk and Sentium *don't care*. Instead of working together to create a contingency plan, our MPC benefactors have decided it more prudent to *wage civil war* over Illal's few remaining resources. If you're a regular reader you know this already. You also know our only chance for long-term survival is spreading the truth. What you don't know is that, from now on, you're going to need to do it *without me*.

On the topic of journalistic integrity, a professor once told me, "A good reporter knows when to fight. A wise reporter knows when to run." And while I'm no fountain of insight, even I know when to fold. The quarantine has all but nixed off-world communications. Reaching an audience here isn't any easier. Broadcasting outside MPC-controlled channels grows harder each day. I need a new hack for every new post, and even when I succeed, most devices simply auto-download a mandatory patch "addressing network vulnerability." This is what it's come to: uncensored news is treated like a virus. Plus, try as I might to retain anonymity, the Illuminator has somehow become a voice of the oppressed masses, which makes yours truly a "documented dissenter" – a label *I didn't want* even before the UTA flew the coop.

Have you seen the flashes on the horizon? The MPC forces have been clashing more frequently than usual for months now. This isn't about Cavorite. Not any more. Illal World News broke the "good" news, remember? They practically wet themselves. Synthetic Nano-Cavorite. A lovely reminder of what the corporate boffins can achieve when scrip is at stake. All the gravity-defying properties of the original ore, with none of the pesky scarcity issues. I'm not even sure which MPC created it and which ripped it off. It happened so fast. One can only wonder how many lives might've been spared if this artificial substitute had surfaced a little sooner.

So if Cavorite *isn't* the cause of this conflict, what is? I think I know. The Hyper-Republic is buzzing right now over the discovery of a brand new miracle fuel called Vitrolium. Potent and expensive, a little Vitrolium goes a VERY long way. And if my source is correct, it's coming from Illal. "But how?" you ask. "What about the quarantine?" Well it's definitely still being enforced. The charred remains of unauthorized ships that attempted to flee this deathtrap are proof. But my source tells me Prosk and Sentium are earning trillions via a special "backdoor export agreement". Bribe the right official and anything is possible. A small transport vessel posing as a VIP taxi loaded to the gills with Vitrolium is worth its weight in scrip. Worse yet, reports from Pelu suggest that this fuel is in actuality a by-product of the very Giga-Structure the MPCs are supposedly fighting to contain. It's a crazy theory, but it all somehow makes terrible sense when you think about it.

And so, it is with a heavy heart that I type my final words for The Illuminator. I endeavored to provide you with the one thing I know you will never get from the MPCs: the truth. And no matter what happens next, I'm proud of what WE accomplished. And don't worry about me. I'm cutting and running, heading away from Prosk and Sentium City. There's whispers of a growing anti-MPC coalition hidden somewhere out there among the ruins. Maybe I'll find them. Maybe I'll just get fat and raise goats. Who knows? Until the next life, my friends. This is Marion Carthright, signing off and reminding you: *Freedom Is Not For Sale.* ■

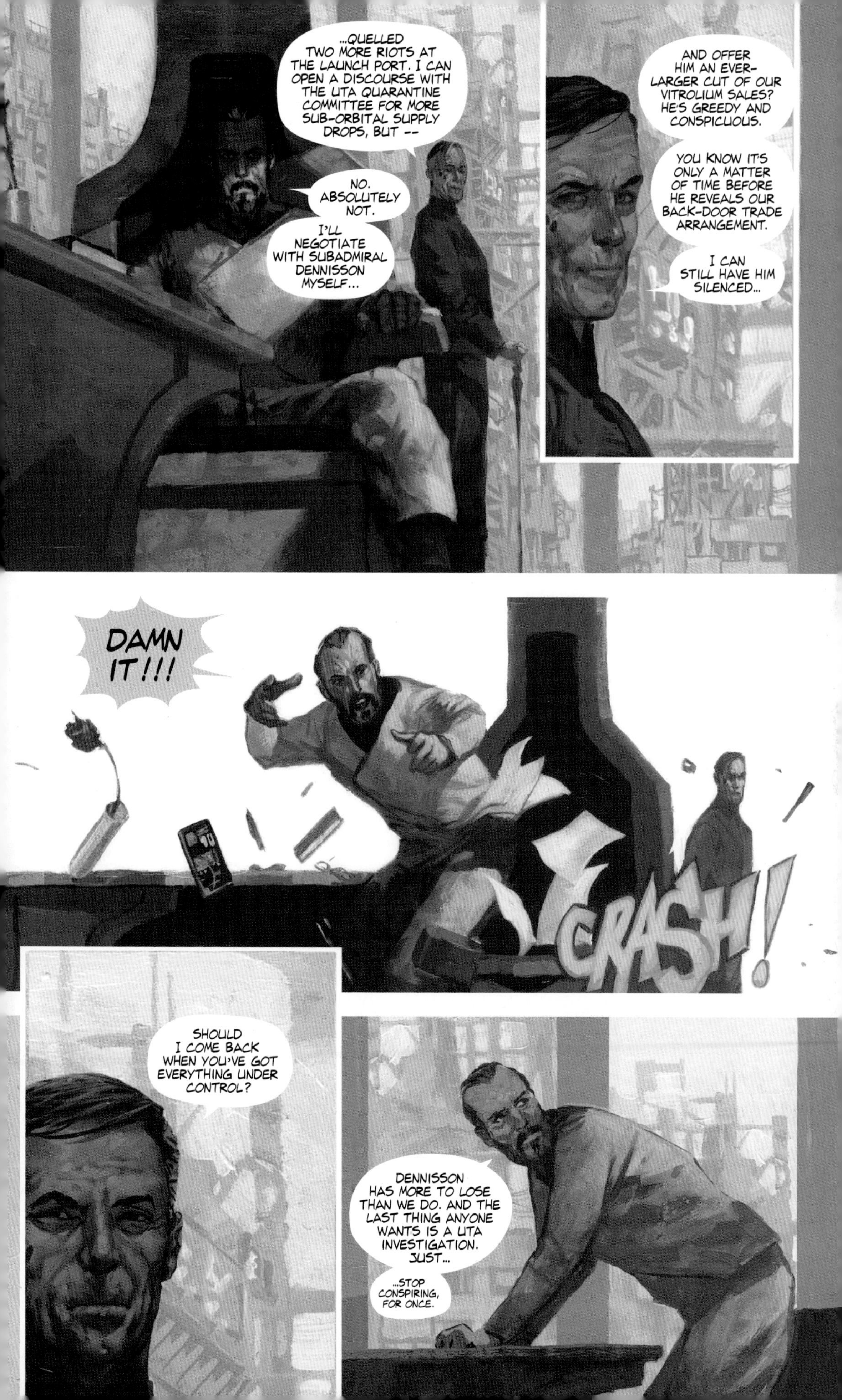
...QUELLED TWO MORE RIOTS AT THE LAUNCH PORT. I CAN OPEN A DISCOURSE WITH THE UTA QUARANTINE COMMITTEE FOR MORE SUB-ORBITAL SUPPLY DROPS, BUT --
NO. ABSOLUTELY NOT.
I'LL NEGOTIATE WITH SUBADMIRAL DENNISSON MYSELF...
AND OFFER HIM AN EVER-LARGER CUT OF OUR VITROLIUM SALES? HE'S GREEDY AND CONSPICUOUS.
YOU KNOW IT'S ONLY A MATTER OF TIME BEFORE HE REVEALS OUR BACK-DOOR TRADE ARRANGEMENT.
I CAN STILL HAVE HIM SILENCED...
DAMN IT!!!
CRASH!
SHOULD I COME BACK WHEN YOU'VE GOT EVERYTHING UNDER CONTROL?
DENNISSON HAS MORE TO LOSE THAN WE DO. AND THE LAST THING ANYONE WANTS IS A UTA INVESTIGATION. JUST...
...STOP CONSPIRING, FOR ONCE.

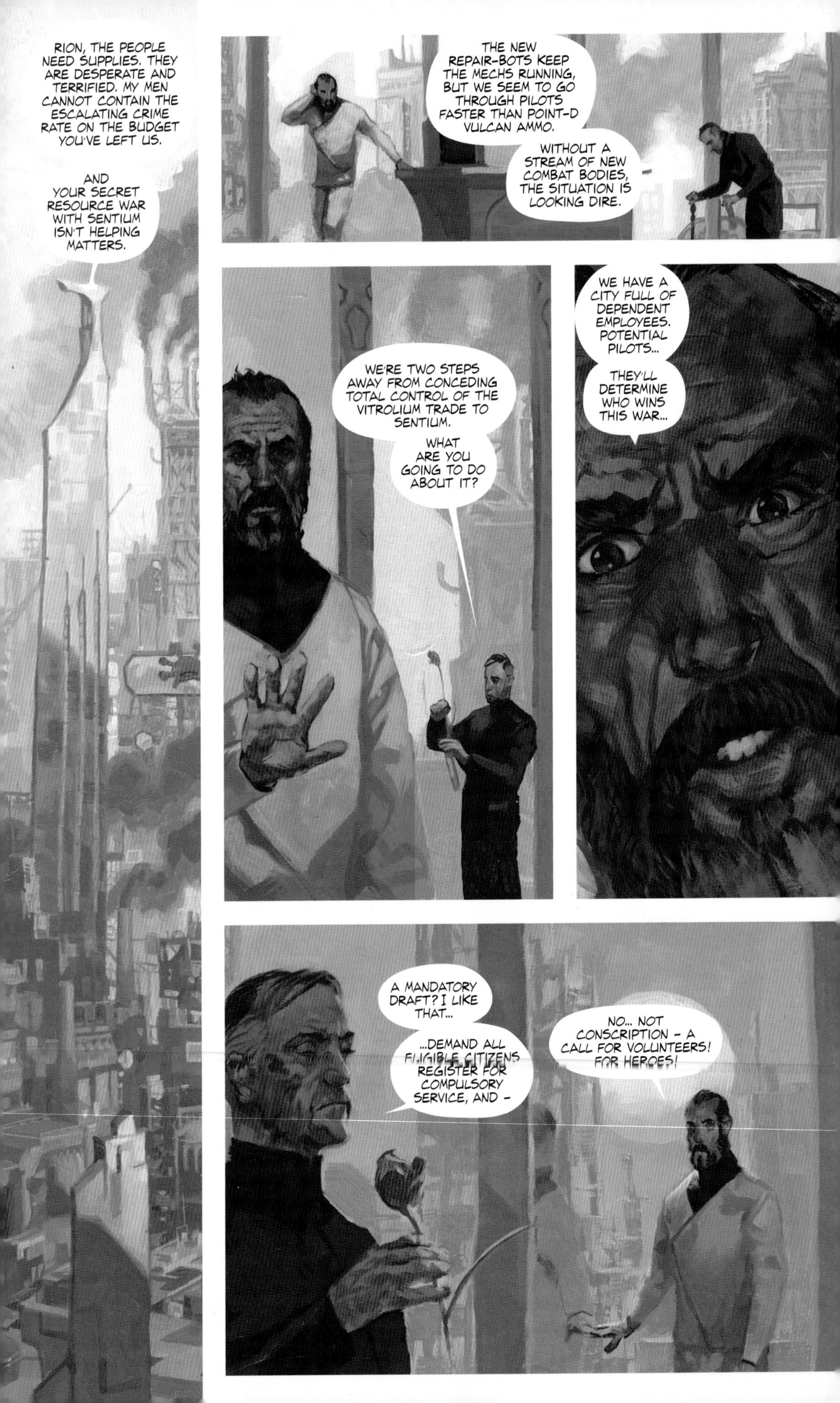
RION, THE PEOPLE NEED SUPPLIES. THEY ARE DESPERATE AND TERRIFIED. MY MEN CANNOT CONTAIN THE ESCALATING CRIME RATE ON THE BUDGET YOU'VE LEFT US.
AND YOUR SECRET RESOURCE WAR WITH SENTIUM ISN'T HELPING MATTERS.
THE NEW REPAIR-BOTS KEEP THE MECHS RUNNING, BUT WE SEEM TO GO THROUGH PILOTS FASTER THAN POINT-D VULCAN AMMO.
WITHOUT A STREAM OF NEW COMBAT BODIES, THE SITUATION IS LOOKING DIRE.
WE'RE TWO STEPS AWAY FROM CONCEDING TOTAL CONTROL OF THE VITROLIUM TRADE TO SENTIUM.
WHAT ARE YOU GOING TO DO ABOUT IT?
WE HAVE A CITY FULL OF DEPENDENT EMPLOYEES. POTENTIAL PILOTS...
THEY'LL DETERMINE WHO WINS THIS WAR...
A MANDATORY DRAFT? I LIKE THAT...
...DEMAND ALL ELIGIBLE CITIZENS REGISTER FOR COMPULSORY SERVICE, AND -
NO... NOT CONSCRIPTION - A CALL FOR VOLUNTEERS! FOR HEROES!

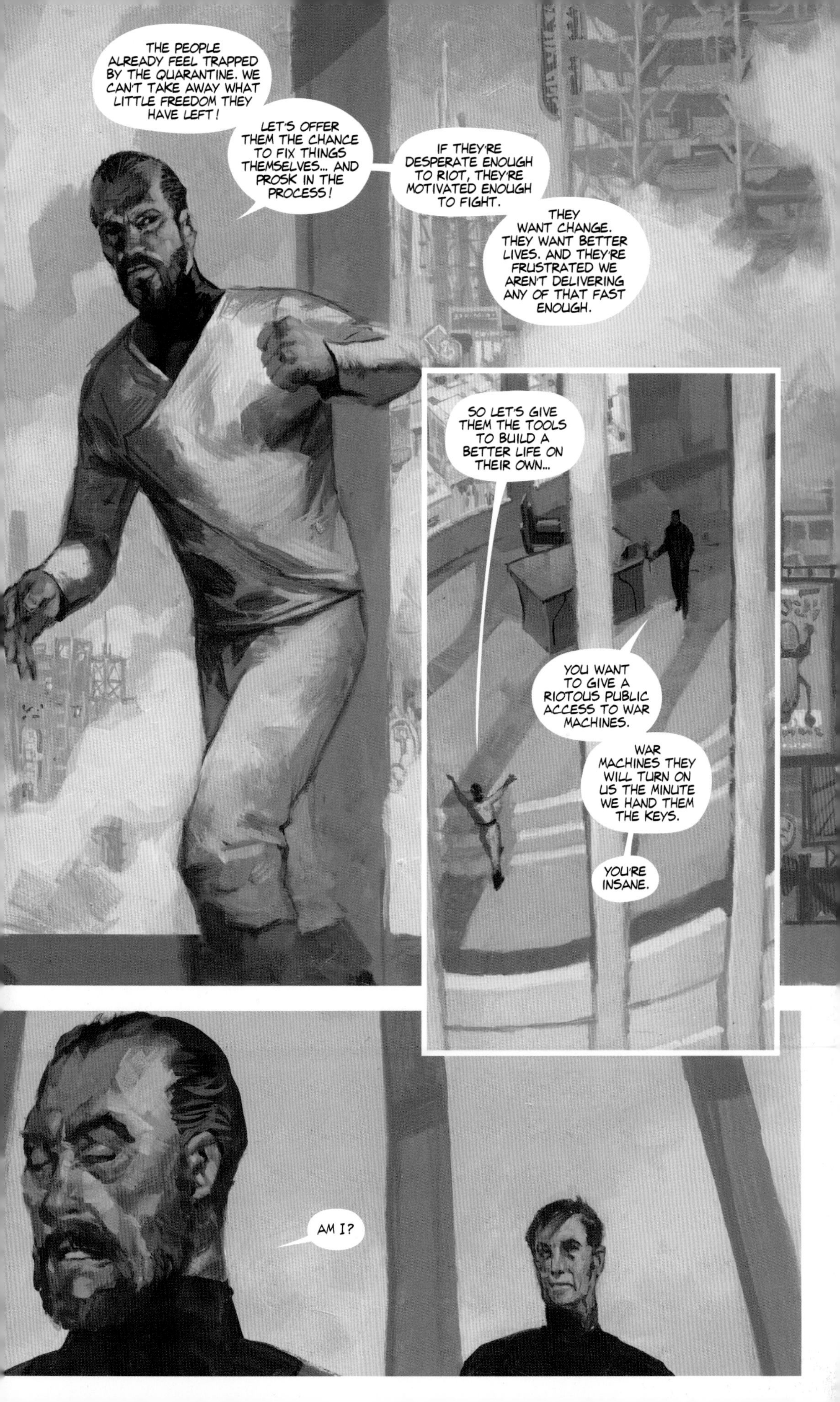
THE PEOPLE ALREADY FEEL TRAPPED BY THE QUARANTINE. WE CAN'T TAKE AWAY WHAT LITTLE FREEDOM THEY HAVE LEFT!
LET'S OFFER THEM THE CHANCE TO FIX THINGS THEMSELVES... AND PROSK IN THE PROCESS!
IF THEY'RE DESPERATE ENOUGH TO RIOT, THEY'RE MOTIVATED ENOUGH TO FIGHT.
THEY WANT CHANGE. THEY WANT BETTER LIVES. AND THEY'RE FRUSTRATED WE AREN'T DELIVERING ANY OF THAT FAST ENOUGH.
SO LET'S GIVE THEM THE TOOLS TO BUILD A BETTER LIFE ON THEIR OWN...
YOU WANT TO GIVE A RIOTOUS PUBLIC ACCESS TO WAR MACHINES.
WAR MACHINES THEY WILL TURN ON US THE MINUTE WE HAND THEM THE KEYS.
YOU'RE INSANE.
AM I?

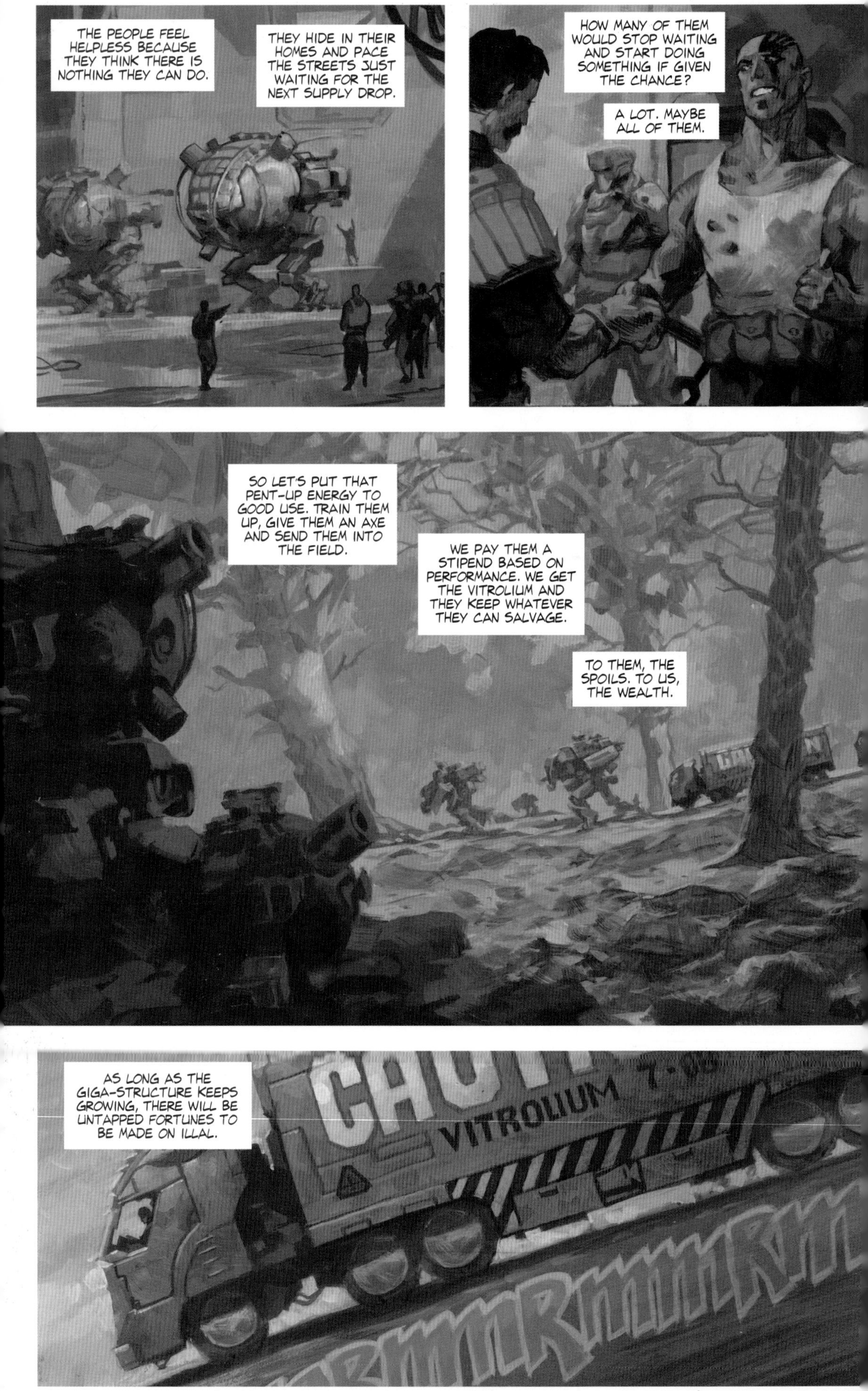
THE PEOPLE FEEL HELPLESS BECAUSE THEY THINK THERE IS NOTHING THEY CAN DO.
THEY HIDE IN THEIR HOMES AND PACE THE STREETS JUST WAITING FOR THE NEXT SUPPLY DROP.
HOW MANY OF THEM WOULD STOP WAITING AND START DOING SOMETHING IF GIVEN THE CHANCE?
A LOT. MAYBE ALL OF THEM.
SO LET'S PUT THAT PENT-UP ENERGY TO GOOD USE. TRAIN THEM UP, GIVE THEM AN AXE AND SEND THEM INTO THE FIELD.
WE PAY THEM A STIPEND BASED ON PERFORMANCE. WE GET THE VITROLIUM AND THEY KEEP WHATEVER THEY CAN SALVAGE.
TO THEM, THE SPOILS. TO US, THE WEALTH.
AS LONG AS THE GIGA-STRUCTURE KEEPS GROWING, THERE WILL BE UNTAPPED FORTUNES TO BE MADE ON ILLAL.
VITROLIUM
VITROLIUM

A FRACTION OF WHICH CAN MAKE AN ORDINARY CITIZEN WEALTHY BEYOND HIS WILDEST DREAMS.

AND WHAT IS MORE MOTIVATING THAN PROVIDING FOR ONE'S FAMILY? STRENGTHENING ONE'S COMMUNITY?

LET'S FOSTER SOME PRIDE IN THEIR CORPORATE CITIZENSHIP.

TREAT THE MOST SUCCESSFUL PILOTS LIKE NATIONAL HEROES.

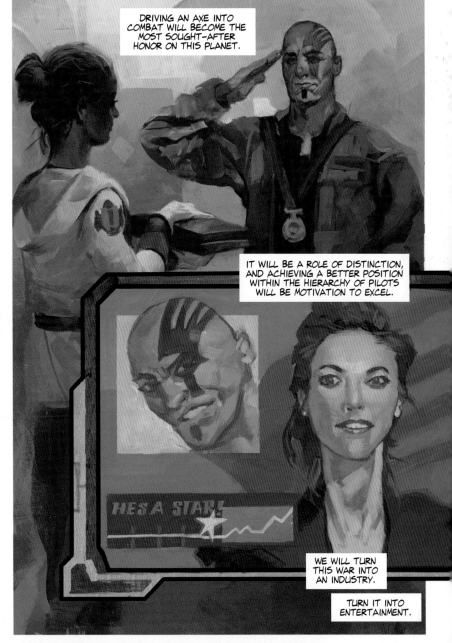

DRIVING AN AXE INTO COMBAT WILL BECOME THE MOST SOUGHT-AFTER HONOR ON THIS PLANET.

IT WILL BE A ROLE OF DISTINCTION, AND ACHIEVING A BETTER POSITION WITHIN THE HIERARCHY OF PILOTS WILL BE MOTIVATION TO EXCEL.

HE'S A STAR!

WE WILL TURN THIS WAR INTO AN INDUSTRY.

TURN IT INTO ENTERTAINMENT.

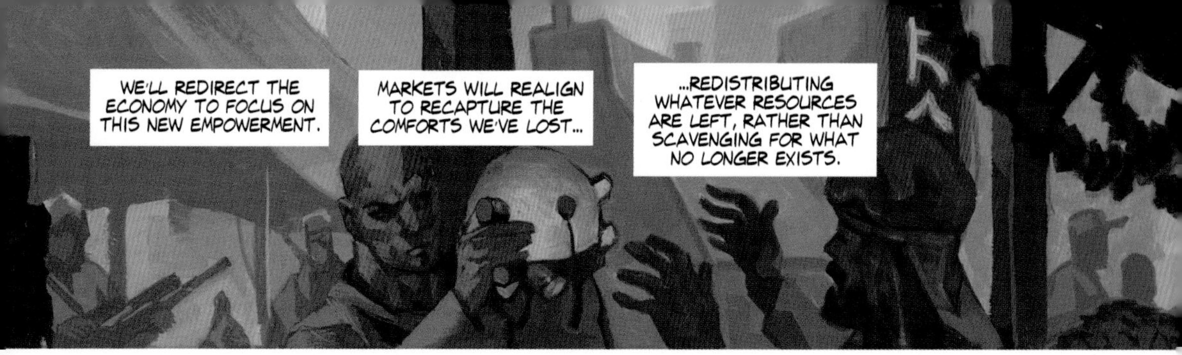
WE'LL REDIRECT THE ECONOMY TO FOCUS ON THIS NEW EMPOWERMENT.
MARKETS WILL REALIGN TO RECAPTURE THE COMFORTS WE'VE LOST...
...REDISTRIBUTING WHATEVER RESOURCES ARE LEFT, RATHER THAN SCAVENGING FOR WHAT NO LONGER EXISTS.

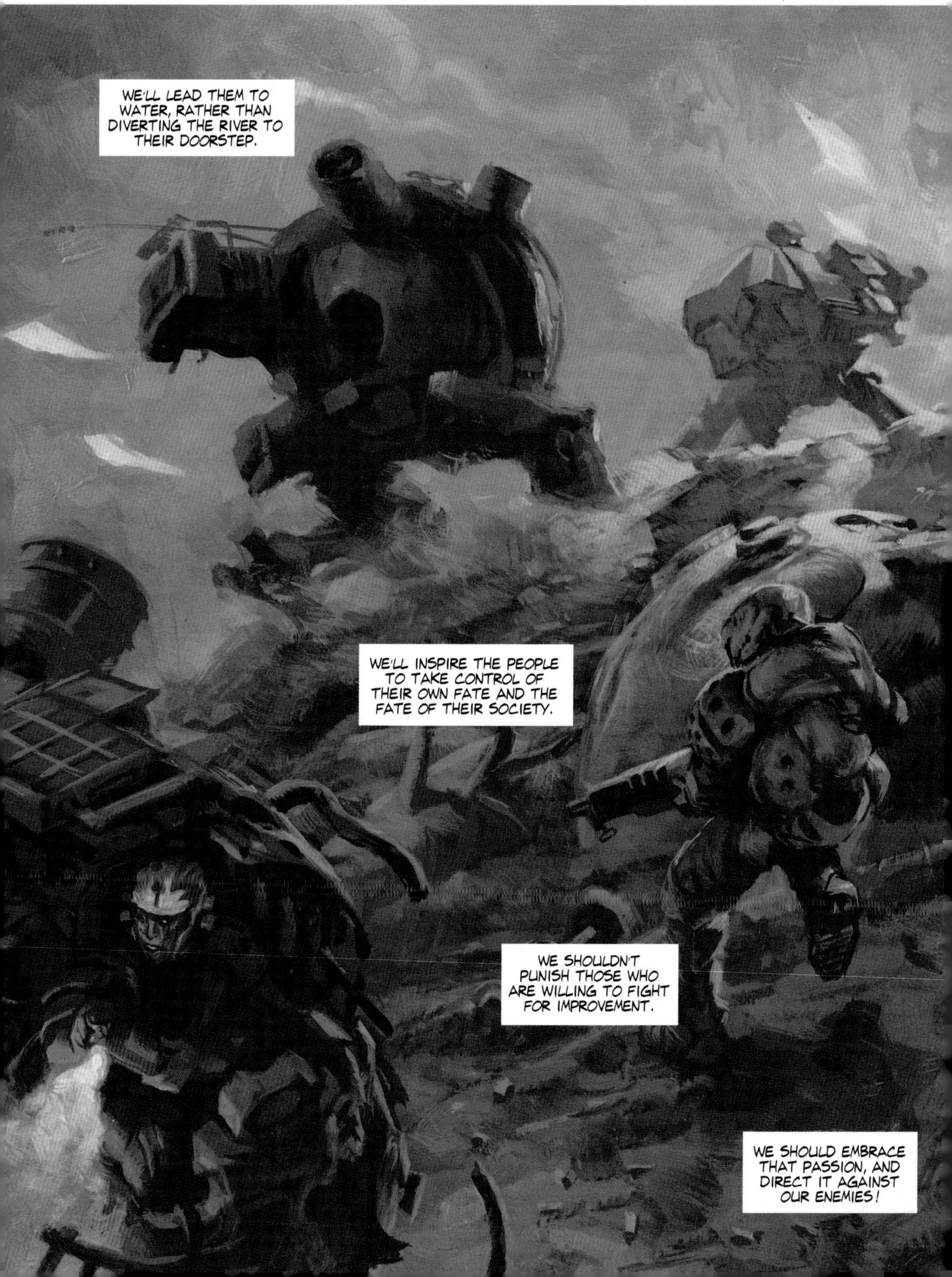
WE'LL LEAD THEM TO WATER, RATHER THAN DIVERTING THE RIVER TO THEIR DOORSTEP.
WE'LL INSPIRE THE PEOPLE TO TAKE CONTROL OF THEIR OWN FATE AND THE FATE OF THEIR SOCIETY.
WE SHOULDN'T PUNISH THOSE WHO ARE WILLING TO FIGHT FOR IMPROVEMENT.
WE SHOULD EMBRACE THAT PASSION, AND DIRECT IT AGAINST OUR ENEMIES!

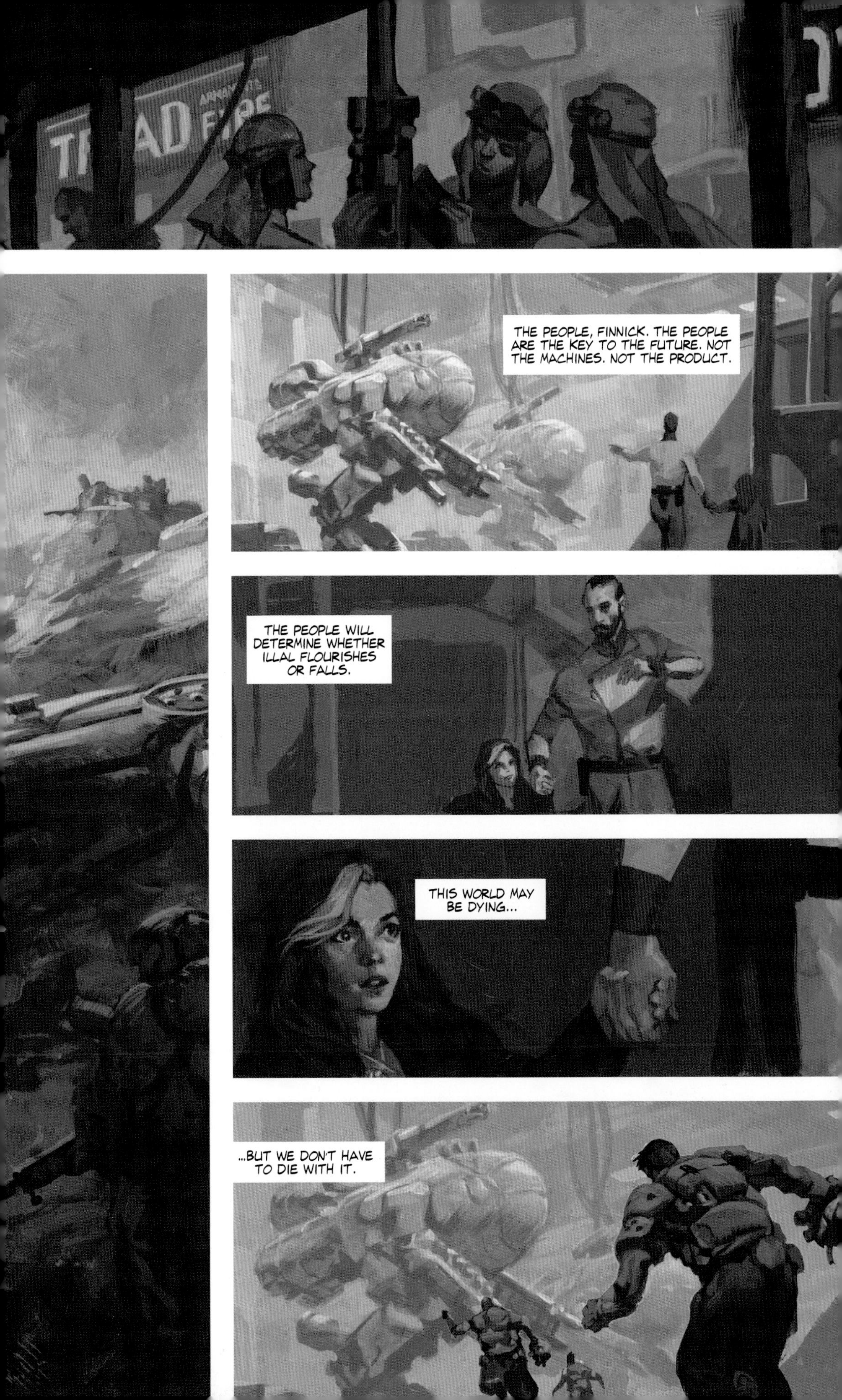
THE PEOPLE, FINNICK. THE PEOPLE ARE THE KEY TO THE FUTURE. NOT THE MACHINES. NOT THE PRODUCT.
THE PEOPLE WILL DETERMINE WHETHER ILLAL FLOURISHES OR FALLS.
THIS WORLD MAY BE DYING...
...BUT WE DON'T HAVE TO DIE WITH IT.

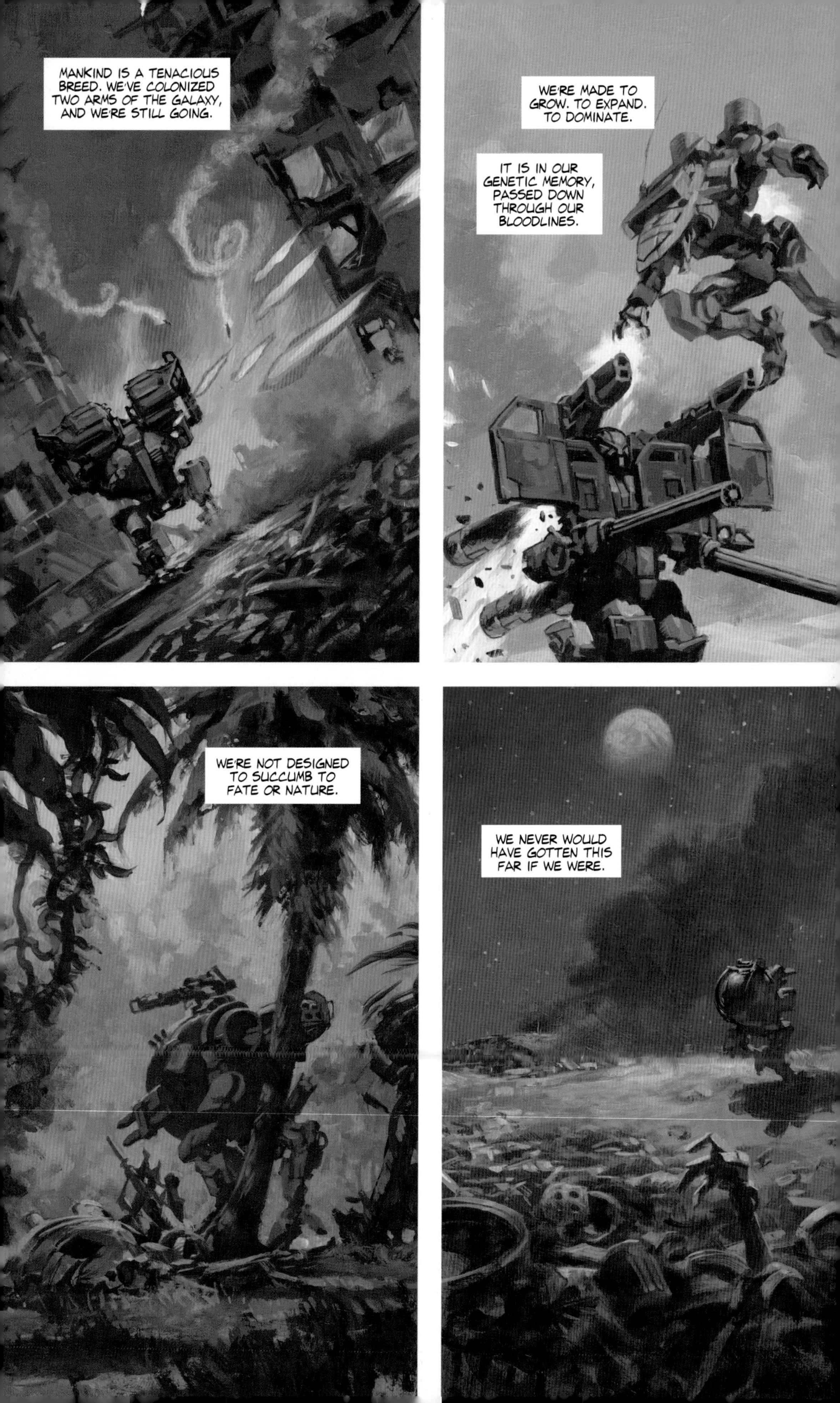
MANKIND IS A TENACIOUS BREED. WE'VE COLONIZED TWO ARMS OF THE GALAXY, AND WE'RE STILL GOING.
WE'RE MADE TO GROW. TO EXPAND. TO DOMINATE.
IT IS IN OUR GENETIC MEMORY, PASSED DOWN THROUGH OUR BLOODLINES.
WE'RE NOT DESIGNED TO SUCCUMB TO FATE OR NATURE.
WE NEVER WOULD HAVE GOTTEN THIS FAR IF WE WERE.

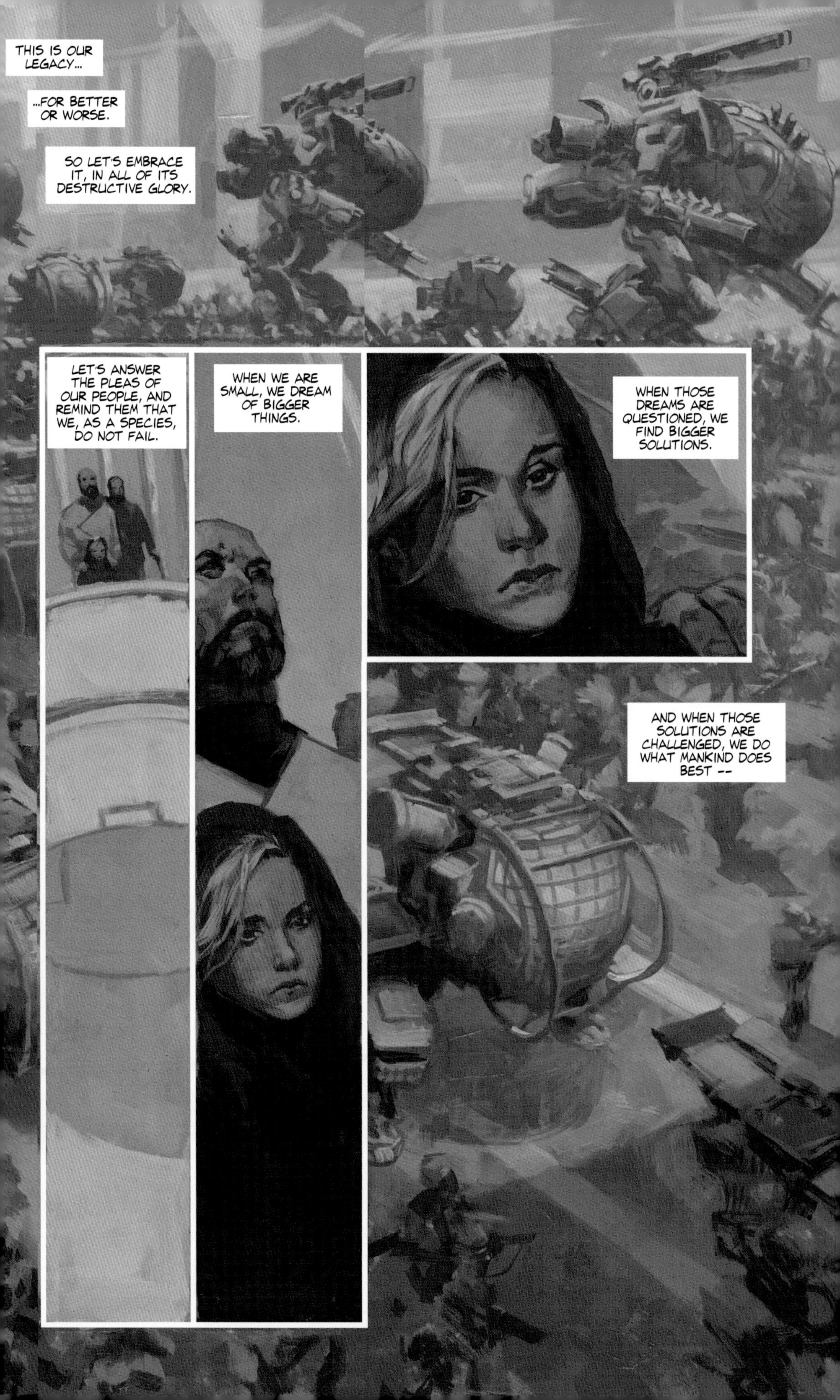
THIS IS OUR LEGACY...
...FOR BETTER OR WORSE.
SO LET'S EMBRACE IT, IN ALL OF ITS DESTRUCTIVE GLORY.
LET'S ANSWER THE PLEAS OF OUR PEOPLE, AND REMIND THEM THAT WE, AS A SPECIES, DO NOT FAIL.
WHEN WE ARE SMALL, WE DREAM OF BIGGER THINGS.
WHEN THOSE DREAMS ARE QUESTIONED, WE FIND BIGGER SOLUTIONS.
AND WHEN THOSE SOLUTIONS ARE CHALLENGED, WE DO WHAT MANKIND DOES BEST --

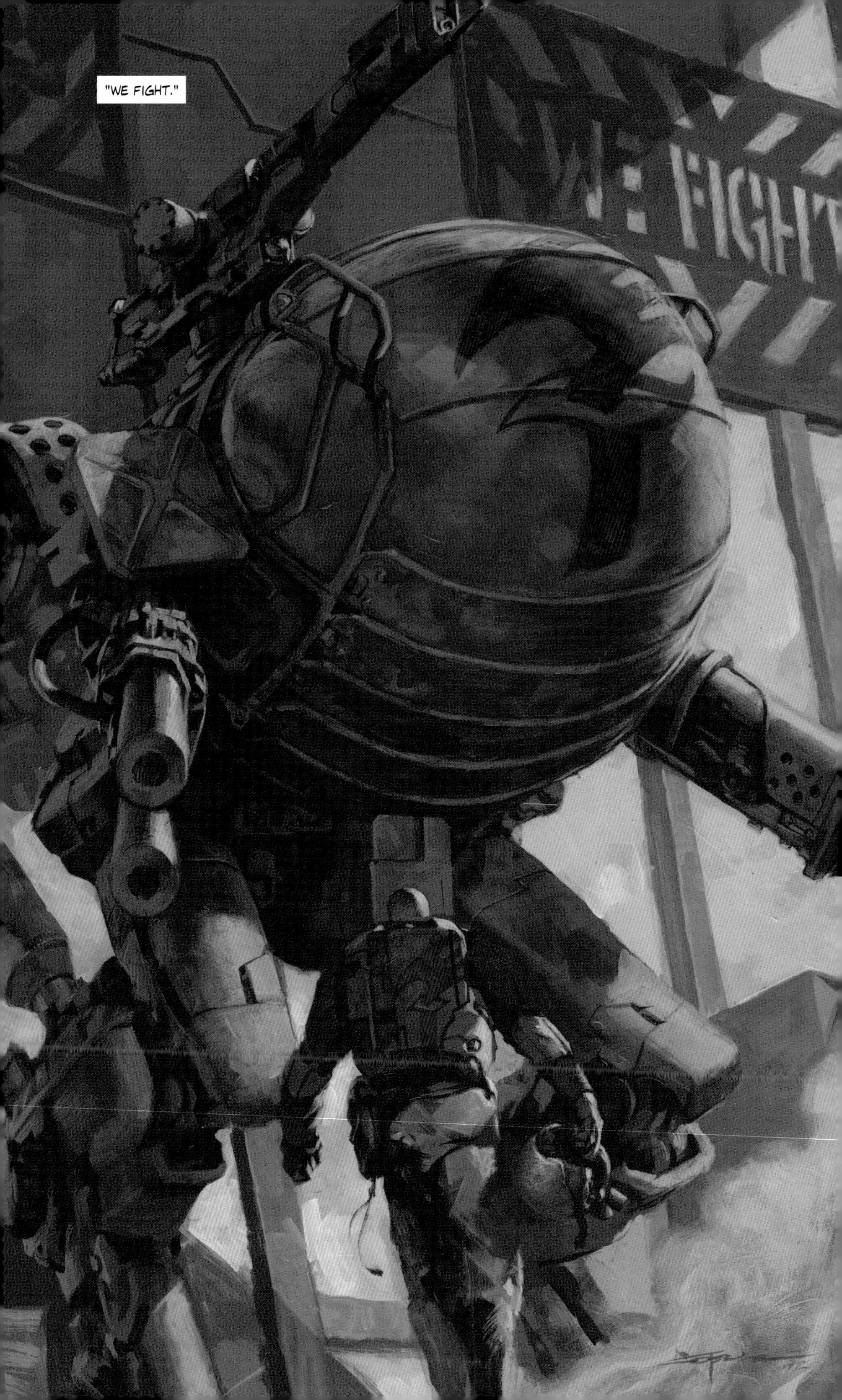
"WE FIGHT."
FIGHT

YOU ARE
FREE TO FIGHT

REGISTER NOW
[playhawken]

HAWKEN GLOSSARY

ANDROMEDA

The largest (and most densely populated) megacity on **ILLAL**. Home to **PROSK**'s corporate HQ, **ANDROMEDA** is a bustling and colorful metropolis, with high poverty and unemployment rates.

ATMOSPHERIC GENERATORS

Environment processors that create and sustain a human-habitable artificial atmosphere (i.e., a replica of Earth's ideal Troposphere, Stratosphere, Mesosphere and Thermosphere) of variable sizes. Typically one facility is needed per 1000 square miles.

AXE

A colloquial term for a weaponized **MECH**. What the initials are actually an acronym for is debated among pilots.

BATTLESHIPS

Relatively slow-moving, heavily-armored air-to-ground carrier/gunships used by **MPC**s to deploy and support **MECH**s in major land-based battles.

CAVORITE

A rare ore that possesses inherent gravity-defying properties. When smelted into other materials the overall weight of the resulting alloy is significantly decreased. See also: **NANOCAVORITE** and **SYNTHETIC NANOCAVORITE**.

CRION SOLUTIONS

Part of the **MPC** Conglomerate that sponsored the **TERRAFORMING** of **ILLAL**, **CRION SOLUTIONS** is a technology-orientated **MPC** that focuses on scientific research and development over manufacturing.

CSD

CSD is an acronym for "Corporate Security Division". Every **MPC** has one. Their role is closer to that of an intelligence agency (like the CIA or MI6) than traditional physical and intellectual corporate protection.

GIGA-STRUCTURE

The scientific name given to the vast inorganic shell left in the wake of the **HAWKEN NANOVIRUS**.

HAWKEN VIRUS

The virus is named after Dr. Hawken primarily because it was his nanotech research project, codenamed **OHMU**, that was in development at **CRION**'s **TYPHUS** facility when the incident occurred, destroying **PRAXIS VALLEY** and releasing the **NANOVIRUS**. The mechanics and machinations of the cataclysmic virus are a mystery to almost everyone.

HV LOADERS

SKU for Heavy Loaders. These open mechanized exoskeletons mimic the anthropomorphic movements of their operators but greatly amplify their strength. They are generally used for non-military purposes such as construction work or emergency services. They are the flagship product of **PROSK**'s and **SENTIUM**'s manufacturing division.

ILLAL

ILLAL is one of six planets orbiting an 8-billion-year-old star named Kepler-11, located about 2,000 light-years away from Earth. **ILALL**'s indigenous atmosphere is poisonous to Earth-based life forms, rendering a human unconscious in about 10 minutes and dead in an hour.

ILLAL DEVELOPMENT INITIATIVE

The **UTA** passed the controversial and historic IDI Act in 2296, allowing a conglomerate of **MPC**s to sponsor the **TERRAFORMING** and colonization of **ILLAL** in exchange for special business-related privileges and exemptions.

KOBALT

The smallest of the three megacities on **ILLAL**. Scarcely populated and more industrial. Home to **CRION SOLUTIONS** HQ.

MPC

Acronym for Multi-Planetary Corporation. Colossal companies with subsidiaries and business spread across the Hyper-Republic.

MECH

A large, typically bipedal, heavily armored, mechanized anthropomorphic tank. Like its precursor, the **HV LOADER**, **MECH**s are designed to imitate the pilot's human movements on a larger-than-life scale in battle.

MECH-OPS

The term for a team of special force **MECH** pilots. First employed on **ILLAL** during the Cavorite Conflict.

MEGA-CARRIERS

The air-bound equivalent of a 21st-century aircraft carrier. Mega-Carriers are essentially floating mini-cities used by **MPC**s to deploy squadrons of **BATTLESHIPS** to the ever-changing battlefield.

NANOBOTS

Individual machines created on a submicroscopic scale (dimensions of a few nanometers or less) that can be programmed for a wide variety of uses in medical, technological, and engineering fields.

NANOCAVORITE

A more efficient refinement of **CAVORITE** (created by Dr. James Hawken and patented by **PROSK**) that boasts a greater weight-to-ore anti-gravity ratio than **SENTIUM**'s equivalent alloy.

NANOVIRUS

NANOBOTS programmed to act collectively as a virus, consuming all matter in its path and reconfiguring its molecular structure to replicate and spread.

OHMU

The working code name for an ambitious **NANOTECH** project that Dr. James Hawken was developing prior to the **CRION** incident. **OHMU**'s objective was never disclosed.

PATRON

Citizens (of age) on **ILLAL** must legally become **PATRONS**. This involves either investing a sizeable amount of money in or being employed by an **MPC**.

PROSK

This **MPC** is the largest blue-collar employer on **ILLAL**. **PROSK** is a mass-market manufacturer known for its large workforce producing vast quantities of low-cost/low-quality product.

PQR

Acronym for Public Quarterly Reports, where each **MPC** announces its most recent earnings, market share, and overall fiscal stability. **PQR**s greatly affect the **SCRIP** rate of each **MPC** and therefore the overall assets of its **PATRONS**.

PRAXIS VALLEY

Similar to 21st-century's San Jose-based Silicon Valley, **PRAXIS VALLEY** is home to **CRION**'s most advanced research facility, **TYPHUS**. Two-thirds of the valley was obliterated in the initial blast that released the **HAWKEN VIRUS**.

SCRAPLAND

The colloquial term for **PRAXIS VALLEY** and any additional area since consumed entirely by the **GIGA-STRUCTURE**.

SCRIP

ILLAL's dominant currency, tied to the valuation of its associated **MPC**. **SCRIP** rates fluctuate daily and are greatly influenced by **PQR**s.

SENTIUM

A benchmark, luxury-goods **MPC**. A brand known throughout the galaxy for exemplary quality and exorbitant costs. Their strict and efficient **ILLAL** factories use a largely automated workforce, managed by personnel of the highest qualifications.

SYNTHETIC NANOCAVORITE (SCV)

Created by Hawken to offset the diminishing supply of **CAVORITE**, **SYNTHETIC NANOCAVORITE** is an artificially replicable alloy that uses **NANOBOTS** to recreate **CAVORITE**'s remarkable anti-gravity properties.

TERRAFORMING

Literally, the "Earth-shaping" of a planet, moon, or other body. The process of deliberately modifying a body's atmosphere, temperature, surface topography or ecology to be similar to those of Earth, in order to make it habitable by terrestrial organisms.

TERRAN HYPER-REPUBLIC

The collective term given to the extended human civilization now spread out across a vast range of star systems, colonizing a countless variety of planets and moons.

TITAN

The second biggest megacity on **ILLAL**. Home to the social elite, and the best architecture, arts and culture Illal has to offer. **SENTIUM**'s HQ, including the two intertwining towers of the iconic Bankson Hall, is located here.

TYPHUS

Cutting edge, $132,000 ft^2$ CRION research facility. When Dr. Hawken defected from **PROSK** to **CRION** he relocated his work here. The facility is infamous for being the epicenter of the "**CRION INCIDENT**."

UNITED TERRAN AUTHORITY

The pan-galactic government of the **TERRAN HYPER-REPUBLIC**. The **UTA** stations embassies, officials and significant peacekeeping forces on all their colonies to enforce consistent intergalactic law (including taxation). However, as a result of the IDI Act, their presence on **ILLAL** is nominal (and later non-existent following the orbital quarantine enacted in response to the unstoppable spread of the **GIGA-STRUCTURE**).

VERMIN

Collective term used for the planet's lower animal life forms. Reviled by the population, they ironically prove valuable when they evolve to feed off the **GIGA-STRUCTURE**.

VITROLIUM

This incredibly potent energy source is refined from the waste matter of the planet's indigenous **VERMIN** populace, whose rapidly evolving digestive systems uniquely enable them to consume the **GIGA-STRUCTURE**.

CONCEPT ART GALLERY

STEPPING OUTSIDE THE MECH

The breathtaking vision of ***HAWKEN: GENESIS*** is inspired by ***HAWKEN*** creator and co-CEO of Adhesive Games, Khang Le. With an esteemed background as a conceptual designer in the entertainment industry, Khang originally crafted this rich visual foundation for Adhesive's first independent game – the free-to-play multiplayer mech shooter HAWKEN. Even though the user would never leave the cockpit of their trusty mech, Khang and his gifted crew of concept artists spent over a year exploring and defining the intricate realm outside of the mech, bringing this incredibly unique and visually striking world to life.

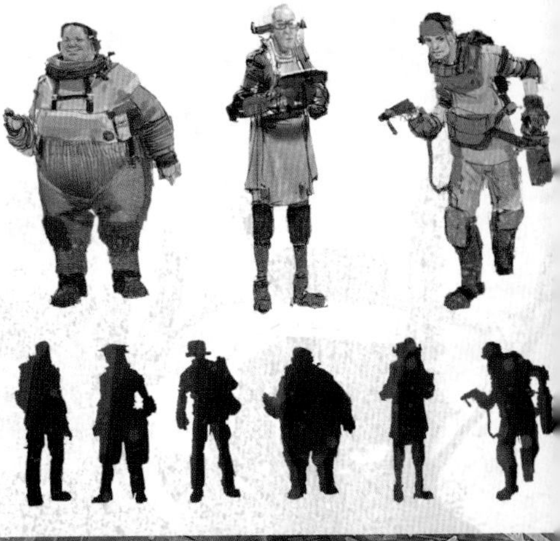

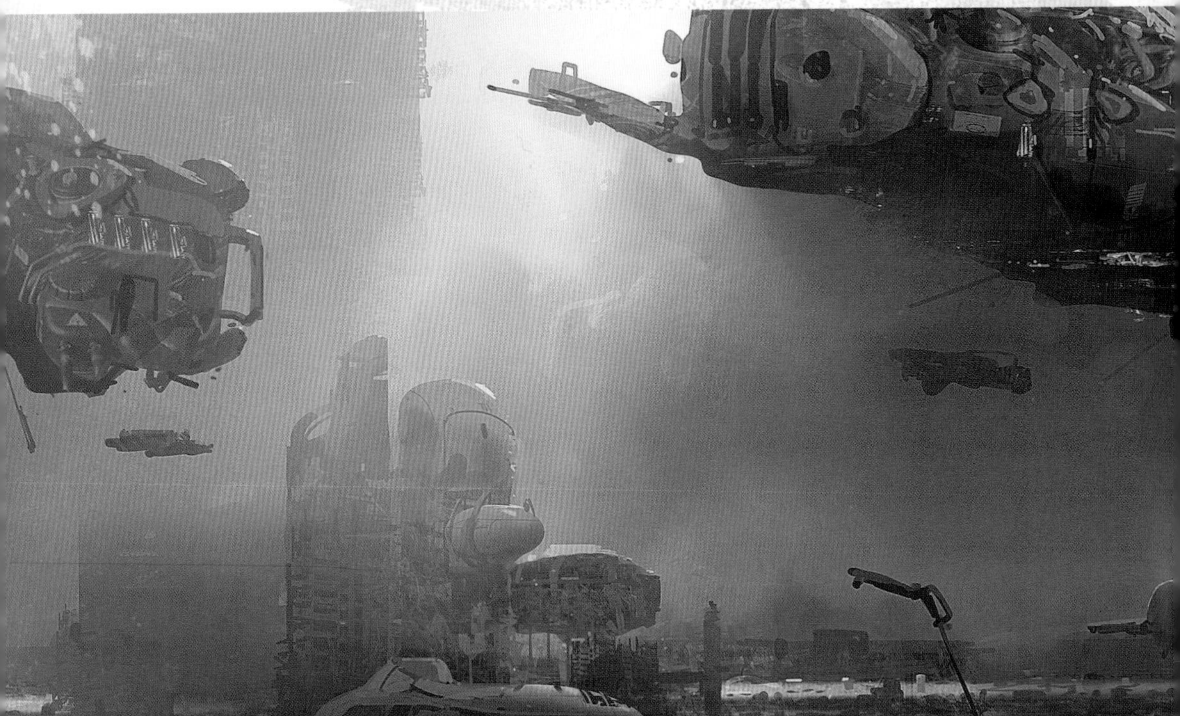

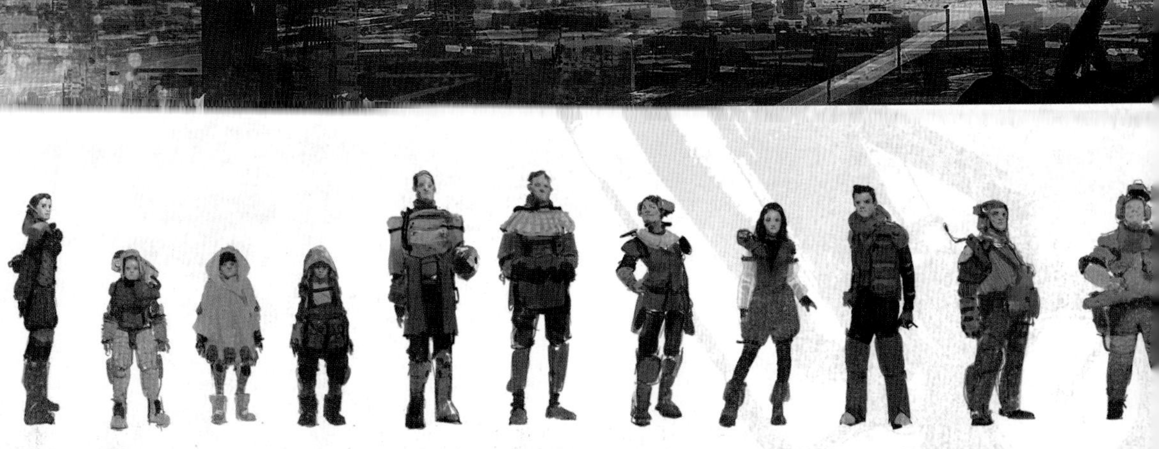

DINER 21
STOP

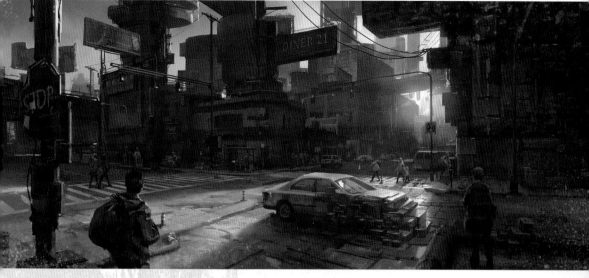

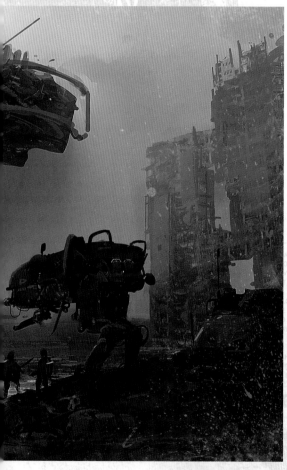

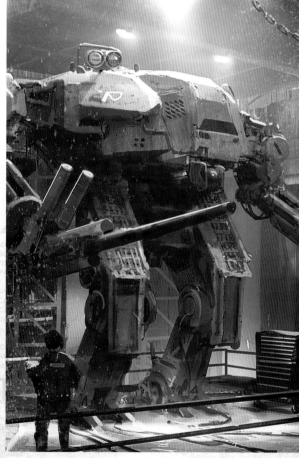

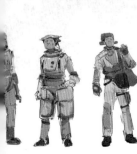

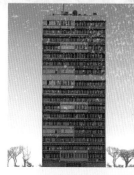

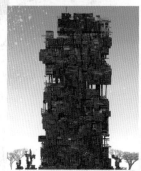

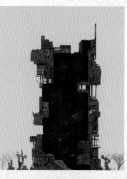

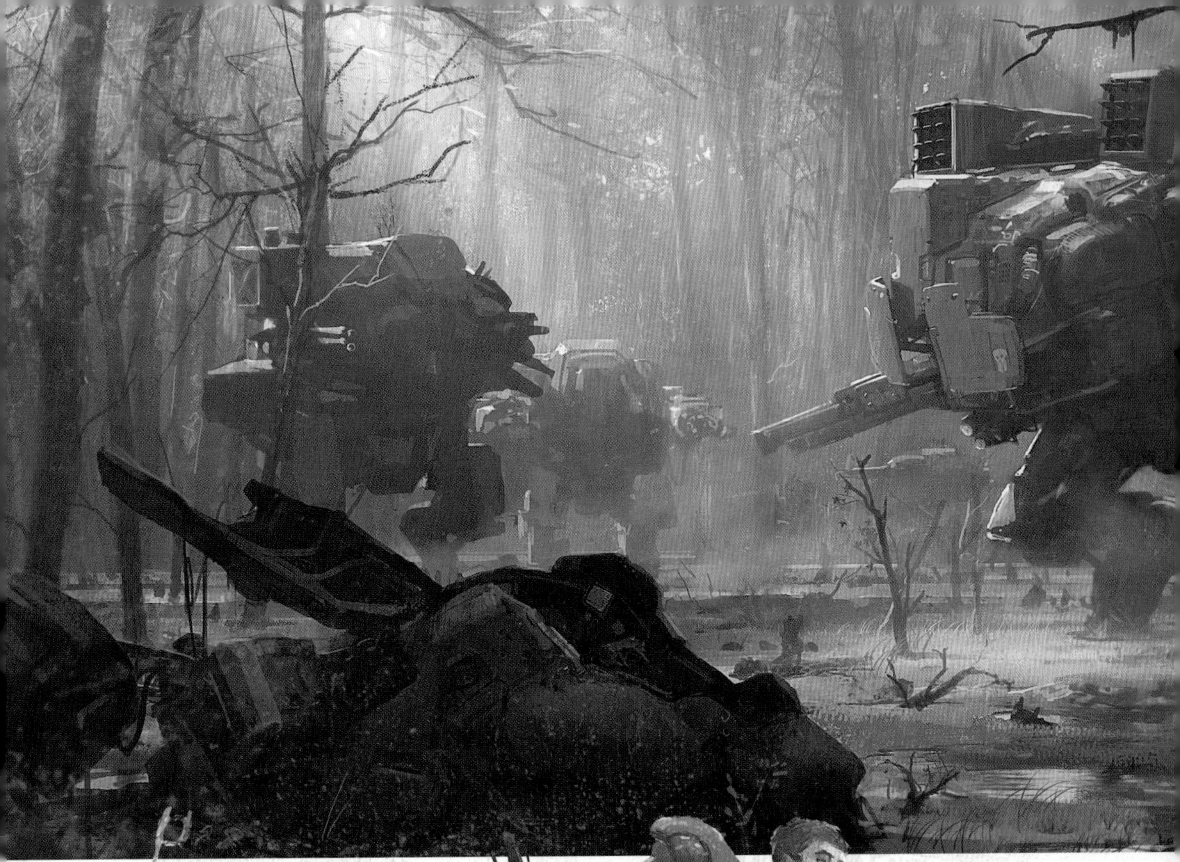

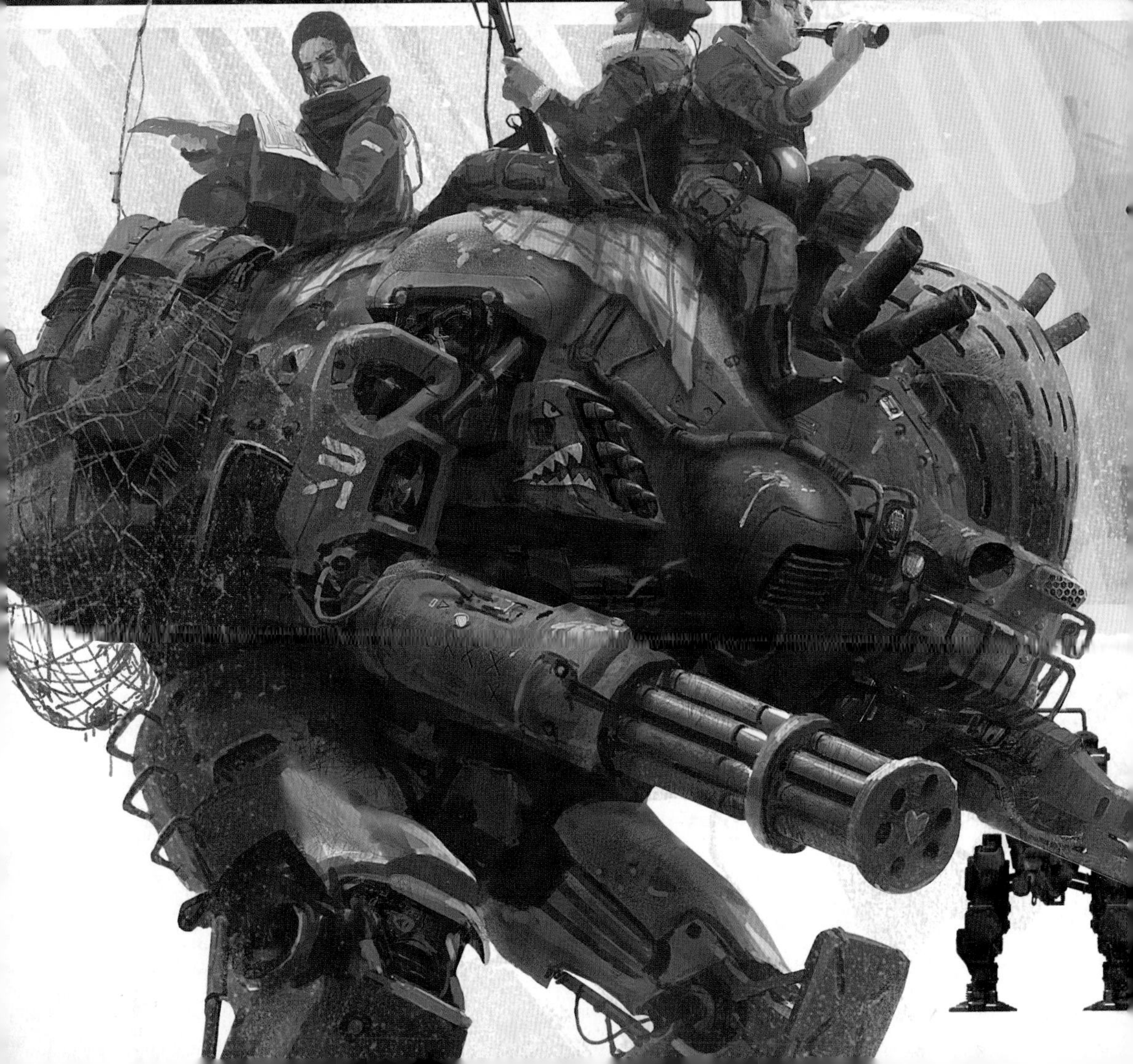

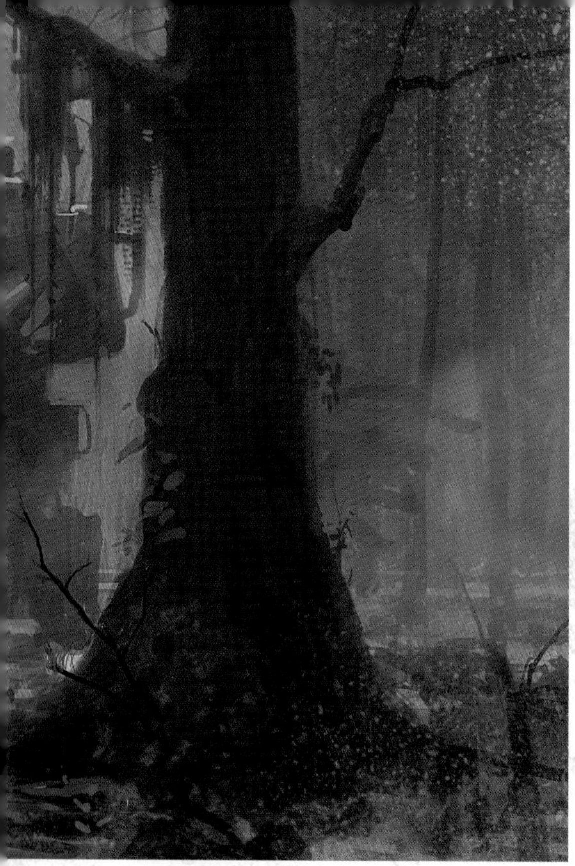

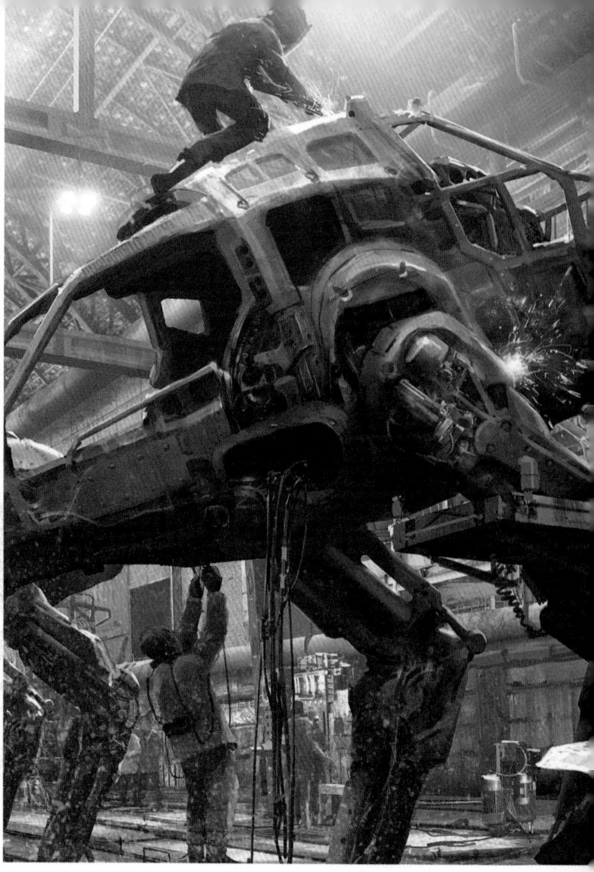

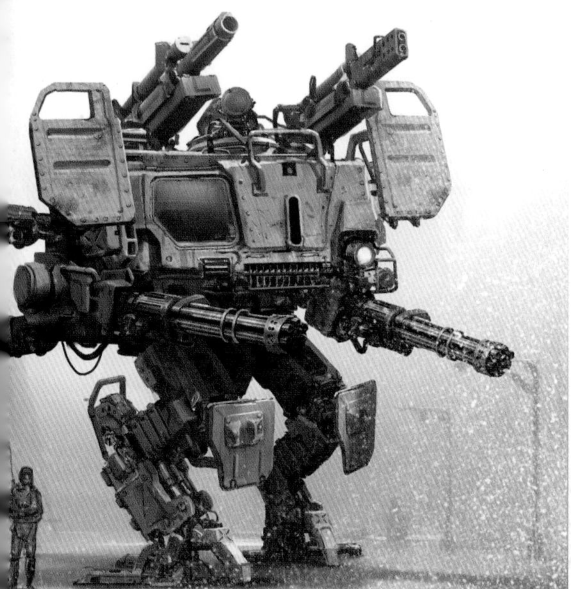

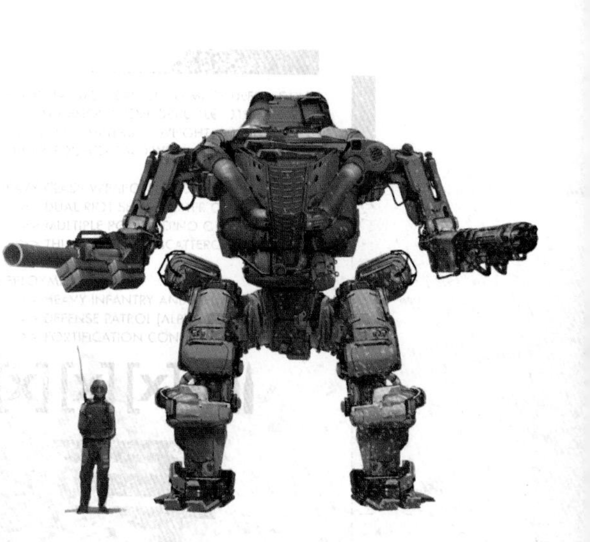

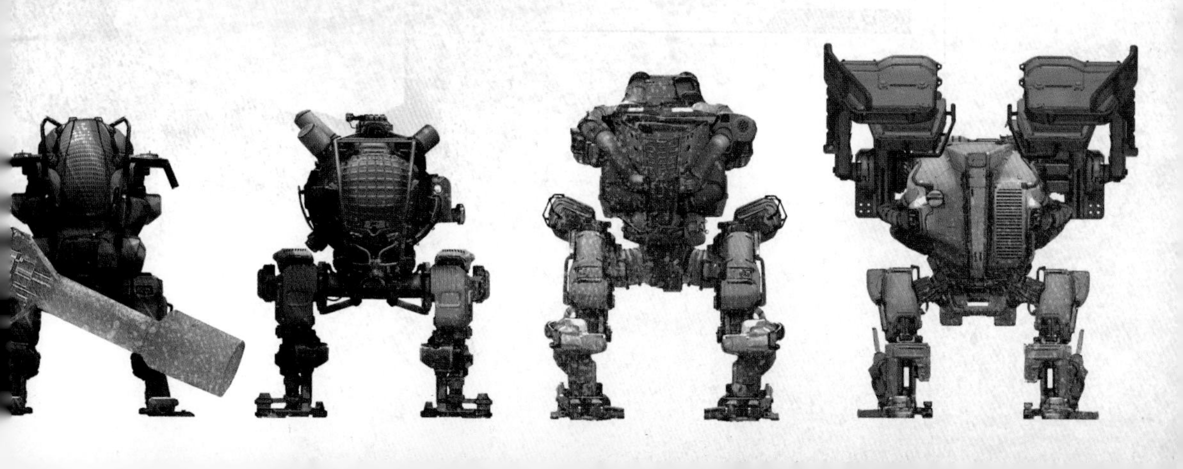

ABOUT THE AUTHORS

KHANG LE

Khang Le received a BFA in illustration from The Pasadena Art Center College of Design in 2005. After doing freelance work for various games, music videos and film companies, he joined Offset Software as Art Director. The company was eventually acquired by Intel in 2008. In 2010, he co-founded Adhesive Games and became the Creative Director on **HAWKEN**, the basis for the Archaia graphic novel, **HAWKEN: GENESIS**. Some of his previous clients for visual development include Steven Spielberg, Roland Emmerich, Robert Zemeckis, Bryan Singer, Alex Aja, Gil Kenan, Linkin Park, Blink 182, Shania Twain, New Found Glory, Microsoft, Activision, NCsoft, Red 5, and Spark.

DAN JEVONS

Dan Jevons is a writer, video game designer and transmedia producer with twenty years of entertainment industry experience. He's written on staff for worldwide print publications (including *Mean Machines*, *Maximum* and *GameFan*), produced and/or designed over a dozen videogames (including *The Darkness*, *The Red Star*, *Enclave*, *Bangai-O* and *Record of Lodoss War*) and is recently responsible for creating the **HAWKEN** Brand Bible, including the fiction that inspired the book you're holding right now. He lives in Santa Monica, California.

JEREMY BARLOW

Jeremy Barlow is a freelance writer and former editor for Dark Horse Comics, whose writing credits include *Star Wars*, *Mass Effect*, *Deathklok*, and *Kult*. As part of Portland, Oregon's Periscope Studio, he partakes and provides inspiration for a veritable gang of cartoonists, illustrators, and graphic novelists who all share a similar love of the medium, and the magic it can produce.

www.jeremybarlow.com

FRANCISCO RUIZ VELASCO

Francisco Ruiz Velasco began illustrating comics in his native country of Mexico, founding Studio F, an art house which provided computer coloring to the comic industry, with clients ranging from Dark Horse to Marvel. His original series *Battlegods* premiered in 2000, which led to the co-creation of *Lone Wolf 2100* and various other licensed projects, including original work for Marvel, BMW, Lucasfilm, and Blizzard. This work led to concept design for such films as *Hellboy 2*, *The Hobbit*, and *Pacific Rim*. He also wrote and directed the award-winning original animated short, *A Gentleman's Duel*, produced at Blur Studios, as well as the live-action sci-fi short *Abandoned*.

fruiz-fruiz.blogspot.com

ALEX SANCHEZ

Alex Sanchez is an illustrator hailing from New York whose work has been featured in publications ranging from *JSA Classified* to *30 Days of Night*. His detailed line art has also brought to life such titles as *Star Wars: The Old Republic*, *Joker's Asylum*, and *Michael Turner's Fathom*. He is currently working on *Katana* for DC with writer Ann Nocenti.

www.Ironhedcomics.com

KODY CHAMBERLAIN

Kody Chamberlain is a writer, artist, and designer who recently created the award-winning original miniseries *Sweets: A New Orleans Crime Story*. He is currently working on a digital comic series titled *Punks: The Comic* published by MTV Comics. In addition to his extensive comic and graphic novel work, Chamberlain is also an accomplished storyboard artist, conceptual artist, graphic designer, and public speaker, whose clients have included 12 Gauge Comics, DC Comics/WildStorm, HarperCollins, LucasArts, Marvel Comics, Sony Pictures, Universal Pictures, and Warner Bros. He lives in Lafayette, Louisiana.

www.kodychamberlain.com

SID KOTIAN

Sid Kotian is an artist who lives in Mumbai, India with his two dogs, Apatchy and Kelli. While they demand a lot of attention, he still finds time to illustrate comics, such as *Odayan* and *Brick Jones, Attorney From Earth*. His past work includes the horror graphic novel *Eat the Dead* and *Twilight Guardian*. He is currently hard at work on his first creator-owned series, if the dogs let him finish.

siddharth-kotian.blogspot.com

BILL SIENKIEWICZ

Bill Sienkiewicz (pronounced sin-KEV-itch) is a multiple-award-winning artist known worldwide for his unique visual style and eclectic use of varying mediums and techniques in his work, be it oils, inks, brush, collage, or pen. He is best known for his work on Marvel's *The New Mutants* and *Elektra: Assassin*, but has created artwork for numerous other titles and media, including album covers for Roger Waters, Kid Cudi, and Bruce Cockburn, as well as various covers for *Entertainment Weekly* and *Spin Magazine*. He operates out of Los Angeles.

www.billsienkiewiczart.com

BAGUS HUTOMO

Bagus Hutomo is a concept artist and painter living in Jakarta, Indonesia. He has been working as a digital artist for the past 6 years for studios including Infinite Frameworks and Imaginary Friends. He has created concept artwork for various projects inspired by cyberpunk and manga titles such as Katsuhiro Otomo's *Akira*. His work has been featured in titles such as Mark Long's *Shrapnel*, *The Darkness*, and *Heavy Metal*. He enjoys exploring mechanical and military concepts in his work, always in search of an undiscovered configuration of shapes and themes.

bagushutomo.blogspot.com

MICHAEL GAYDOS

A painter, draftsman, and printmaker, **Michael Gaydos's** work has been the subject of a number of solo exhibitions and is in private collections worldwide. He has established himself in various other artistic channels, including several renowned graphic novels, such as Brian Michael Bendis's *Alias*, for which he received two Eisner nominations. His list of credits include work for Marvel, DC, Virgin, Dark Horse, Fox Atomic, Image, IDW, NBC, Tundra, NBM, Caliber, and White Wolf, among others. He is a graduate of the Cleveland Institute of Art, and currently resides in New York.

michaelgaydos.com

FEDERICO DALLOCCHIO

Federico Dallocchio is an Argentinian artist who has worked for DC, Wildstorm, Marvel, Dark Horse, and Archaia. He has been gaming since he was five years old, starting with a Sinclair 1500, and has experienced the evolution of the video game industry firsthand. He enjoys creating original universes and witnessing the growth of his favorite genre... being a mecha pilot!

www.federicodallocchio.com

NATHAN FOX

Nathan Fox is an editorial illustrator and artist whose work has been featured in *The New York Times*, *Interview Magazine*, *The New Yorker*, *Rolling Stone*, *Wired*, *Entertainment Weekly*, *Spin*, and *ESPN Magazine*. His comic book work has included *Pigeons From Hell*, *DMZ*, *Haunt*, and *Flourescent Black*, an original co-creation which was serialized in *Heavy Metal Magazine*. His clients have included MTV, Subaru, DC, Marvel, and Dark Horse. He is a graduate of the Kansas City Art Institute and The School of Visual Arts Illustration in New York, and now is the Chair of the MFA Visual Narrative Department at the School of Visual Arts in New York.

www.foxnathan.com

CHRISTOPHER MOELLER

Since his 1991 debut graphic novel *Rocketman: King of the Rocketmen*, **Christopher Moeller** has emerged as one of the world's top writer-painters of graphic novels, best known for his creator-owned series *Iron Empires*, which also spawned a popular RPG. His body of work includes *JLA: A League of One*, *JLA: Cold Steel*, and regular covers for series such as *Lucifer* and *Batman: Shadow of the Bat*. His prolific career has provided illustrations for a wide range of publishers, including Marvel, IDW, Virgin, FASA Publications, Topps, West End Games, Wizards of the Coast, Blizzard Entertainment, WizKids, and White Wolf Games. He is currently completing a third volume in the *Iron Empires* series.

www.moellerillustrations.com

SPECIAL THANKS

Special thanks to our invaluable collaborators at Meteor Entertainment, Adhesive Games, DJ2 Entertainment, and Quixotic Transmedia, as well as **M. Zachary Sherman**, and all of the *HAWKEN* fans who supported us from around the globe.

At Meteor Entertainment, we would like to thank **Mark Tanjutco**, **Lloyd Bennack**, **Kim Harle**, and **Paul Loynd**.

At DJ2, we would like to thank **Mohnish Saraswat**, **Sirus Ahmadi**, and **Gary Harrod**.

And we want to thank all of the brilliant individuals at Adhesive Games for their inspiring creativity.

YOU ARE **FREE** TO **FIGHT**.

Enter the world of *HAWKEN*, an award-winning multiplayer first-person shooter that puts you in the pilot seat of a giant robotic war machine. Best of all, *HAWKEN* is free to play.

Customize and upgrade your mech the way you want, then join your friends on the battlefield to rain destruction across the planet of Illal. For FREE.

"HAWKEN looks to be the king of free-to-play gaming"
—Destructoid.com, Best PC Game, E3 2012

PLAY NOW

Register at **www.playhawken.com/genesis** to download
HAWKEN for free and join the fight!

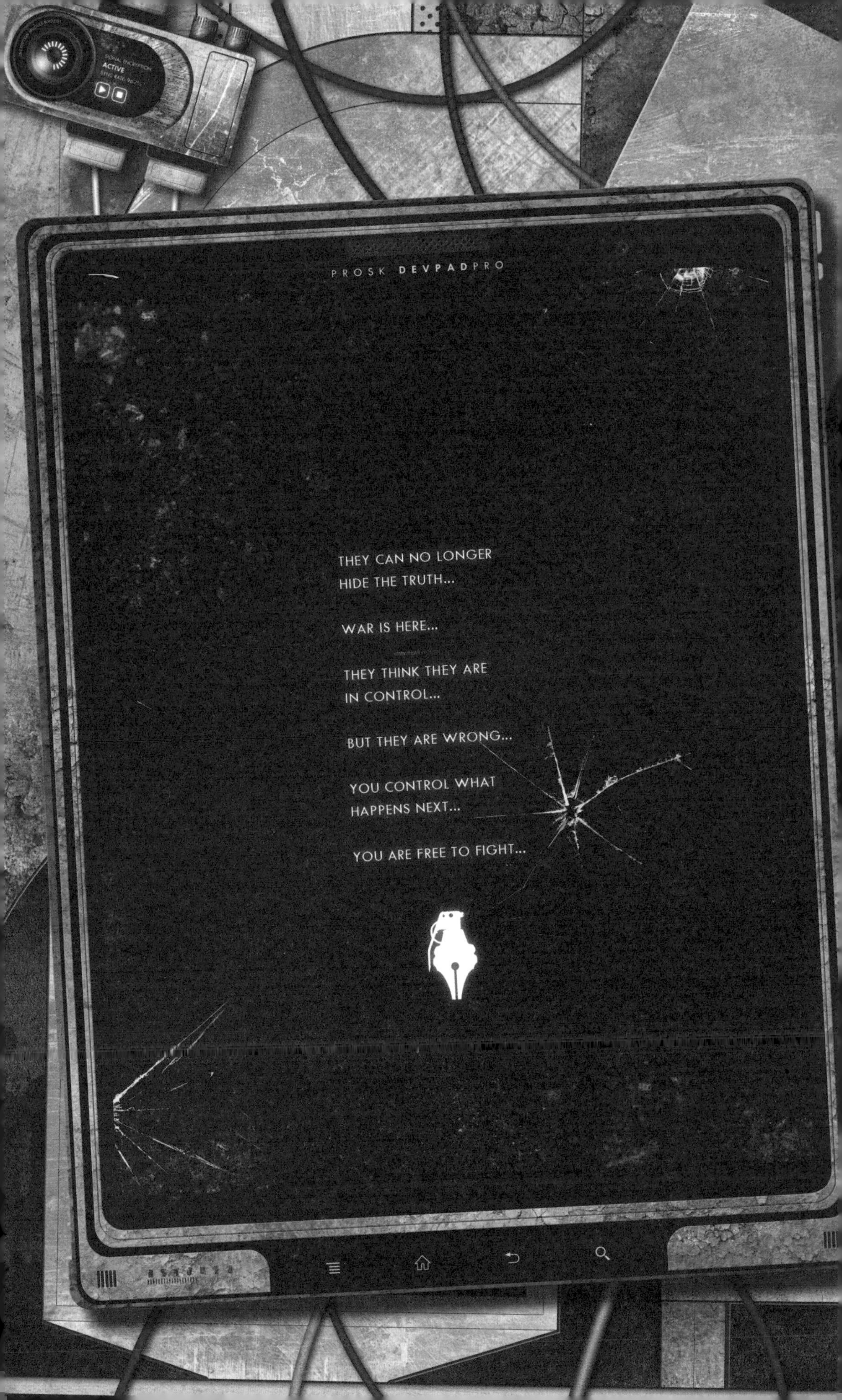
PROSK DEVPADPRO
THEY CAN NO LONGER
HIDE THE TRUTH...
WAR IS HERE...
THEY THINK THEY ARE
IN CONTROL...
BUT THEY ARE WRONG...
YOU CONTROL WHAT
HAPPENS NEXT...
YOU ARE FREE TO FIGHT...